25 Years of Lifting

Steve Foxall

This book is available for special discounts on bulk purchases.
For more information visit 25years.ca

Painted Door Publishing
Hamilton, Ontario
www.25years.ca

25 Years of Lifting -- 1st edition

ISBN 10: 0995812403
ISBN 13: 978-0995812406

I wrote this for my family,
the source of all my strength

Contents

The Reason

The Switch

Part 3:   How We Lift

Conclusion

Steve Foxall

The Reason

"I learned many great lessons from my father, not the least of which was that you could fail at what you don't love, so you might as well take a chance on doing what you love."

Jim Carrey

It sure as hell doesn't feel like twenty-five years have passed since I first started lifting but I remember everything, even that first month. Looking back, it's an understatement to say it was a different world. There was no YouTube, no websites, and our only phone was hanging on the wall in the kitchen. Protein powder was all you had and it tasted like shit, but it didn't matter. The gyms were full of weights, not treadmills, and the walls weren't covered with posters of skinny people holding up their "fat" jeans. You were there to lift and aside from the football team, not too many others did. There just wasn't much available for bodybuilders back then. We had Flex Magazine, and every month I'd keep an eye out for the latest copy at the gas station down the street. I'd always chuckle at the creative comments the cashier would make about the guy on the cover, just to be polite.

Back then, if you wanted to know who won the Mr. Olympia contest you had to wait two months for the story to come out in print.

It's been a long time since I first took it up, but year after year I've always found time to lift and to keep learning. I've trained at dozens of gyms all over the country, always natural, no drugs. At five foot ten and a hundred and ninety pounds I laugh when people question me on that. I'm not sure why I have the passion for it that I do, it's just there and I don't think it will ever go away. You could say it's part of who I am, as much as anything else.

The gym is a constant, in a world that kicks you in the ass week after week. The room might change but the bench is always there waiting and as Henry Rollins says, 'a hundred pounds is always a hundred pounds.'

For years now, I've had the desire to help others and contribute, to have an impact on the industry. A while ago I sent a package out to some supplement companies in the States to see if I could help them expand their product lines up here in Canada. Without a single response, I soon realized that resumes don't go too far in today's world of marketing. What counts today is followers, likes…the sum of your social media audience. It makes sense: hand out a bunch of your product, then have them tell thousands how wonderful you are. With about thirty friends max on Facebook, I soon realized that anything I decided to do would have to be done on my own. As with most 'side projects,' the desire just sat on a shelf in my head as the years passed by. And then desire turned into a commitment, both to me and to my wife.

Sometimes it takes a big event in our lives to push us into doing something. For me, it was losing my job. It frustrated the hell out of me to know that someone else had the ability to change my path, and put what my wife and I have at risk. So I started putting some serious thought into my dream. I thought about how the industry has evolved, and will continue to do so, and about how certain elements haven't changed at all. When I first started training, I did everything wrong, completely wrong. My form sucked, I used too much weight, I overtrained and never ate enough of the right foods. Getting to a point where I could consider myself an expert lifter took years, and it shouldn't have. Now, when I go to the gym, I see my story being told over and over again. I stand in a room full of people struggling to get it right. The effort is certainly there but the knowledge isn't. I've handed out thousands of tips to help people get on the right track but over and over, it's the same mistakes being made.

My goal with this book is to help you become an experienced lifter in a lot less time than it took me. Be prepared: lifting is a shitload of work, but if you're passionate about it, this book will save you years of frustration. This book is NOT about fast-track secrets or shortcuts to getting big. If that's what you want, there's a whole industry waiting to take your money.

**I will do everything I can to teach you how to lift,
how to use your mind and make the most of your time training.
This is day 1, so let's get after it.**

Steve Foxall

The Switch

"I have a big ego, and I'm a confident person, but when it comes down to being a jerk, that doesn't work for me, I tried it... for about ten years."

Harry Connick, Jr.

The training in this book is broken down into two main sections: the mental side and the physical side. After studying the material, you will know exactly what you need to do in the gym to make progress and how to go about doing it. You can skip the mistake-riddled break-in period we all go through during which we slowly try and figure things out. Learning to lift properly can be a very frustrating experience but I'm here to help. I learned it all the hard way, maybe so I could write this book and spare you the same experience.

Before we get deep into that education, I can't begin to teach you anything without first dealing with what is by far the biggest problem out there. This particular problem applies to men, and only men. My female readers will definitely be entertained by it and further convinced they rank a little higher on the smart scale.

Why do women ask for directions?

It's a simple question but it's the perfect analogy. Time and time again when couples are heading somewhere and lose track of where they are, instincts take over. Women will immediately admit to being lost and begin looking for someone to ask for directions, while men remain fully convinced that this simple task can be handled without any outside assistance.

How could a man possibly admit defeat? It would be like driving around and yelling out the window 'I've failed!' God forbid you were forced to ask another man for directions...the shame of it all.

It's a story that dates back to the invention of the automobile—maybe even before!—and it still happens. Why is that? Well, there's something else that dates back even further: it's the male ego and it is on display every single day at your local gym.

I could fill a book with nothing but examples of guys looking like id-iots using too much weight to impress themselves and all of those around them. I think I've made my point, so let's get to it.

Here's what I want to cover...

1. Why using too much weight will stop you from achieving any amount of progress

2. Effective practice

3. The all-important switch from impressing with weight, to impressing with technique

There will be quite a few areas in the book where I compare lifting to golf. I know what you're thinking, the two cultures couldn't be more different. Surprisingly, there are several key parallels. The two are also unique from other sports in that individuals will commit hours and hours of their time, buckets of their hard-earned money, and still fail to improve year after year. The same way I see mistakes every time I go to train, I see plenty of swing mistakes when I go for a round at the golf course. And in the same way the male ego gets in the way of lifting, it definitely gets in the way of effective golf.

Being in sales, I've played a fair bit of golf. I'm far from good, which is fine. You can't commit a mere few days a year to something and expect to improve. Regardless of whether you play or not, there's a good chance you've been to a driving range. It's a place to practice, to learn, to focus on one or two key points and become better. The majority of people don't seem to see it that way. To most, it is simply a firing range. Pull out the driver, swing as hard as you can and see if you can out-distance your friends. This is done for a good half hour before heading home, essentially accomplishing nothing.

Are these individuals going to make progress? Are they going to improve on the fundamentals of the swing? The takeaway, the shoulder turn, the weight shift, the hip turn, impact or the follow through? Not a chance. Well guess what? When you lift with too much weight, you are that person. You are the guy at the range trying to smack the ball as hard as he can to impress his friends and anyone else who's watching.

For the exact same reason, you will not make progress or improve. The thing about golf is that anybody can grab a club and swing at a ball as hard as they can, the same way pretty much anybody can walk into a gym and bench press their max. If your goal was to become a great golf player, you would quickly realize that it is a very difficult game to learn, and that becoming great takes hours and hours of practice. If serious about your goal, you'd likely take lessons from a coach or golf pro to help develop the fundamentals. Even after weeks or months or even years of practice and training, there will still be days of struggle and a need for further guidance.

Lifting weights is no different. The challenge is that nobody ever considers the fact that they have to learn how to lift through effective practice. To become great at lifting, you need to learn proper form and create lasting muscle memory. Understand and appreciate the *need* to learn in order to create a scenario where you *can* learn.

Consider this next year of training as practice. You're not lifting, you're learning how to lift.

Now when it comes to practice, I mentioned something called "effective practice". There's a book I really enjoyed called *Talent is Overrated*, by Geoff Colvin. I recommend it. Basically it says that we are not born with greatness or excellence, it is always learnt. It says that on average it takes ten thousand hours of practice to become truly great at something. It also explains that the practice must be effective. If you are not practicing correctly, you are wasting your time, and you are certainly not on your way to becoming great. This applies to any sport. You need to learn the fundamentals and how to practice them, and then you need to repeat that practice over and over again, always striving to find ways to improve.

When I first started lifting, my friends and I immediately began focusing on *how much* we could lift. No effort was put into learning proper technique. There was never a thought of 'how to lift', just how much.

The number one goal of this book is to help you learn how to lift weights properly, even if you've been working out for years. From here on out, your next year in the gym is practice. If that practice is done effectively, you *will* become better, but in order for it to be effective, you have to stop using too much weight.

Let's keep talking about weight, because, how much you use in any exercise is crucial, and I mean the exact amount of weight. It is the most important factor that you have to get a handle on. You might argue and say that technique is the most important but I assure you that proper technique can only truly be mastered by using the right amount of weight.

Back to golf. At some point, I made the decision to become a better golfer. I am definitely a perfectionist and was tired of being frustrated on the course all the time. Now, if you want to get really good at something, it makes sense to study those who are the best in the world. If you want to be a good salesperson then replicate the habits of the best salespeople. If your job is in management, study the top business leaders and read their books on leadership. Simply put, learn from the best.

So I went out and I bought some books. I grabbed one on Tiger Woods' short game and Nick Price's book on the swing. I studied them on TV, their technique and their stance. I then studied how they hit different shots and managed the course. The result was that I became fairly good at golf even though I only played a handful of rounds a year.

When I was learning how to lift, I wasn't able to watch the pros train. That wasn't an option, so it was very difficult to copy them or know exactly what they were doing. Any books I found just told you what to do, but not how to do it. Today, you have videos. I wish I'd had this when I was trying to figure things out. I actually remember when I first started watching them and how exciting it was. I ordered Dorian Yates' video "Blood and Guts." I watched it over and over, in awe of what I was seeing. I then studied Ronnie Coleman's series and Jay Cutler's chronicles.

Now you also have all the "tribute" videos on YouTube and compilations set to music. Quite recently, the supplement companies began handing out contracts to the pros, and bodybuilding websites now post endless videos and commercials for their products. These videos are good for two things, one is that they show you how lifting should be done and two, they will motivate the hell out of you.

Steve Foxall

So let's apply my belief in learning from the pros, the best in the world. What do *they* do? What can we learn from watching them to answer our weight question?

The first thing you will notice is pretty obvious. The pros all use great technique. Pro lifters move the weight in a perfect fashion. It is the direct result of years in the gym practicing. But even the pros wouldn't be able to perform those exercises in that manner if they used too much weight. The reason for that is that too much weight prevents you from placing the entire load on the intended muscles throughout the complete range of motion. I'll use an example because "placing the weight on the intended muscle" is a term you need to understand.

Let's look at squats. A good squat demands that you lean forward just a touch, stick your butt way out and lower your body to the point where your thighs are parallel to the floor. In that position, your quads are forced to carry almost the entire load. The reason you hardly ever see people in the gym go to parallel is because with too much weight, they don't have the strength to put it all on their quads and so they have to rely on their backs to carry the weight.

Many years ago I went to see Jay Cutler give a seminar close to Toronto shortly after winning the Mr. Olympia. I'd never met a professional bodybuilder before and what I saw shocked me. Jay was massive, beyond comprehension. I'd been looking at muscle mags for years and watching videos but to see this guy in person shed a whole new light on the amount of muscle that can be packed onto a human frame.

This reinforced the importance of what I already knew. What I can do in the gym, and what the pros can do may be the same in terms of technique, form, and after years of training, intensity, but I can't lift anywhere near what they lift. Some people seem to be a little confused in that area. They have this odd belief that they can squat 500 pounds or bench 400. There is no comparison, and while social media is full of extremely strong individuals, you will hurt yourself trying. You can't dunk like Lebron, tackle like Clay Matthews or skate like Sidney Crosby, and you sure as hell can't lift like Jay Cutler!

Here is one simple switch you can make to stop training with your ego: *impress with technique!* That's a lesson I learnt back in university. I was training legs one day and trying to squat too much weight. I probably had close to three plates a side and was using what I'm sure was terrible form. After one of my sets, one of the linemen on the football team walked over. "Lower the fucking weight, you look like an idiot," he said, and then he turned around and went back to his training.

This one statement had a pretty big effect. Maybe the direct approach works best. My training changed that day, and with that change came progress. I did start lowering the weight and I did stop looking like an idiot. I made the switch.

See this is the key, if you still think the amount of weight on the bar is what impresses people you couldn't be more wrong. Anyone who knows what they are doing is impressed by proper technique. Think about it. You see two guys doing squats. One guy is using three plates, and as his legs shake, he lowers it about a foot before working his way back up. The other guy has two plates, and in full control, he lowers down to parallel and smoothly raises the bar while contracting all of his quad muscles. If you were watching, which one of the two would impress you the most? It better be the fella with two plates. If I had to guess, I would say 60% of the people I see squatting fall into the first category, leaving around forty that actually know what they're doing. Fall into the forty percent, and that my friend is when you will start impressing those around you, if you still feel the need.

Train as if you are the only person in the gym.

Using too much weight...

1. Prevents you from having the strength to place all of the weight on the muscles you are working, and therefore, prevents you from using proper form

2. Forces you to use your joints and supporting muscles to carry a lot of the weight

3. Does not let you develop rhythm, which all the best lifters in the world prove is essential

4. Means that you are not able to reach or surpass muscular failure

5. Forces you to use momentum to move the weight which increases the risk of injury

6. Prevents you from getting a good contraction

7. Can, if you are using a spotter, force them to do the majority of the work

8. Stops you from effectively practicing, meaning you are not creating a scenario where your body can learn how to lift properly and build the correct muscle memory

9. Prevents you from training your mind how to reach failure and therefore learning how to break the mental barriers we all face in the gym

10. Means you are lifting with your ego which prevents all progress and makes you look like an idiot to all those other people in the gym that for some reason, even though you don't know them, you feel the need to impress

<u>Part One</u>

How We Think

Steve Foxall

Chapter 1: A Strong Mind

"Players today put too much emphasis on lifting weights, low body fat and big muscles that they think...make them look good – all that bullshit. What you need to play hockey is heart and determination, and the ability to stay mentally strong. Mental strength beats physical strength any day."

Phil Esposito

In 2009, UFC fighter George St. Pierre defeated Thiago Alves. In the third round of the fight, George tore a ligament in his abductor muscle. This basically left him with one leg. Imagine going up against a top UFC athlete with only one leg to stand on. After telling his trainer and being told to keep going, he did. He kept going, through an immense amount of pain, he kept fighting, kept moving forward, and he defeated Alves. When the fight was over, he could barely stand.

In Game 5 of the 1997 NBA finals, or what is now known as "the flu game," Chicago was playing Utah and Michael Jordan was battling a severe case of the flu. He had been throwing up all day and night, he was dehydrated and completely exhausted. For most of us, we wouldn't even have the strength to climb out of bed. But Michael went on to score 38 points and lead his team to victory. Watch the high-lights, it's an amazing thing. When it was over, he said that he really wanted it, he really wanted the win, and then he collapsed.

In the 2003 Tour De France, Tyler Hamilton, an American rider with a good chance of defeating Lance Armstrong, crashed in the first stage and broke his collarbone in two places. It's a common injury in cycling and 99.9% of the time, the rider packs his bags and goes home. Tyler didn't see it as a problem and kept going. He climbed mountains, and if you've ever cycled and done hills, you know how much you have to pull on the handle bars. He finished what could eas-ily be called the toughest single sporting event on earth while in agony. Not only did he finish, he finished 4th overall six minutes be-hind Lance. He defeated hundreds of the best riders in the world with one arm. He said "I don't know that I've worked harder for anything in my life."

I could give you pages and pages of similar examples, lists of indi-viduals who overcame significant challenges by having a strong mind. My examples were all sports related but the same applies to all areas of life. Why do we consistently see this in sports? Competition is one of the best environments in which to train our minds. It is essential when you go up against the best in the world. Focus, concentration, confidence, the ability to manage emotions and pain can be phenom-enal. It is that mental strength that is on display in the three examples above.

Let's take a look at Tiger Woods, an athlete well known for having one of the strongest mental games in the history of sport. His late father Earl wrote a book called "Training a Tiger." It's an excellent book for any parent with children in competitive sports. Starting on page 147, the discussion turns to the specific portion of Tiger's train-ing that relates to mental toughness, which began at age twelve.

The training was to be so intense that Earl set up a code word that Tiger could use in the event that he couldn't take it anymore. Once established, they set out to train as they usually did, but now, Earl would do everything he could to break Tiger's concentration. He thought of everything that could happen on the golf course and dished it out. He would throw the golf bag in the middle of the backswing, make animal noises as he tried to putt, roll balls all over the green. He would even heckle him and taunt him. To make it even worse every time Tiger complained, he would scold him for not focusing on his shot.

Earl goes on to say that Tiger would not have wished this type of training on anyone—keep in mind he was *twelve*. As a result, Earl's son's mental toughness was unparalleled. He routinely won tournaments and major tournaments with impossible putts on the 18th hole, and while most people would just watch and think, nice putt, there is a great deal more to it. Tiger raised the bar in his sport to a level that was not yet even conceived to be possible.

In the NFL, quite often a place kicker has to hit a field goal to win the game, let's say forty yards. He gets ready to go and then the opposing team's coach usually calls a time out to "ice" him. They snap the ball and most of the time it goes through the uprights but it's not all that rare for him to miss. Either way the announcers always talk about the pressure.

Think about this, in practice that kicker could probably hit that field goal fifty times in a row, he could probably hit it blindfolded. Tiger Woods has won several huge tournaments by sinking crazy winding 30 foot putts on the last several holes. Now in practice, any pro on tour might make that putt once out of ten tries, maybe. Tiger would do it in the heat of the moment under incredible, unimaginable pressure. How did he do it?

The training he was given at such a young age created a foundation on which he further built an amazing ability to focus. If you watch, you can actually see him blocking out every single fan, reporter, camera man and even the other golfers. He completely empties his mind in order to create a scenario where it's just him and the course, and then he goes to work. He analyses the green and he visualizes the putt, he gets to a point where he knows exactly what the ball is going to do and how hard he has to hit it to keep it on the necessary path. By the time he stands over the ball to take the shot, he has firmly convinced himself that he will make the putt, and then he executes the fundamentals that are ingrained in him.

Here's another result of his Dad's training. In his prime, when another golfer went up against Tiger, he would not only lose, but he would lose big. He would shoot six to eight shots higher than he did on the previous day. It was to the point where players would consider purposely giving up a shot to be in the second last group rather than sharing the lead with Tiger. Why would they play so poorly? There is absolutely nothing physical about it, they just couldn't focus on their game. At twelve years old, when other players were still learning how to swing, Tiger was learning how to deal with the crowds and the cheering and the cameras going off. He was training to deal with the distractions that would come with being the best, with being a sensation followed around the course by thousands. He knew very well that his competitors weren't prepared to handle that level of distraction and he would use the crowd to his advantage. The announcers would always assume Tiger had this great ability to intimidate his opponents, but all he did was focus, in any environment, better than anyone else.

Now let's look at another example. Former heavyweight champ Mike Tyson also raised the bar in his sport to a new level, but as far as mental training goes, you'll see the polar opposite.

Mike grew up in Brooklyn where his father was rarely around and his mother passed away when he was 16. That's when he started training with Cus D'Amato. He went on to set a new standard for what the Heavyweight Champ should be, a monster. While it wasn't his intent, he developed this amazing ability to instantly send fear and doubt into his opponent's mind, you could see it when they stood toe to toe before the first round even started. I remember watching all of his fights as he was working his way up. I was fascinated—he won before even stepping in the ring.

Mike didn't have all that training Tiger had, his strength was physical. He was a product of the environment he grew up in, as most of us are. When he first came to Cus, he had very little confidence, he had this huge need to be loved and constantly re-assured. As he worked his way up through the Olympics, he would actually walk around crying before a lot of his fights. In his documentaries, he talks about how he had this overwhelming fear of failure, and not because of how it would affect him, but how he would disappoint those around him who had helped him and taken him in. He didn't want to let down his new family.

Once the first round began he would take all of that fear and just unload it with everything he had. That's what Cus taught him, how to project his fear onto his opponent. At the beginning, he wasn't fighting to win, he was fighting so he wouldn't lose. That's what fueled the fierceness and the aggression, that's what no other fighter had, that's how he raised the bar. It was amazing to watch, fighters over a foot taller with five or six more inches in reach that didn't stand a chance. They weren't just knocked out, they were sent flying across the ring, usually within the first two rounds. The best fighters in the world, beaten down like it was their first time in the ring.

So what does this have to do with you or me? Even though most of us don't compete on a worldwide stage, we each have our own challenges and we compete against life on a daily basis. Most of the time, it's not a fair fight. What I'm trying to demonstrate is the all-important role your mind plays in helping determine your level of success in every aspect of your life.

It can be hard to relate these stories to our own lives and situations, but let's try, let's look at how a strong mind can help all of us no matter who we are or what we do. We're all different. Some of us are students but most of us work, and most of us aren't all that happy at work. I think a big reason a lot of us aren't happy is because our jobs don't tap into a great deal of what we are capable of and what we're passionate about. Instead, they put us to sleep.

Let me show you one way in which having a strong mind has helped me. I've never considered myself normal, not by any stretch of the imagination. "Normal" is probably my least favorite word in the dictionary. Normal is average, boring. "Normal" exists in the absence of creativity and passion. Unfortunately, in today's world, not being normal can sometimes be a disadvantage.

I spent 16 years in banking. I started as a part-time teller cashing cheques and quickly worked my way up to financing multi-million dollar operations. For most of that time I really enjoyed my work, and the opportunity I always had to progress. As I moved up the ladder my customer base became more and more interesting and wealthy and I was always curious as to why this group was so successful, why were they all millionaires? Nothing made me feel better than these customers asking for my advice and then acting on it and thanking me later.

Unfortunately, something always seems to get in the way of a good thing. In 2008, Lehman Brothers filed for bankruptcy. And soon after, the trickledown effect changed corporate culture for years to come. In the post-collapse world, companies don't seem to focus on the client anymore, they don't promote a sales environment and they certainly don't build a team atmosphere, basically all the elements I believe are necessary for success in business. The reason is simple: money. After the collapse, every big company in North America had to cut budgets, tighten the purse strings and increase margins on decreasing revenue.

On the spending side, expenses had to go down. No more golfing, no more expensive sushi lunches, no more big conferences. Basically, no more fun. In a lot of companies, including the one I worked for and likely the ones that some of you work for, they stopped hiring Sales Managers. In my case, the big boys and girls in Toronto felt that these managers were too reckless and liked to spend too much money. Worst of all, they fought for their sales teams, which interfered with the new culture. They were replaced with watchdogs, managers who did what they were told and were not the type to build buddy relationships with their sales teams. They didn't spend money and more importantly, senior management had these folks in their back pockets and that allowed them to cover their asses. That basically sums up the new corporate culture. Cover your ass and keep your job.

Now I happen to like when bosses consider themselves to be on the same level as the whole team, and I like when they actually want to be my colleague because then I have respect for them and I want to impress them. I always said you could gauge the effectiveness of any manager by how hard their team worked to impress them. The same goes for coaches in sports. Think of all the "good" coaches you've had and how much you wanted to impress them and earn their respect. Now think of the bad ones—we've all had at least one—did you care what they thought? Probably not.

Good managers, coaches or teachers know that we all don't learn the same way because our brains don't think the same way. Without that skill set, a manager tends to paint everyone with the same brush and take the "it's my way or the highway" approach. To make things worse, many tend to combine it with the "manage by fear" approach. Here's a tip, as soon as someone tries to manage you by using fear, they're making it clear that they don't know what they're doing.

Managing by fear assumes that everyone is afraid. It does the opposite of what every good book on successful management suggests and recommends. This really upset me and I would always get my back up. It's like this, in the schoolyard, someone wants to take a run at you and you have choices. You can stand up for yourself and push back or walk away, it's up to you. In the corporate world, those options disappear. When your boss wants to take a run at you, there's no fighting back because you can't win, and you can't risk the pay-cheque. Maybe they were bullied as kids and this is their chance to get back at the world, maybe it's a woman who's fighting back after taking shit from men year after year. Either way, it's cowardly, it's weak and every time it happened I'd stare at them with a look that told them just that.

So long story short, I ultimately got fired because lifting gave me the confidence not to be afraid, not to take their shit. While you might be saying that's probably not a good thing, it was. People tend to stay unhappy in jobs for years without doing anything about it. Don't be that person.

The confidence that lifting can give you will help you at work, in your relationships, in creating and achieving goals and getting what you want out of life.

So why? Why does all that lifting get rid of your fears and give you the ability to get out of a horrible situation? How can the gym change the way you think, the way you interact with people and the way you look at goals and what you're capable of? Because it gives you mental strength. It makes you believe that you can do anything. You will welcome challenges and you will need to be challenged. You will always look for ways to improve and thrive on being good at what it is you do. Why? Because in the gym, once you discover your ability to control your mind and push your body to the limit, you will amaze yourself. The impact that lifting has on who you are as a person can be immense, it is a massive reward that bleeds into so many other areas of your life.

However, and this is the key, in order for it to change the way you think and how you approach life, you have to actually learn the mental side of lifting, and it is crucial that you do.

Typically, everyone learns to lift and then slowly figures out the thinking side of it after. This is a mistake. Learn what it takes mentally before learning the physical side and you will taste success. That is what Earl Woods did, he prepared his son Tiger by teaching him how to deal with the distractions of being the best in the world when he was only twelve years old.

I'm going to teach you how to build a strong mind.

Steve Foxall

Chapter 2: Learning to Fail

Bruce Lee *From the Art of Expressing the Human Body*

"Bruce had me up to three miles a day, really at a good pace. We'd run the three miles in twenty-one or twenty-two minutes. Just under eight minutes a mile. Note: when running on his own in 1968, Lee would get his time down to six-and-a half minutes per mile. So this morning he said to me "We're going to go five." I said, "Bruce, I can't go five. I'm a helluva lot older than you are, and I can't do five." He said, "When we get to three, we'll shift gears and it's only two more and you'll do it." I said "Okay, hell, I'll go for it."

So we get to three, we go into the fourth mile and I'm okay for three or four minutes, and then I really begin to give out. I'm tired, my heart's pounding, I can't go any more and so I say to him, "Bruce if I run anymore," and we're still running "if I run any more I'm liable to have a heart attack and die." He said, "Then die."

It made me so mad that I went the full five miles. After-
ward I went to the shower and then I wanted to talk to
him about it. I said, you know, "Why did you say that?" He
said, "Because you might as well be dead. Seriously, if you
always put limits on what you can do, physical or any-
thing else, it'll spread over into the rest of your life. It'll
spread into your work, into your morality, into your entire
being. There are no limits. There are plateaus, but you
must not stay there, you must go beyond them. If it kills
you, it kills you. A man must constantly exceed his level."

That's a great story, and an important one. Bruce Lee's work on the mental side of fighting was groundbreaking, and while there's no opponent in the gym, mental strength is needed in taking your body to and past failure. When we all start lifting, the concept of failure equates to "doing as many as you can." As you gain more experience and devote time to your new hobby you will learn that failure is a concept that goes way beyond that simple definition.

WHY WE NEED TO FAIL IN ORDER TO GROW

First let's quickly look at why "failure" is important. Why can't we just do ten reps and move on? It all has to do with our survival mechanism. Our bodies come equipped with it, to protect us, it's our house alarm that tells the brain when something is wrong. It prepares us for what's to come and is the basis for adaptation. In a nutshell, our bodies believe that whatever we do, we will have to do again.

I'll give you an example, if you want to lose fat and, like so many others, you decide to starve yourself and eat salad all day, here's what happens. Your body will assume that you are stuck in the middle of nowhere and have no access to food.

Seeing as you constantly need energy to allow your organs and brain to function, your body will start breaking down the protein in your muscles in order to use it for energy. Why? Within this mechanism is a belief that fat is essential, far more essential than muscle. If you're stuck somewhere and starving, fat will keep you alive, what do you need muscle for? As a result, your salad diet will result in less muscle and the same amount of fat. Also, once you do eat fat, say a late night pizza, your body will purposely store every ounce of fat from that pizza because it thinks you will continue to starve.

Here's another example. If you've got a big night out coming and you want to look good, it helps to make sure you're not holding water, that you're not "bloated." How do we get rid of water? *Drink lots of water.* The more you drink, the more your body thinks you will drink, and it will make room for all that water by getting rid of what you already have. When you don't drink a lot of water, your body does the opposite and hangs on to what it has because you need water to live.

You get the idea. So what does this have to do with muscle growth? Here it is. When we lift weight, we actually damage our muscles, we cause the fibers within them to tear. The better you become at lifting, the more efficient you will become at making this happen. How do our bodies react? They repair the muscle using the protein we eat, because protein is basically what muscles are made of. That's fine and post repair you will have the same amount of muscle. But, remember our principle, your body believes that what you do in the gym today, you will likely have to do again. If you go to failure, or beyond failure, your body should think that the muscle you have now is not capable of handling the stress that it will be dealing with. In that case, once the muscle is repaired, it will want to build more.

There is a constant debate in bodybuilding as to how hard you have to work a muscle to trigger this process and it's pretty tough for any scientist to nail it down. I've always trained with the mindset that your brain should believe that you "failed", It's the way most lifters think and it will certainly work. Unless your body has a reason to want more muscle, why would it force growth?

So if you do your sets of bicep curls and manage to take it all the way to the point where your mind believes that you couldn't complete what you needed to do, and more importantly, what you will continue to be required to do, it will build you a bigger bicep. Assuming of course that you eat properly and get adequate rest.

That's it, that's why we grow. That's why cyclists have massive legs and no upper body, that's why gymnasts have huge shoulders and triceps and that's why the world arm wrestling champ has one big-ass forearm. Our bodies evolve in order to perform the physical activity they are continually asked to complete.

WHAT OUR MINDS NEED TO DO IN THE GYM

When it comes to training the mind, your goal should be to increase your ability to focus on the task at hand. In order to increase your focus, you have to essentially shut down your mind, you have to learn how to turn it off, not on. You want to eliminate your thoughts from the equation. Our thoughts create limits, they distract us and can easily control the outcome of any situation. Bruce Lee wrote constantly about not thinking and emptying your mind while fighting. When Tiger sinks that putt to win a tournament it's because of his ability to eliminate all of his thoughts about the pressure, the crowd, the cameras, the "what ifs." What if I miss? What if I fail? Think of the place kicker trying to win the game for all his teammates. The soccer player taking a penalty kick to win the world cup and the goalie trying to stop it. Having the ability to block everything out and not have it affect your performance is crucial for any top athlete, or successful business person or salesperson for that matter.

It doesn't take long in the gym to realize how negative thoughts can take over your workout, especially when you use too much weight. You take the bar off the rack and immediately you doubt your ability to lift it, you can't help it, those thoughts just creep in. You discover that once those thoughts of doubt creep in your set is basically over. You didn't come anywhere close to reaching physical failure.

Back when I started, I trained with my buddy Jeff. Did we make the mistake of using too much weight? Of course, we made every mistake. We would go to the gym and hop on the bench press, probably every third workout. We had this goal of pressing two plates (225 pounds) and we tried over and over and over. Why did we keep failing? Because neither of us believed we could lift it. Another mistake we made was using that specific exercise. The bench press is probably the toughest lift for the mind to crack. Especially when you're trying to reach a certain weight instead of just focusing on getting good strong muscle contractions. You start to bring the bar down and those negative thoughts creep in, the doubt starts and by the time the bar hits your chest, you don't have a chance. Want proof? Once we managed to lift it, with a whole bunch of squirming and kicking, we quickly got up to 235 and 245. Look at powerlifters, talk about having the ability to block out those negative thoughts, they've mastered it!

Arnold once said, "The mind always gives up before the body." It's a pretty simple quote and it's been repeated thousands of times. Why am I using it? Because I don't agree with it. I used to, it made perfect sense because at the gym, my mind always gave up first, as will yours. One of the biggest mistakes we make is not realizing soon enough that we have to learn to control our minds before we can use it to go past failure and build muscle.

So while Arnold is 99% right, we don't ever want to limit ourselves and ignore what we are capable of, it's a mistake. Think about it, your body does what your brain tells it to and doubt creates fear in your mind, and fear always gets in the way of lifting. So what's possible? How far you can take it? Can your body really outlast your mind, can it win the battle?

The answer is yes, but it's very rate and never easy. Have you ever watched a triathlon on TV, maybe the Ironman in Hawaii? I always watch it whenever it happens to be on. When they get to the end of the race and start showing competitors approaching the finish line you see exactly what I'm talking about. It's called hitting the wall, bonking, and it happens to the best of them. It's basically the body giving up because the mind is shutting it down. It's the self-defense mechanism saying "No more!" Some competitors call it a day but some keep going. They crawl to that finish line, they try and walk on legs of jello. They are in incredible pain but they simply refuse to let their minds stop even though their bodies are physically unable to function. They find a way to block it all out and get into this magical zone that many athletes speak of. The networks love to show it because it speaks to how hard the race is.

I watch the Tour de France every year, especially the climbing stages. It just blows me away that they can climb mountains at that speed, with so little oxygen for hours. Drugs or no drugs, it's remarkable. But again, you see instances where the legs just stop and the rider overcomes it. The mental strength of these athletes is as trained and developed as their skills on the bike.

Anyone who competes and is among the best in the world at what they do will tell you that the mental training is crucial and extremely demanding, it makes them the athlete they are.

On a much lower scale, I experienced this in a mountain bike race that's held in the town where I live. It's called the Paris to Ancaster race. It's kind of a famous race among riders and we always get top racers and Olympians competing. It's 70 km through crazy terrain and because it's held at the end of winter you can get snow, hail, cold rain and always lots and lots of mud. I like riding so I've done it a few times. The race ends with a nasty climb that finishes right across the street from where I live. On this Sunday I was trying to break three hours and knew I was close. The weather was terrible. At one point, it was snowing sideways. I was covered in mud from head to toe, cold and wet and of course, tired and hungry! But I knew my son and daughter were waiting for me at the top of the hill with cameras in hand ready to congratulate their dad. As I approached the start of the climb my right leg cramped up and it hurt like hell, I couldn't move it. This is usually where most riders get off their bikes and start walking and the ones with cramps just move to the side and stretch. If my hobby didn't happen to be lifting, then I'm sure I would've done the same. Instead, I did what I do in the gym, I blocked out the pain and I somehow forced my body to work, I imagined a set of leg presses and needing to get more reps. I looked at the ground in front of me and just pedaled. There was no way my kids were going to see me walk up that hill, not on this day, failure in my mind was not an option. As painful as it was, I made it to the top and beat my three hour target. We can all amaze ourselves, every single one of us.

Chapter 3: Create Your Environment

"I'm not out there sweating for three hours every day just to find out what it feels like to sweat."

Michael Jordan

I like this quote. MJ was a very unique athlete in that he too raised the bar in his sport. He wrote a small book titled, "I Can't Accept Not Trying." I've had a copy for years. A couple of weeks ago I gave it to my son Matthew and sat down with him to read it. It's a reminder of what hard work gets you and how you need to set goals and be focused on what it takes to achieve them. It's about the importance of practice, hours and hours of practice. It's a great little book.

You want to know how to increase your ability to focus, to control your thoughts and in turn, your body? Lots and lots of practice, but as I mentioned before, you need "effective" practice in order to get better. The best coaches all know how to have 'effective" practices, but in the gym, you're the coach, so let's talk about how to make your practice effective.

The first step I want to talk about is creating an environment where effective practice is possible. Look at the pros in all of sport, where do they practice? On the court or out on the ice, the field, the track, the road or in the ring. It's just them, the coaches and their teammates. Where do we practice? In a gym full of all kinds of people and all kinds of distractions.

People talking, walking around texting, grabbing weight off your rack while you're doing your heaviest set, asking for a spot, trying to pick up and even dancing. It's a gong show! Imagine Lebron having to practice in that environment, he'd lose his mind! So how do you have a hope in hell of blocking all of that out?

If you're going to devote time to working out and spend your hard-earned money on supplements and food, then this is essential to ensuring your time and money aren't being wasted. It may seem intense, but if you're going to set aggressive goals for yourself and you want to see significant progress, then this is what it takes.

1. Partners and Friends
2. Crowds
3. Music
4. Phones
5. Talking
6. Clothes
7. Plan Ahead

Partners and Friends

Ever since my first year of working out, I've trained alone. I think that's one of the reasons I've had a lot of success making progress. While it's a pretty standard practice to have a training partner or to work out with your friends, it can be very difficult to find someone who is equally driven, as experienced and whose schedule matches yours. The gym, at least to me, is an escape, a place where I can focus on the weights and nothing else. A partner means talking, it means lots of talking and it can be very distracting. Some will say a partner is motivating because you drive each other but you shouldn't need anyone else to drive you, it should come from within. The other issue is that we are all very competitive, especially guys, and with a partner or group of friends, we tend to try and out-lift each other. If you can bench 240, then so can I, etc. This takes you back to lifting with your ego and that gets you nowhere.

If you look at the positives and negatives, it should be pretty clear that a partner will only hurt your ability to focus and become better.

Crowds

When do you train? I ask because it makes a big difference. That list of distractions above is no exaggeration, and it varies depending on what time you're at the gym. If you're at a busy gym, then any time after work until around nine in the evening the distraction level is maxed out. Lunch time? Better, but probably pretty high then too. Ninety percent of the time I'm at the gym between six and nine in the morning. Sure the gym might be a little busy but the folks that get up early and go are more serious about lifting, they're more driven and they are there to train, not to socialize, not to impress.

I can't stand training when it's packed, it drives me crazy because I have to work that much harder to focus, to block everything out. I can't rely on any machine being available so I can't plan my workout. Dumbbells are everywhere and there are groups of friends just hanging out talking and laughing. I can't imagine having to lift in that environment every day, it would be hopeless. The bottom line is that if you are serious about making any progress with your lifting, then you're going to have to get your ass out of bed in the morning or find another time when it's quiet.

Music

This is a no-brainer, you need your headphones and here's why. First, you're trying to block everything out in a room full of people and sounds you can't control. You don't want to hear that idiot talking behind you about the girl he supposedly picked up on the weekend or that woman complaining about her job. You would be surprised by how little it takes to stop your set far too early. Once your mind focuses on that sound, just for a split second, it's not focusing on the task at hand.

Second, you're trying to learn how to empty your mind and stop those negative thoughts from creeping in. One of my tricks is to focus on the music. I don't mean just listen, I mean focus, hear every note, every lyric, the beat, the sounds in the background. I get in complete sync with the song and then I lift. When my mind is that focused on the song, it's not thinking about being tired or how many reps I can do. You shut down your brain and just lift.

Now I've been lifting for a while so the technique is automatic. I know it's tougher for exercises where you're still building muscle memory.

Consider your playlist carefully. If you look on the bodybuilding forums you see guys listing all of their favorite workout tunes. Typically is pretty hardcore rock. Sure, we have our favorite songs that get us going and motivate us but keep in mind that your music needs to help you focus, take you to a place where you can excel and take your muscles to their limit. The rhythm in the songs can help the rhythm in your lifting. Some of my favorites are ones that were used in tribute videos on YouTube because my mind associates the song with the motivating videos. There are days when I'll listen to slower music for the whole session and it is just as effective. I also like to throw in some of those motivational speech compilations. All I'm saying is that you can try different types of songs rather than just relying on the hardest music you have

One last tip, get headphones that stay on your head. I could never get used to the ear buds, maybe it's just the shape of my ears but they would never stay in. Now I wear a set that covers my whole ear. This is better for me as I never have to worry about them falling out and they do a much better job of blocking out the noise in the gym. Try it out.

Phones

For me, this is an easy one. Unless you need to check if for important calls, leave it in the gym bag or even better, in the car. I see people constantly texting between sets and I just don't get it. Your time in the gym should always be an escape, and once you make it an escape it becomes much more rewarding.

I depend on it to help get rid of stress, to shut out the world for an hour and just lift. As long as you're texting, you aren't putting anything on hold.

Pro athletes wouldn't think of texting while practicing. Act like a pro. Your mind needs to be focused on the next set, your form, which weight you should use. You need to spend that time convincing yourself that you can lift the weight, you need to remove any doubt. Think about what golfers do before every shot, they all go through their routine, of course, but in their heads they're convincing themselves that they can make the shot, they're visualizing the flight of the ball and where it will land. They're eliminating doubt. They do this before every single shot in every round. Imagine if instead of going through that mental routine they spent the time checking their messages—that's essentially what everyone in the gym is doing with their phone. Just try leaving it in the car, and you'll see a major difference in your workout.

Talking

Headphones help, but it's still worth mentioning the issue of talking. When I go to the gym it's usually at the same time early in the morning. As a result, I tend to always see the same people. At the start of my workout I look around and nod to the people I always nod to. I say hi to whoever is in my area, make a couple funny comments and take some abuse from the boys. I get it done right at the start before I put my headphones on. I do this because once I start training, it's all business, and the last thing I want to do is strike up a conversation with someone halfway through my back workout. You might say to yourself "Oh, I'll just go say hi to Joey in between sets" and before you know it, he's telling you this ten minute story about how someone rear-ended his car. I'll see guys go up to women and start talking to them and they go on and on and on while she's in the middle of her workout. Then when that guy leaves another one pops up. It always amazes me how polite women are and how inconsiderate these guys are. All I'm saying is one long conversation can easily ruin a good workout so get it out of the way, put on your head-phones and train. If someone says something, just make like you're really pushed for time.

Clothing

Here's a constant I've witnessed in all my years of training: stupid outfits. Now I'm not about to tell you I never took part. In university I wore some crazy shit and I must have looked like an idiot. Remember, It's the mistakes you make that teach you how to do things right. Your task is to focus on the lifting and nothing else, so don't wear something that will distract your thoughts. There was this guy at my gym wearing a t-shirt that he cut up from the armpit to the waist, you could see his whole upper body. Some guys wear sweatshirts with big holes all over them, or tiny bright yellow tank tops.

Now you can wear whatever you want but what I'm saying is that if you're thinking about what you're wearing and what other peo-ple think of it, then you're not focusing on the weights. I'm not going to get into what the girls wear (or what they don't wear for that matter) but the same rule definitely applies to you. If you're comfortable in it then fine, otherwise stick to the basics.

Plan Ahead

It's a fifteen minute drive to my gym. I already know what body part I'm working because I'm pretty strict about following my split. What I need to determine is exactly what I'm going to do that day. You should have it planned out in your head. This way you're not in there walking around staring at machines to see what looks good. This is another crucial reason to train when the gym isn't too busy.

When you know exactly what you want to accomplish, you can walk in and get at it. If something isn't available then find an alternative and focus on getting it done. I see people get frustrated when a machine is taken and it's six o'clock at night, what do you expect? They walk around waiting for ten minutes all flustered when they should be training.

Know what muscle group you want to train and what types of moves you want to focus on. Don't let yourself get distracted or frustrated, just get it done.

With these tips under your belt, you can easily create the right environment for your mind to get to work.

Chapter 4: Discover Your Zone

"There were probably about five games in my career where everything was moving in slow motion and you could be out there all day, totally in the zone, and you don't even know where you are on the field, everything is just totally blocked out."

Lawrence Taylor

Only a handful of bodybuilders have won the Mr. Olympia contest, and they all trained with different styles. Dorian Yates created the "Blood and Guts" style of training, which involves working your way up to one heavy set to failure per exercise. He believed that once you took a muscle to failure with one good set, the job was done and there was no point in repeating it, doing so would just hamper your recovery. His workouts were short but certainly did the job. Jay Cutler swears by the opposite, he trains at a very fast pace, completing dozens of sets and exercises without going extremely heavy. Ronnie Coleman was also different, he believed that while many lifters contemplated between volume and heavy weights, he did both. He lifted mind boggling amounts and still managed to keep his reps fairly high. Back in the day, Arnold and his buddies would train for hours working every body part twice a week.

The point here is that there is no set way to get big, and don't listen to anyone who tells you there is. In a world where everyone is selling the latest and greatest 'secret' to get big, people eventually find what works for them and a large part of why it works is their consistent commitment, not some magic formula.

There are however, several common elements to all the different styles and one of them is "the zone." When you watch the videos of these guys and girls lifting, you can see them get into that zone, you can see the focus and the concentration. It's no different than watching Usain Bolt getting ready to run the two hundred or J.J. Watt in pregame warm-up. This is something you can practice—it's not just for the pros.

Discovering your zone is like discovering your favorite way to train, it's what works for you. The only advice I can give you is that it is crucial. Create a mental state that allows you to push your body to where it normally wouldn't be able to go. This isn't something you do on every set, it would be far too taxing. Typically, in a given workout, you might have four to six sets where you want to do everything possible to reach physical failure.

Here's an example from my own routine. Let's say I'm doing leg press. It takes me quite a few sets to work my way up as I try to avoid large weight increases between sets. The sets aren't very difficult physically. Mentally I'm just focusing on engaging the outside of my quads both on the positive and negative portions of each rep.

Once I've worked my way up to a heavy weight, I'll do two very intense sets, the latter being a drop set. Both take incredible concentration.

So here we go, I have my headphones on and turned up, I grab a drink and then I sit down somewhere close to the press and I stare at it. I know I can lift the chosen weight—that should never be an issue, my focus is on *not* stopping. I visualize getting into a good rhythm and then I remind myself why I'm doing this, why I want to keep going. I convince myself that I'm stronger than the weight and that I can do as many reps as I want. I stand up, hop in the sled and get ready.

I usually let out a big "YUP" as I take control of the weight and I start the set. I pick a spot on the wall and I stare at it. The weight keeps moving and all I'm focused on is keeping my body very tight, and making my legs do all the work. As I reach five or six reps and I'm in a good rhythm, I distract my mind. I usually do this by continuing to stare at the spot and focusing on the music. I'll start listening to the vocals and the instruments as if I was right there at the concert. It might sound strange but as I already mentioned, if I'm focusing on the music, I'm not thinking of stopping, I'm not thinking about the pain and how many reps I should be able to do. I block out all of those negative thoughts and I just keep contracting the muscles. This goes on for as long as it can, until something in my mind breaks and my legs just stop moving. At that point I have no idea how many reps I did, only that I did as many as I could.

When I do the drop set, everything is the same only it's much harder because I have to get up and strip some weight, hop back in and find my zone again. The leg press drop set is one of the hardest things I do in the gym. It's a lot harder to do twenty reps with 10 plates than it is 10 reps with 12. Distracting your mind is definitely a key element. The leg press is a great move for practicing this because there isn't a whole lot of technique involved, or risk, as opposed to the squat for example.

Use simple exercises with manageable weight to practice getting into a zone where you can stay positive and experience reaching mental failure.

Think about marathon runners and how they take their minds completely away from the running. They don't have to focus on running because their bodies are so used to it. By taking their minds out of the equation, they aren't thinking about how tired they are or how much farther they have to run, or the pain in their legs and feet. If they concentrated on just running for all that time they would never last.

There are a lot of times when I finish one of those sets and I just sit there in awe of what I did, in awe of how far I took myself and that I did reach complete failure. It's not an easy thing to learn by any means, it is the summation of many parts, a recipe with a big list of ingredients. Once you master this, you will have a come a long way, and you will be in a much better position to control your progress. Find your zone, your escape, and push it, push it at some point every single time you train.

Block out negative thoughts or doubt for as long as you can. Eventually, when you can block them out completely, you will have a chance to reach complete muscular failure, as opposed to just mental failure.

Chapter 5: Build Your Confidence

"You have to feel confident. I you don't, then you're going to be hesitant and defensive, and there will be a lot of things working against you."

Clint Eastwood

Not too long ago, The Toronto Maple Leafs were in the playoffs, a rarity. It was a do-or-die game 7 against the Bruins in what would become a heart breaker for Leafs fans everywhere. Before the game started I was in the kitchen making dinner and Canadian sports commentator Ron MacLean was talking to his co-host Don Cherry about pressure. He brought up the final round of the Player's Championship from the day before. Tiger Woods was leading and Sergio Garcia was right there with him. Up comes the famous 17th green that is surrounded by water, one of the biggest and most interesting tests in golf. Sergio proceeds to put two shots in the water and blow any chance of winning. Tiger nails it and wins the tournament. What caught my ear was Ron's comment:

**"Under pressure, you will always
sink to the level of your training."**

I thought it was a great line because he wasn't talking about physical training. Sergio can hit a golf ball better than most with his eyes closed. MacLean was referring to the mental game. How well your mind is trained determines how well you perform under pressure.

It was some pretty impressive foresight as the game to follow demonstrated his point to a tee. Toronto had a three goal lead half way through the third period, pretty much a slam dunk in hockey. As Boston scored the first of their comeback goals, a very young Leafs team was suddenly under tremendous pressure and they essentially choked. Boston went on to win 5-4 in overtime. Back to Tiger, a main reason he was always so tough to beat was that he created that pressure, mounds of it. He brought everyone's game down to a level of their training, and nobody's mental training was as good as his.

One of the main things that having that mental training can give you is confidence. Why? Because it teaches you how to focus under pressure, how to block everything out and how to rely on the fundamentals, the foundation you know you have. Sergio could hit that shot and get it on the green 99 times out of 100, but take away the confidence, even for a few seconds, and doubt creeps in, then you question those fundamentals and you don't perform at your best. Confidence under pressure separates us.

If lifting for all these years has taught me anything, it's the impact having confidence in yourself can have. It determines so much in every part of our lives. School, work, relationships, parenting, it can determine the outcome of all our pursuits. Having confidence means you won't limit yourself, you will set tougher goals for yourself and your family, and perhaps your employees. It means you can get up in front of five hundred people and give a kick-ass presentation. It means you can land the job when the other three candidates are better qualified. It means you can lose weight, run a half-marathon, start a company or even enter a bodybuilding contest. It is an invaluable tool that I keep drilling into my children's minds.

So how do we get it? Where does it come from? Early on in life it's labeled as self-esteem. It controls how we feel about ourselves and these days it's tough. Social media and bullying can take it away in an instant, and it can take years to rebuild. I honestly can't imagine going through school in today's world.

Most of my confidence was built and tested at the gym. In my earlier life it was an even bigger escape for me and in university especially I trained every day of the week. We all have a natural tendency to migrate to the environments where we feel confident in ourselves because it's where we feel good. Sometimes I wonder how I managed to stay away from steroids back then but when you don't talk to the other lifters and you don't have any money to try things then I guess you just stick to what you know. I can't emphasize enough how you need to develop this confidence, and I'm sure it's harder today than ever. I believe that you too can find yours in the gym. Just working out constantly won't do it, though. Confidence builds when we succeed and it breaks down when we fail. In order to succeed we need targets, we need goals, something to measure our success by. In sales, targets are always set, weekly, monthly, annually. You are always measured against your peers in order to build motivation, reward top producers and punish those who fall short. Jack Welsh, long time CEO of General Electric used to fire the bottom five percent of his workforce every year, regardless of how good they were. He felt that this way, his team would continually get better and stronger. Every year it became harder and harder to do, but as a result of the practice, everyone got better.

Now this is the tricky part. Most would say that their targets are to bench or curl a certain amount of weight but that leads to "ego" training. What's the point in squirming your way to a two plate bench when your technique sucks? Success should be measured by how well you lift, not how much.

Here are some sample goals that I once set for myself:

Do five sets of deadlifts for at least six reps keeping perfect form.

Do one hundred reps of squats to parallel, in as many sets as it takes.

Master using your abs to help when doing chest, so that they're sore the next day.

Do two drop sets after five sets on the Leg Press.

Consistently train hamstrings before quads using at least twelve sets.

Have an amazing arm workout using light weight.

Train your front and rear delts with as much intensity as you use in your chest workouts.

Eliminate all negative thoughts in a workout.

Convince yourself you can complete every set before it starts.

Don't get distracted, throughout your whole workout, not for a second.

Learn how to pull with the different parts of your back.

Any goals you set for yourself in life need to be challenging, yet achievable. They need to be set consistently so that they allow for success but require that you push yourself in order to realize it. None of the goals involve weight, but they all have something in common, if achieved they will all make you better, and that's progress. The weight you lift should always be considered a result of how good you are, not how strong you are. In other words...

Your physical strength is a by-product of your skill and your ability to focus your mind.

I'm asked all the time about weight loss and I always tell people not to set weight goals because they're self-defeating. You're trying to lose fat, not weight. Your goals should be how far you walk or run, how many days a week you can follow your diet. Making it all the way to your cheat meal without one dessert. If you meet all of these goals, you'll lose fat and your tight jeans won't be as tight. Your progress will push you to keep setting goals and doing what it takes to meet them.

Now that you have some proper goals, you have a purpose in the gym, you're not just there to look good and impress those around you. Achieving these goals will build your confidence, as a result, you will set tougher goals, you will start to really push yourself. We all feed off of our successes and it motivates us to work harder, to see what we're capable of. So how do we achieve the goals?

1. Knowledge
2. The Weight
3. Visualization
4. Focus

Knowledge

Learn how to do things right, do your research. You can be studying for school, at work managing a project or at home trying to lose ten pounds—always find out what you need to do and then determine the best possible way to go about doing it.

Dorian Yates won the Mr. Olympia title six times, but the first thing he did before he even started training seriously was spend a year researching everything he could in order to learn how to train properly. Routines, technique, nutrition, anatomy, muscle growth. He knew that without the research, he would be blind. Once he had the knowledge, he committed 100% and his progress was constant taking him right to the top. He even created his own training style based on his research. In anything we try to accomplish, knowledge is always the base of our confidence, it is the foundation we build on.

The Weight

Creating confidence means lifting in a way that allows you to maintain positive thoughts, even when performing your heaviest sets. Put another way, you need to eliminate doubt, doubting your ability in any situation will significantly diminish any chance of success. There are a number of tips I can give you that will allow you to train in a way that best allows your mind to stay positive.

Remember the environment you need to create in order to practice lifting effectively? This is very similar only it deals with your mind. We need to create an environment where your mind can stay positive. One where you can practice blocking out and eliminating those negative thoughts and the accompanying doubt. After, we'll push it a step farther and talk more about creating a "Zone" where you can then find out exactly what you're capable of by putting your mind in a place where your body can perform at its best.

By far the most important factor in creating this environment is the weight you use. I know I've talked about eliminating your ego and always using manageable weight but this is much more specific, it's about the exact amount of weight you need to use. Starting from your warm-up set you need to immediately eliminate your ego's need to use as many 45 pound plates as possible. The plates you use need to be determined by feel, and not be packed on for show.

How the weight "feels" is crucial in believing you can move it, if it feels too heavy, then doubt will immediately set in. Most of the time, the weight feels too heavy because of the increase from the last set. Let me explain.

We've all seen the strongman competitions on TV. When they lift the big round stones they start small and go up in small increments until they reach the biggest stone. In your mind, each stone is only a little bit heavier than the last so there's no reason you can't lift it. It also doesn't feel a lot heavier than the previous stone and sometimes it even feels the same. Now if they were suddenly asked to start with the smallest and then immediately move to the heaviest, a lot of them wouldn't be able to lift it. The big stone would feel extremely heavy and there would be more doubt because it is such a big jump from the previous one.

Relating that to our own workouts, we're going to look at squats. I see it all the time, people use great technique for their warm-up set and the following set but then they start to pack on the weight, they throw on two plates a side and then three plates a side. As soon as there is a big jump in weight they're unable to take it down to parallel. They don't trust their legs to do it because the bar feels far too heavy. They give up good technique in exchange for using big weight. Now if you work your way up in small increments, ensuring you can always get down to parallel like you did in your warm-up, then you're starting to push your quads and you are definitely having a better training session.

Every time I train I'm always grabbing ten pound plates. Aside from the leg press and deadlifts, I almost always go up in ten pound increments. I don't care how many sets it takes me to reach my maximum, that gradual method ensures I'll keep positive and never doubt my ability to move the weight. Try it the next time you train, start small and go up small increments, no big jumps. You'll experience a huge difference.

I know what you're thinking, in order to get big you have to lift big, you have to move crazy weight like the pros do. How can you get big legs from squatting only two plates? Tell you what, try to find one video where a pro does half-squats. Getting big is a result of pushing your muscle fibers, and in order to do that you have to use proper form. If you don't, your joints are getting the workout, not your muscles, and your joints are big enough already.

The second you give up form for weight,
you immediately begin wasting your time.

Visualization

One of the best sprinters we've ever seen was known for his concentration. American Michael Johnson would stand behind the blocks, as they all do, and visualize the whole race, every step. You could see his mind working, it was impressive. Then he would get into the blocks and keep visualizing, his head would lift and all you saw were these two incredibly focused eyes. Once he visualized what he was about to do and he had 100% confidence in his ability to do it, there was a pretty good chance he was winning that race.

In the gym, this is very often a missed opportunity. What do you do between sets? Look around, get a drink, talk to your buddy. What you should be doing is focusing on the next set, setting up the bar, machine or grabbing your dumbbells and getting them ready. Go through it all in your mind. How far can you push your muscles? What part of your form are you focusing on, picture yourself actually lifting and imagine the rhythm. Arnold always referred to his bicep workouts where he would imagine they were as big as mountains. He would close his eyes and picture these massive arms in between sets and even during sets. Lately, I always focus on keeping my body tight, my core, my legs, everything, so that only the muscles I want to work are working. It's almost like I'm a machine, an engine, and my muscles move like pistons in perfect rhythm. I hate when sets get sloppy, staying tight makes me feel strong, solid, and always in control of the weight.

Visualization can be a very powerful tool that you should be accustomed to using consistently when you train. Say you're between sets on the bench press. One day, you decide to check your phone and answer some texts or emails and your mind focuses on whatever it is you're typing, or what the person on the other end wants. Then you put it down, grab some more weight, hop on the bench and lift. The next set, you leave your phone on the floor. Between sets you immediately increase the weight, grab a drink and then focus. You take a deep breath and you visualize yourself lifting the weight in rhythm.

You imagine strength and power, you picture yourself in total control of the weight. Without breaking your concentration, you lie down and lift the weights. Training is all about routine so if you choose option A or B and repeat it over and over again, I guarantee you will experience significantly more progress with option B. The more time you spend picturing yourself doing it, the better you will get at convincing your mind you are capable of it, and the better you will get at eliminating those negative thoughts and building confidence. Remember, we are always practicing in the gym, always learning, and always improving. Visualization should be a key component of your practice, and a key contributor to your improvement.

Focus

Here's a good question: how do *you* track your progress with the mental side of training? We all want to track our progress and see improvement, it's what keeps us going. At the end of every set we fail, we get to a point where we can't go on. Either you lost your form, you used too much weight, you didn't focus between sets or you got distracted. You improve by first acknowledging what caused you to fail and then working to eliminate it.

If your form got lost then practice with lighter weight, figure out what you did wrong. If you got distracted then work on your focus, work on getting your mind to lock into the task at hand. If the weight was wrong then get mad at yourself for wasting a set, drop the weight, keep going and don't let it happen again. If you grabbed your phone and texted for ten minutes, you know what I'm going to say next: turn your damn phone off!

If you keep this up and challenge yourself then following the steps will help you develop a stronger mind. Slowly but surely you will get to a point where your sets end because your muscles actually reached, or almost reached failure. Short of some guy tapping on my shoulder with a stupid question, the majority of my sets now end that way.

Improving the mental side of training results in a better ability to focus, more confidence, fewer negative thoughts and fewer mistakes.

Steve Foxall

Chapter 6: Drive, Rage and Deliberate Lifting

``All I want to tell young people is that you're not going to be anything in life unless you learn to commit to a goal. You have to reach deep within yourself to see if you are willing to make the sacrifices."

Louis Zamperini, Devil at My Heels

What drives you to do what you do? Money? That's what drives most of us to work. Life's not cheap and that's what gets us up in the morning. For most sports or hobbies, we do it for pleasure but we also want to improve, we all want to be better. We decide to enter a competition or a race to prove something to ourselves, to feel alive, to have purpose, to say I'm here to do more than just pay bills and die. This drives us to work hard, to train, to sacrifice. The only way I could write this book is to give up sleep, only so many hours in the day. Now when we're done we have this great sense of accomplishment but then we go back to our Netflix and naps on the couch. Well, what about those who always work hard?

There was an NBA All Star game in Toronto, which was great for the city. NBA players are known for having as much fun as anyone in sports and at this event, it was easy to see. Look behind all that fun and what you might see is a court full of the hardest working players in the league. They're not there because they were born with talent, they all busted their ass for years. They work hard all the time...my question is why? Where does it come from? Getting up at 4 to practice before practice and pushing themselves to exhaustion...why? It isn't just the money, I can guarantee you that. It's *drive*, and drive is a huge part of bodybuilding.

Now if we're going to talk drive and work ethic in a book about lifting, we're going to talk about Dwayne Johnson. The Rock is the walking and talking personification of hard work. We all know the story: the dream of playing pro football cut short by injury and being almost good enough. A father on the road wrestling while his mother struggled to keep up, moving them from home to home. Having the car repossessed and a week later, coming home to an eviction notice.

At that point, Dwayne had a couple options. He could let life knock him down for the count, or he could get his ass up and start fighting back. He took option B and the fighting started, and with that, a commitment was made. Since, everything possible was done NOT to fail, to NOT ever be in that situation again. To him that meant never being out-worked.

In 1995 he had $7 in his pocket. In 2015, The Rock brought in somewhere around $30 million. Think about that, if you had a good paying job, a hundred thousand a year, it would take you 300 years to make all that coin. It's more than enough to live off of even with a whole fleet of badass pick-up trucks and a real nice fishing boat. So why *keep* getting up a 4 a.m. to do cardio? Why bust your ass in the gym every day even after working 15 hours straight or flying all night? Why do that last set of heavy squats when most people would have left an hour ago? There's a pretty good chance it's that eviction notice, it's that coach saying sorry, not this year, it's everything that happened. Just imagine the anger, the rage, having some guy kick your mother out of her home. That shit doesn't go away.

There's a reason desperation and the anger it comes with can often lead to great accomplishments. It doesn't just create drive in the moment, it fuels it for years to come. Even after the bad shit is over, you can keep calling on it to keep the fire going. Dwayne isn't the only one to do it, there are thousands of untold stories, just take a look around in the gym and you'll see them, the ones truly getting after it. All you have to do is look at their faces.

What The Rock did was simply take it to a whole new level. There's setting the bar high and then there's climbing a fucking mountain and jammin that sumbitch into the peak, and you can't help but respect the hell out of it. Might not be a bad idea to follow his advice:

"Be humble,
Be hungry,
and always be the
hardest worker in the room."

So let's look around the gym. These guys (and gals) are right there beside you. The ones that constantly lift with a level of intensity that exhausts them, that has them crawling back to their cars—those are the ones who are driven. I'm not talking about the pros here, I'm talking about the ones that are there every Sunday morning at six bangin out sets in the squat rack. What drives *them*? Are you one of them?

Ronnie Coleman is considered by many to be the "best" Mr. Olympia ever. He was just massive and ridiculously strong. In 2004, Ronnie released his second training video, "The Cost of Redemption." In that video he squatted 800 pounds for two reps. Look it up, if you train, you know what a feat that is.

Kai Greene is one of the top bodybuilders to ever compete. I really like Kai, his drive is also a by-product of desperation. I like the way he trains and the professional manner in which he presents himself. He is very philosophical and I can certainly relate to the way he commits himself to the lifestyle. He also teaches others about the tremendous mental commitment required to succeed both in and out of the gym. Kai was being interviewed one day and he talked about Ronnie's squat.

``Ronnie Coleman to me is definitely someone who, you know, is worthy of a tremendous amount of respect. I think the real Ronnie Coleman, though, we most definitely will never be privileged enough to know. Where does a man have to go to put 800 pounds on his back and say "I'm going to squat down to the floor and stand up as many times as I can before I pass out or blow something out, you know, just the rage that would have to be there, in there, inside, that you know, to begin to open up and talk about...*

You tell me where this guy has to go...I said there's violence in there, there's rage. You asked me, "is it violent? Is there rage?" I'm saying I believe there has to be.

There's something else that needs to be motivating you to do that cause there's no way I could do that and say "I'm a nice guy" I might be a real nasty mother behind the scene and I might be ready to really be able to call on that when I need to and that's what makes me proficient at my job, should it be a linebacker, should it be a man outside on the line fighting for the country, should it make me a good cop?, or would it make me a good athlete right now.

I think there's a psychological profiling, if you really explore it, it would probably alarm people to think about it, you know, who this guy must really be, because you can't be just a very normal person to explain, a simple person to understand, with that kind of ability.``

Kai's thoughts are exactly in line with what I believe. Bodybuilding—and powerlifting—require something extra, something deeper that you need to be able to call upon. It's not the work ethic and it's not desire, those are only parts of the equation. To excel, to exceed your expectations and surprise yourself, you need that final piece of the puzzle, and it's in all of us.

In my opinion, to lift and progress you have to bring that something out, whatever it is in your life, your situation, you have to call on it. In today's society, quite often we see people's desperation and anger taken out on other people, everywhere from the highways to the hallways. I guarantee you, unleashing it in the weight room is a much better option. I think it boils down to who you are as a person and why you train in the first place. Outside of the gym I'm one of the most laid back people you will ever meet. In the gym, I need that emotional fuel.

I trained with a lot of rage for years. The stress I had in my life gave me that extra something, it gave me somewhere to go mentally. I befriended the battle. The way a runner loves to run, I loved to lift, but I fought the iron. I'd call upon it again and again, it's what made me do ten reps when I was done after eight, it's what made me add more weight and push myself again and again. It's what made me grow.

This rage can come from all sorts of places and the thing about it is that nobody knows what's inside you, what stories you have to tell. Do you have a bad boss you can't stand? Your parents drive you crazy or your marriage sucks? Tired of having no money, waiting for that paycheck that never goes far enough? The rage I have today is completely different than it was three years ago or ten years ago, it's always evolving. Today I'm happy in my relationship, happy with my work, and amazed by my three children, so what do I have to be angry about? Sometimes now it's hard to get out of bed on those Sunday mornings to train because there's no anger, I'd rather make pancakes and read the paper...so I created some.

Being divorced, as some of you probably know, makes life a whole lot tougher from a financial point of view. I used to have all kinds of money and now we live paycheck to paycheck, and it sucks. So I created a connection. It might not take rage to make you shoot hoops all night or practice your slap shot for hours, but when you're staring at a stacked leg press and you're ready to go home, you need something to get you back in there, so you think about it. You think about how your daughter wanted to go see Taylor Swift but the tickets were too expensive, you think about that cabin you want to rent in the summer to get away with your wife but you can't afford it. You hear everyone else talking about their trips south and you get all kinds of angry and then you lift. You lift with everything you have because you need to do a show for your book, and the book is your shot. It's plan a, b, c and d...it's all you have, and you can't fail and sleep is something you are definitely willing to give up.

So where does your rage come from? My point is that we all have it, we all have something. Life's a bitch and you need to be able to bring it out. As Kai said, "Where does a man have to go?" What he means is, where do you have to go mentally in order to do what you have to do to achieve your goals? This applies to everyone, even if all you want to do is build some bigger arms or lose ten pounds, write a book or get that promotion at work. I see so many people in the gym that lift with no enthusiasm or intent. They do ten reps when they could probably do thirty.

I use the term *deliberate lifting*. It's an attitude, it's something I try to use every time I train. It's focusing 100% on beating the weight, it's pushing as hard as you can push to keep it moving. It's an attitude that you can't be defeated, that you're stronger than the machine or the bar. Simply put, you're the boss, you decide when you can't lift anymore, you don't answer to the weight, it answers to you. Lifting this way is very hard, it drains you both physically and mentally, and to do it consistently requires drive, drive that's fueled by some kind of emotion, and for many, that emotion is rage, it's anger, it's the desperation in all of us.

I encourage you to try it, to get angry, find that rage, let it build and then take it out on the weight, you will surprise yourself, and you will feel amazing after you do it, I guarantee it. Befriend the battle!

Steve Foxall

Chapter 7: Challenge Yourself

Kobe Bryant - *This is such BS! All the training and sacrifice just flew out the window with one step that I've done millions of times! The frustration is unbearable. The anger is rage. Why the hell did this happen?!? Makes no damn sense. Now I'm supposed to come back from this and be the same player Or better at 35?!? How in the world am I supposed to do that?? I have NO CLUE. Do I have the consistent will to overcome this thing? Maybe I should break out the rocking chair and reminisce on the career that was. Maybe this is how my book ends. Maybe Father Time has defeated me...Then again maybe not!*

Stop feeling sorry for yourself, find the silver lining and get to work with the same belief, same drive and same conviction as ever. One day, the beginning of a new career journey will commence. Today is NOT that day.

"If you see me in a fight with a bear, prey for the bear". I've always loved that quote. That's "mamba mentality" we don't quit, we don't cower, we don't run. We endure and conquer.

Kobe Bryant tore his Achilles during a game. It was, as he puts it, a step he'd taken millions of times. He turned to social media and posted the great paragraph above. What I love about his quote is that it provides us with insight into how he is thinking. It is one of the few things I can appreciate about social media, one of the very few things. Maybe this is the end and maybe it's not. For an average player, this injury just means six to nine months of recovery, but for Kobe, it means having to work twice as hard to get back to a level that he demands of himself, a level that makes him the best. That's twice as hard for someone who already works harder than anyone else. That's the challenge, that's the mentality.

If you see me in a fight with a bear, pray for the bear, don't quit, don't cower, don't run, endure and conquer.

So far we covered off how you need to fail in order to grow, how failure convinces your mind that you need more muscle to cope with the workouts. We talked about creating an environment where you can focus, how to build the confidence you need to learn and improve. We talked about the zone and what it takes to push yourself through sets, and lastly, we covered the drive and how you need to learn how to take your mind to a place where you can do what needs to be done.

Now by this time, you're either so motivated to get your ass to the gym and get after it with some mad rage...or you're saying to yourself, "Great, but I just like working out."

The thing is, anybody can just work out. There are plenty of people going through the motions and looking the part, I see them every day. The question is, do you want progress, do you want to make change? I'm going to guess that if you're reading a book about bodybuilding, you're aiming to change the way you look and feel.

I can tell you this with 100% certainty, your goals will remain goals until you decide to challenge yourself. I'm doing everything within my power to give you the tools you need to do it, but you still have to do it.

It's a lesson that follows us all through life. If you want to accomplish anything, you need to make that commitment. One of my close friends growing up always struggled with math. He hated it, because it always took so much more work and thought. All through school he struggled until he'd had enough. One day he challenged himself. He was going to conquer math in order to get the degree he needed and the job he wanted. He lived in the library for months while everyone else was partying. He just kept studying the formulas until his brain had no choice but to understand the logic, he basically taught his brain how to think in numbers. He went on to graduate and is now a top city planner in New Brunswick.

Challenging yourself means that you've made a decision to focus on something and put all of your energy into it. It can only come from genuine desire, if you don't really want something, and I mean really want it, then your commitment won't last, you'll give up, you'll give fifty percent instead of one hundred. Here's the key: you have to want it for yourself.

So much of what society does today is based on impressing others. I was having lunch at a restaurant and the woman next to me spent half an hour taking pictures of herself...why? To impress others. Well, the problem with trying to impress others is that you can never win, nowadays everyone judges. It's like when a woman creates an amazing physique and someone says, "She's got too much muscle, I don't find that attractive."'

Do you really think she gives a shit if you find her attractive? Just appreciate what she's done and respect the hard work it took to do it.

People struggle to lose weight because they diet for other people. Ask anyone who actually did it, and they'll all tell you it started the day they decided to do it for themselves, the day it became important to them.

Lifting so you look good for your selfies is a joke. Nobody gives a shit that you work out. Do whatever it is you do because you love it, because you have passion for it, because it makes you feel alive, then, you will welcome the challenge and you will blow yourself away.

Whether it's adding muscle, losing fat, running a marathon or getting that degree, it's all about your commitment. You don't skip workouts or meals, you don't binge on ice cream and if you're scheduled to study, you study. If you're just here to show off bigger arms, then buy tighter t-shirts. If you want to make some serious progress in the gym and you have the desire then I'm telling you what it takes: do it for yourself. Now challenge yourself, put everything you have into it. Then and only then will you get everything you can out of it.

It's funny, you think about someone writing a book and you picture this guy typing away in a sweater sitting in his cabin smoking a pipe. You picture a woman and her Mac sitting in Starbucks drinking a latte. For me, writing a book is a second job. It means getting up at 6 to try to get a few paragraphs in before work and it means passing out at night with my hands on the keyboard. It means taking a pre-workout drink just to get my mind going and sitting on a bench with my laptop while my son has football practice. You give up time, you give up sleep and you give up the all things you'd rather be doing, it's all a matter of what's important to you. I'm going to make this work, period! So I kept pushing, and I kept writing, one page at a time, that was my commitment...what's yours?

Steve Foxall

Chapter 8: Bad Advice

There is no shortage of advice in the fitness industry. More than any other sport, everybody has an opinion, they've all read some article that said you have to do something a certain way in order to get results. There is a constant overload of information that will make your head spin. The problem is that the majority of it won't help you, and the reason it won't help you is that it's usually not based on facts or data. Most articles are written in a way that doesn't let you understand the reasoning behind it. Being in banking for so long, I've always worked with women, and I've listened to them chat about weight loss day after day after day. They would always come in with these new strategies, they'd say they read an article and it said to eat grapefruit every day and they would shed the pounds. I would always ask them why? Why grapefruit? They never had an answer, not once in 16 years could any of them explain the science. Every bit of advice I give you in this book comes from my own experiences, and I try and back it up by explaining why it makes sense. That way, if you tell a friend that you read in my book that something should be done a certain way, you should at least be able to answer the question. Bad advice has become standard, it's become the norm. I'll do this again in the physical section of the book, but for now, let's look at bodybuilding from a mental stand-point.

1. Stick to the Basics
2. Counting Reps
3. Spot Me
4. Muscle Confusion
5. The Journal
6. Overtraining

Stick to the basics

This is probably the most important item on the list. Almost every article out there on "getting big" will tell you that in order to pack on muscle, you have to stick to the basic lifts. These would include the bench press, deadlift, squat and military press. This is true, BUT, only if you are an experienced lifter. If I asked you to rate how difficult a 'basic' exercise is, on a scale of one to ten, how would you rate that exercise? They're pretty simple, grab the bar and lift. You'd probably rate it pretty low. Now if I asked you to rate them on how difficult they are mentally, what would you say? The number should go up.

The basic "powerlifting" exercises are easily the toughest moves you will ever do for your mind. What I mean by that is there will be a greater chance of you doubting your ability to lift the weight than if you were doing a machine for example. This whole section is on how you need to train your mind how to lift. Before you can make any serious improvements, you need con-fidence and the ability to block out negative thoughts.

When Tiger Woods learned to golf he started with the putter and worked his way up to the driver, which he learned how to hit last. Most hackers start with the driver and ignore the putter. While a golf swing is a golf swing, the driver is the toughest shot to hit mentally and usually brings on the highest level of doubt. Once you have the confidence you need to hit your wedges and irons, then you move up to the fairway woods and then the driver. It's the same in any sport, you learn to hit a free throw before you try and master the three point shot, you learn a wrist shot in hockey before you practice the slap shot. Well the squat is like that three pointer, the slap shot and that big bad driver in the golf bag.

There is absolutely no rush to master these moves, remember why your muscles grow? They grow in response to you pushing them to their limit. This can be accomplished using a number of different exercises. Why not train your mind on leg extensions and the leg press? Why not use a good hammer strength chest press or shoulder press? Do pulldowns and seated rows for your back. You need to learn to use the proper weight, contract the muscle and train the mind to focus and have confidence in your ability. All of that can be far better accomplished while staying away from the powerlifting moves. Once you build a foundation, once you master some fundamentals, then you should start bringing the big moves into your repertoire.

Counting Reps

Bodybuilding is very much about limits, at least that's how I see it. Limits exist and are pushed in every sport and every competition. Every time I train my main goal is to push those limits, to improve in some way and to be better than I was the last time I trained. Back when I was trying to learn the fundamentals I would read, but there was a massive amount of repetition in all of the articles I read. I couldn't understand why the pros didn't want to write more, give more insight into what it is they did and why they did it. There was very little depth. It was tough to find anything on the mental side of lifting, the challenges, mistakes being made, what they went through and how to overcome obstacles.

It made sense to me that if something was being repeated over and over then it must be right. Well it wasn't. Counting reps is a perfect example. I can't imagine how many articles I've read on training that recommend doing three sets of ten reps. Over and over and over again.

Here's a story, two summers ago I did a lot of running, Melissa loved to run so even though I found it ridiculously boring, I ran too. I entered a couple races and did horribly. Every time I went out to train I would have a route planned with five, seven or ten kilometers. Each time I ran, regardless of the distance, the last kilometer would always be the same, I would run out of gas. Eventually my gym habits took over and I decided to just run with no route, no plan. I got in the groove, had good rhythm and just kept running, and guess what, I didn't run out of gas. I ran fifteen kilometers and could have easily done twenty except I had to get home and change to pick up the kids. Moral of the story...when you tell your brain you want to do ten reps, you will very rarely do eleven.

Think about this, do you spot people? I haven't given anyone in the gym a spot in a very long time, basically because I have headphones on and always look pretty busy and unavailable. For years I had trouble getting through a session without lending a hand. The one common element when spotting was that every time, the guy would tell me they should be able to squeeze out around five or seven, and that's always as far as they could go. It's the ones that didn't count their reps and just did as many as they could do that would exceed their expectations.

There is a place for counting reps, but until you know how your set is going and how you are managing the weight, you don't know how far you can take it, so why set limits?

Here's what I do. When I start a set, I don't have a number in mind. All of my focus is on ensuring that the intended muscles are doing the work and my body is tight which helps me maintain my form. I focus on getting into a rhythm in order to create a scenario where I can push those limits and do as many reps as possible.

Once I've accomplished all of that, I wait until I reach a point where I'm close to the end, then I start counting. I'll tell myself "three more" and do everything humanly possible to complete those three reps. This way, you aren't starting your set with your mind already convinced of what you can or can't do. This scenario lets you complete your sets without limits, but also uses counting at the end to help push your muscles and your mind as far as they can both go. The bottom line is that three sets of ten to twelve reps is far too simple and neglects all of the crucial elements that any athlete incorporates into repeating and exceeding their previous accomplishments. Give it a shot.

Spot me

This is another big one, and it's unique to the sport. Forced reps. This is something I see all the time, especially with young people. There's a common practice when people workout together or in groups, they always spot each other. Now I'm not saying that safety needs to be ignored, but let me make this simple and clear.

You will not learn to take your muscles to failure while someone else is finishing off your sets for you.

I work out alone and I have for the majority of my years in the gym. I hate having someone spot me and I purposely lift in a manner that helps me avoid it. Think about it, you're trying to learn how to focus your mind so you can squeeze out those last couple of reps once your muscles give-up. When someone helps you with those last reps, then you aren't learning anything. I just don't see how this will help you in any way. If you are doing an exercise that requires a spot for safety reasons then a) You're probably using too much weight and b) they shouldn't touch the bar until you fail, then they should have their hands close to the bar while you try and get another rep or two. For some reason, and again, the magazine articles don't help at all, everyone thinks you need forced reps to grow, it's crazy. If you are just learning how to lift then chances are your buddy is too, and therefore he or she wouldn't know how to properly spot you anyways. Another point is that a lot of times, there is so much weight on the bar that if something did go wrong, there is little that person would be able to do to help.

Experienced lifters use spotters who know exactly how to use forced reps to help their partner push their muscles, and it's not an easy thing to do. You really need to know your partner, and how far they can go. If you watch videos of Dorian Yates, he always used forced reps, but he had an excellent training partner and they were in complete sync. That's a tall order.

As far as mental training goes, developing your ability to focus and block out negative thoughts requires that you be 100% responsible for finishing your sets right to the end. This is where you need to focus the most and it's another reason to learn on exercises that don't require a spot.

Muscle Confusion

This is a well-known principle that I do agree with but in a lot of cases, it's used incorrectly. The concept is that you need to mix things up as your body gets used to the same exercises and routines. I definitely agree that you should mix things up to avoid too much of a routine which can lead to complacency. Where you can go wrong is by constantly trying to find new exercises in order to confuse the muscles, different machines, and all kinds of weird moves with dumbbells and cables. Here's how you should mix things up:

1. Stick to the exercises you know because your body knows them, that will help you develop muscle memory, a comfort zone and a confidence in doing them.

2. In order to mix things up, change the order in which you do them, change the angle on the bench, do seated instead of standing, free weight instead of the Smith machine.

3. Incorporate other principles, like drop sets, pauses, heavy sets of three or four or low weight high rep sets. This is a great way to challenge your muscles,

for example, do a hundred squats in however many sets it takes you with a given weight.

4. When you're performing exercises you know, you're able to mix it up and still push them to failure, or very close to it. With new exercises, you will tend to focus more on technique and form which will impact your focus and limit your success.

The Journal

This is an interesting one, and you might be thinking that there's no way I could have a problem with keeping a journal, well I do. I see it all the time, both guys and girls taking notes in between sets. Many pros will confess that in their early years they wrote everything down. Here's the thing, what are you getting out of that information? More importantly, what are you giving up to get that information. You might think it's no big deal to jot down the numbers but it is actually a very big deal.

From the people I've spoken to at the gym, the journal helps them set out what they want to lift, it keeps a record and helps make sure they are progressing with regards to the weight they are using. Remember one of my common themes of this book, the amount of weight you lift isn't that important, it's how you lift it, how well you contract and engage the intended muscle groups and how well you learn to take those muscles to failure. Once you start using too much weight, you lose control and rely more on your joints and other supporting muscles. The amount of weight you use should always depend on how you feel as you slowly work your way up. As you may already know, on some days you are stronger than others. This is due to the amount of sleep you managed to get, how you ate, how stressed you are and how tired your muscles are from your last workout.

So trying to force yourself to lift a weight in order to get a check mark in your book doesn't make much sense to me and it doesn't make for effective workouts. You should take advantage of your time between sets to focus and visualize your next set, working on your book takes you out of that zone, and it can be a disadvantage. If you're only writing it down so you have a track record then let me suggest this. First things first, if you're going to keep a journal, why not write about your workout?

1. How was your workout? Describe it, if it was great then why was it great?

2. Don't worry about the numbers, write down what you learned, how did you improve?

3. Maybe you got some good advice, maybe you fixed a problem you were having. Write about it for next time...we all forget.

4. How about your focus, were you distracted, did you have a hard time concentrating?

5. Keep a journal of what you eat, that information is way more valuable than how much weight you used or what exercises you did.

6. If you read a good article in a magazine or find a good video on the internet, jot down some notes, see how you can incorporate that info into your next workout.

This information is all useful because it helps you improve, it helps you remember what you've learnt while practicing in the gym. Then, the night before your big leg workout, read what you wrote from last week's leg session, this will remind you of what you learned, and how you can keep using it. Knowing how much I squatted last week doesn't help me in anyway.

Overtraining

If you are new to lifting then go to the gym all you want and learn, get used to the exercises using light weight and build muscle memory. I'll repeat it over and over, you need to learn how to lift weights before you can start lifting heavy and punishing your body. You want to learn how to kick a field goal? You practice it, over and over and over. You want to learn how to do bent over rows properly, same thing, repetition. Eventually you will get it, you'll know how to lift and like everyone else, you'll start overtraining.

This is a topic I will be covering in great detail as part of the physical portion of the book. What I want to do here is address the mental side and how overtraining has become the norm due to constant repetition in all of the articles we read. It's no different than all those bodybuilders way back when telling me to start with the basics and count your reps, they all suggested similar training splits. Over and over I read about training five or six times a week, three on and one off, four on and one off. Train each body part twice a week. As with everything else I followed the advice and basically trained almost every day.

I trained on days I was tired, stressed, sick and even injured. I'm pretty sure that if you asked around in the gym most people would tell you that's what it takes, that it's the only way to make progress. Once again, bad advice.

Back in university, not much got in the way of my training. I didn't live on campus so I would have to spend all day there and always had time to kill. I trained out of pure boredom some days and would even go in for a second session before the day was done.

Once I graduated things changed, I moved around the country to find work, I can't even count the number of places I've lived in. Priorities changed. School was always easy but work and paying the bills was a different story. There were days when I couldn't get near the gym. I went from working out every day to three or four days a week. As upset as I was about it not being able to lift, I noticed something, I was growing.

While muscle recovery is physical, recovery in general definitely has a mental component to it. Imagine going to the gym on a day when you didn't sleep, you had a horrible day at work and found out that your car is screwed and it's going to cost a grand to fix it. Now imagine the opposite, you slept great, you feel good, you just got a raise and life couldn't be better. From a mental standpoint, you would be in for two very different workouts. Consider what shape your mind is in when you decide on whether you should be lifting or not. What you should also do is rate your workouts. I'm sure if I asked most people to rate their workout they would point to how much weight they lifted, we do that because it's easy to measure. I benched two hundred or squatted two plates.

Here's a thought, rank your session on a scale of 1 to 10. I just gave you some ideas of what to write in your journal and those are exactly the questions you should be asking yourself, how was my workout from a mental standpoint? How was my focus, was I tired, did I fade at the end, was I able to take a couple sets right to failure? There are a lot of physical symptoms of overtraining but these mental cues are also crucial indicators.

What I noticed when I started taking more days off was that my ability to focus and my desire to train both increased significantly. This was extremely evident in the second half of my sessions. I would walk into the gym and attack the weights with crazy intensity. At the same time I would see the usual gang and some of them would always be yawning, they're tired or they're coughing or they're just out of it. I'd ask them why they were training that day and they would just shake their heads as if to say "I have to train." It just seems like it's been drilled into everyone's head. Here's my rule, and I don't always follow it to a tee but I try. Never train more than three days in a row and never take more than two days off in a row, unless you're sick or injured, of course. It's pretty simple, but like a lot of the advice I'm handing out in this book, all I can ask is that you try and see if it works for you. In this case, the better you become at lifting, the more important this advice becomes. Nobody can argue that if you work out when you are well rested and fully recovered, your ability to focus and concentrate is far better than if you're tired and still recovering from last night's workout.

Once you learn how to lift and are capable of really punishing yourself you simply need to push back against that constant urge to hit the weights, you need to ignore that guilt that creeps up when you take a day off. An effective hour to an hour and a half in the gym can do a significant amount of damage to your body and tire you out mentally, that's what you need to appreciate. I'll talk more specifically about recovery and muscle repair later but here is what I want you to get out of this. And just in case you're wondering, NO, 2 scoops of your pre-workout supplement will not alleviate the need to rest your nervous system!

**The amount of weight you lift does not determine
the effectiveness of your workout,
it's your ability to focus, to push and punish your muscles.
How well you can do that depends on
how rested your mind is.**

Steve Foxall

Chapter 9: Support

"When I was doing 'Scarface,' I remember being in love at that time. One of the few times in my life. And I was so glad it was at that time. I would come home and she would tell me about her life that day and all her problems and I remember saying to her, look, you really got me through this picture because I would shed everything when I came home."

Al Pacino

Throughout the book, I talk about how the gym can be a very important escape. For years, the gym was my escape from a bad marriage, now things have completely changed. Nobody wants a life or a relationship they need to escape from, but unfortunately, it's what many of us deal with.

Here's a great indicator of whether or not you're in a good relationship. Ask yourself if spending time with that person is one of your escapes, or something you want to escape from. If you have a terrible day at work, maybe your boss came down on you, what are you thinking when you drive home? Are you thinking how you can't wait to give that someone a big hug, lie on the couch together and watch a movie or sit outside on the deck with a few drinks? Does that instantly make you forget about your bad day? Or does it make things worse? So much so that you drive home thinking of excuses to get out of the house and go see your buddies?

Melissa is a huge escape for me, she just has this way of making stress disappear. It makes no sense to be with someone that you need to get away from in order to cope with the stressful parts of your life, either get out, or change your mind set, the two scenarios are night and day, one's wonderful, and one will drive you mad.

Now this section applies to all sorts of hobbies and is important because it speaks to how crucial having support is to increasing the probability of your success. Lifting can be very selfish, and at times, incredibly selfish. First of all there's time, you want to go to the gym and train at night and on the weekends. There's your diet, you'll only eat certain meals and you always need a fridge full of food. There's money for all of that food, supplements, clothes, shoes and for some, steroids, which I don't imagine are too cheap. Then there's the toll it takes on you, you do legs in the morning and then you're exhausted all day. Many of the people I know that are into fitness tend to only date those with a similar passion, this makes it pretty easy but as hard as it is to find "the one," it's a lot tougher when you narrow it down to that small percentage of the population that trains. That person has to accept who you are, believe in you and support what you love to do.

Melissa was just starting to get into fitness when we met, she loved to run and was training for a half-marathon. She was on this crazy diet of salmon and almonds and would run every day.

Her parents live up north and when Mel would go to visit, her mom Carolyn would follow her in the truck while she ran every day just in case the bears came out.

She challenged herself and committed to doing everything she could to succeed. She finished the race which was a huge accomplishment and I think even she amazed herself with her dedication and the result. Now she's fallen in love with Cross-Fit. She comes home from the workouts drenched and her face is always red, she just loves it.

I support her one hundred percent because I know the benefits of her being able to escape and do something she loves, and I also know the benefits of being healthy and happy about what you've accomplished. But what if I didn't? What if I bitched every time she wanted to go and said it was a waste of her time. From people I've talked to at work over the years, It seems very common in relationships for the man to "not allow" the woman to go to the gym. This can be for a few reasons but the big one seems to be insecurity. Maybe they just imagine their girlfriend or wife being hit on by all these fit guys at the gym. Maybe they don't want them getting too fit and then thinking they deserve someone better. It can certainly happen, there are a number of scenarios where someone has lost fifty or even a hundred pounds and changed their lifestyle, and their partner.

The bottom line is that in any relationship, the second you stop letting someone be who it is they want to be, you stop supporting them, and you stop believing in them, you quickly become someone that they want to escape from.

It might not seem like a big deal but believe me, it will forever change the relationship you have. Your partner should work out as much as they want, or run, or cycle. In fact, go buy them a few outfits and some shoes and show them how proud you are of their success. Be a positive influence and understand that people will naturally pick up new hobbies throughout life, they will want to try new things and believe me, nobody likes to be told what they are "allowed" to do. Do you?

Finding the right partner will empower you to accomplish great things, and being that person for someone else can be incredibly rewarding.

Here are some important tips on how you can be more accommodating to your partner with your lifting:

1. Schedule
2. Money
3. Take a Break
4. Focus

Schedule

This is crucial, for both of you. For yourself, you need to know if you're going to the gym or not and when you're going. You need to eat property around your workouts and be able to give yourself enough time to have the workout you want. If you both agree on a set schedule of when you want to work out each week then it becomes a routine and it's expected, just like work. You eliminate the scenario where the other person feels like you're going just to get away from them.

Money

This is another big one, depending on your situation. If you are doing quite well financially then it probably isn't a big deal but for most of us, it is. The money you will spend on this hobby can add up quickly. You need to set a budget and be smart. You can't be reckless and just say "I need it". What I mean by being smart is put some effort into saving money. I always check the flyers to make sure we're getting the best deal on chicken, steak or fish. We buy a lot of meat at Costco too which helps. I'm dieting for a show now so whenever I see Tilapia on sale, we stock up and put it in the freezer because it can be expensive. With supplements, don't be an idiot, if you don't have hundreds to spend every month then don't. Stick to the basics, and buy what's on sale. Protein Powder used to be thirty bucks for 5 pounds, now it can anywhere from sixty to a hundred, always look for a deal. Vitamins are great for you and if you're old and tired like me, a good pre-workout drink can help. That's all you really need. During contest prep you may need a lot more so save up. You don't need a new pair of fancy shoes every few months, leave that to those with the deep pockets, get a good pair for the gym and take care of them, they'll last a long time. Hit the outlets every once and a while a grab a couple of outfits on clearance.

A great deal of what we do becomes habit, routine, and if you routinely shop in a way that saves money, it will add up to hundreds.

Take a break

This is so important, always remember that lifting is a hobby, it's a lifestyle, it's not your life. I'm sure you've heard the saying, work to live don't live to work, well it applies here too. Like with any hobby, you have to stop yourself from becoming obsessed with it. In other words, be a meathead in the gym, but when you're out, go back to being somewhat normal.

We've all seen the guys outside of the gym looking pretty foolish, and I'm always shaking my head. Mel and I will go out for dinner or to the movies and I'll always point them out, the ones wearing a size medium t-shirt when they should have grabbed a large. Walking around with flexed arms. I shake my head sometimes and I'll ask Mel "I don't look like that guy right?" It's funny that I love bodybuilding but I don't want to look like a bodybuilder.

Hey, if you're single then do what you want but my point here is that if you want your partner to support you, I think it's healthy to just relax and not be so concerned with how "big" you look and how in awe of your size everyone else is. Remember, nobody gives a shit that you lift.

Maybe your girlfriend likes it when you get attention and maybe she's embarrassed, I have no idea. If she doesn't, which is likely the case, then relax, loosen up the shirt and just have some fun. Eat a dessert now and then and don't hassle the waiter with how you want your fish prepared. Women like attention, so take a break from looking at your refection in the car window and stare at her instead. Obsessing over size can be a very dangerous thing, and can quickly lead you down a dark path.

Finding someone who believes in you makes all the difference in the world

Steve Foxall

Chapter 10: The Addiction That Saved Me

"The Iron never lies to you. You can walk outside and listen to all kinds of talk, get told that you're a god or a total bastard. The Iron will always kick you the real deal. The Iron Is the great reference point, the all-knowing perspective giver. Always there like a beacon in the pitch black. I have found the Iron to be my greatest friend. It never freaks out on me, never runs. Friends may come and go. But two hundred pounds is always two hundred pounds."

Henry Rollins

In today's world of fitness and muscle there are extremes. There are those that take lifting to a level of obsession, they eat ridiculous amounts of food and ingest buckets of supplements all in search of size, bigger arms, a wider back and sweeping quads. They live bodybuilding 24 hours a day and I guess there are worst things to be addicted to. I was never addicted to the physical side of it, I never became obsessed with size, but I was still incredibly addicted. Before I wrap up this whole part on the mind, I want to quickly share my story with you.

When I was in grade ten I had to have surgery, they made an incision under my left ear along my jaw line. As the stitches slowly dissolved I quickly learned that I have a condition where my body doesn't heal well from these cuts, it overcompensates with the scar tissue and I get what's called Keloids.

As a result I've got some pretty nasty scars. Imagine you're going into high school and all of a sudden you have this thick two inch scar along the side of your face. It definitely had an effect on me, it took all of my confidence away, my self-esteem. Now I wasn't picked on for it or made fun of because I was a pretty good guy and I had an amazing group of friends. Where it affected me the most was with dating, that's where you need confidence in High School. Chicks may dig scars but not this one. I completely shut down that side of my life for all of high school. I avoided every girl I liked because I knew I wasn't an option for them. When I was older and we started going to bars I figured I had a shot, I figured it was too dark for them to notice, I felt equal, even if it was just for a few hours. I'd be out early in the morning so I could avoid the situation.

The result? Anger, mounds of it. Now I was still playing hockey at this point and that's where I would get it out of my system, one game at a time. I'd ram people into the boards or drop the gloves and go at it whenever I could. I remember one game, I knocked this guy out cold, biggest guy on their team, and I did it right in front of their bench. Later that night I wondered why, I could have just hit him and knocked him down but I put everything I had into it and then looked at their bench as if to challenge the entire team. I was probably the most easy-going guy you could meet with absolutely no interest in fighting anyone but on the ice it all came out. I worried what would happen if I just lost it on someone off the ice. Hockey was perfect because you had the helmet and mask on and you could sort of escape into your own world out on the ice and all the violence was just part of the game and pretty much expected.

Soon though, my hockey career would come to an end, I could hit as good as any of them but my skating was nowhere near good enough to continue into the NHL farm teams. Now I had a problem, a big problem.

What I was left with was this massive void, the anger was still there but I had no arena where I could let it out, no other players to hit, I had no escape. I kept working out just out of boredom in university and it didn't take long for me to figure out that the iron would soon become my new best friend. I'd already been lifting for a while but not very seriously, that would change. I wasn't just lifting anymore, I immersed myself into the world of bodybuilding. I started reading everything I could get my hands on and studying how to become better. I started paying attention to my diet, I gave up pizza for eggs and chicken.

Bodybuilding became everything, not because I wanted to be this huge guy and compete, it just gave my mind a place to go, and it was a place where I could lash out. I would think about it every night in bed and during class. It was the ultimate escape from reality. If I was thinking about the gym, I wasn't thinking about everything else. It provided an identity. I'd go to parties and pretend to drink because I didn't want to be hungover for the next day's workout. I'd sneak out early, walk home and read FLEX magazine in bed. In the gym was where I found peace, I loved it. When I trained I would walk around with my head down and purposely not make eye contact with anyone, especially

Steve Foxall

women. I would just lift, for hours, until every ounce of anger was gone. Then I would do it again the next day. There were days when I would just do squats or deadlifts so that I could stay in one corner, away from the crowd.

In my third year of university, I decided to do a show. It was a local novice show and it gave me an excuse to commit even further to the training, it was a challenge. I knew whoever else did it would likely be on steroids and much bigger than me but I didn't care. Although I did everything wrong and lost way too much weight, I still did well and came in third. It was something I did completely by myself. I remember my parents were away for three weeks, in South America I think. I'd work out during the day and drive back to school for cardio at night. I went to the show by myself and I don't think anyone in the whole place knew who I was. The funny thing is, back then nobody even knew what bodybuilding was, I'd go to parties and bring containers of food and throw them in the fridge. I'd be sitting on the stairs eating chicken and rice and people would come up to me all hammered asking what I was doing, "just hungry" I'd say. Most of my friends didn't know I was competing until after the show.

I remember the day after, I still went to the gym. I was working out and a friend came over and said "you must be loving this." I didn't know what he was talking about until he explained that everyone in the gym was watching me. I looked around and realized he was right. I was all tanned, pumped up and around 5% body fat. There was only one other bodybuilder in the whole university so it wasn't all that common. To me it was just another day to escape into my own world. It's difficult to describe the level to which I alienated myself. While other guys would work out to socialize or to find a date for the weekend, I would walk around wishing everyone would leave so I could have the gym to myself.

Now I had lots of friends and always had somewhere to go on the weekends because I was able to hide all of my anger from them. Outside of the gym I was just like everyone else. I can't remember the last time I thought about those years, and looking back, the extremity of it blows me away.

That's the main reason I never had any interest in steroids, I trained for sanity, not size, size was a side effect.

Thinking back, I remember specific workouts I had after getting bad news. I remember the workout I had after learning that my younger brother had cancer and would have to undergo chemo. I remember picking up a bar with 250 pounds on it and throwing it at the wall. I remember when the doctor told me I had skin cancer and that he would get back to me in two weeks to let me know if I was going to live. I went straight to the gym and trained for three hours ramming the plates onto the bar, I trained until I couldn't lift my arms. I honestly can't imagine what life would have been like without the gym.

I had this one friend that worked out and he used to get a kick out of how I shut out the world. He would do this thing where he'd stand right behind me and see how long it would take me to notice him, the record was four minutes. The gym really is the perfect place to get rid of it, you don't just lift the weights, you attack them, swear at them, challenge them and defeat them. You can put on your headphones and shut out the world for an hour and when you're done, you leave your anger in the gym, all of it. Your story obviously won't be the same as mine but there are sure to be parallels, everyone has their own reasons to be angry at the world and I'm telling you this so that you too may find a way to deal with it. It doesn't matter how bad things get, the gym always helps, it might not fix things or make them go away, but it helps you deal with them, it gives you confidence and makes you a stronger person. The gym clears your head and helps put everything into perspective, it helps you think and it helps you resolve.

I say it's the addiction that saved me because the alternative escapes people turn to in high school can lead you down a very dangerous path, and those paths might not have me here today writing.

<u>Part Two</u>

How We Train

Steve Foxall

Chapter 11: Contracting the Muscle vs. Moving the Weight

"My movement is the demonstration of my muscles contracting."

Kai Greene

So now it's time to start discussing the 'physical' aspects of lifting. In the next few chapters, I'm going to go over some key advice that applies to all of your workouts. This is the stuff that can only come from years of experience, you need to study it and like anything, give it a try. I hope you find it useful.

Let's start things out by continuing with my earlier bit on "The Switch". There I talked about NOT training with your ego. This section represents the physical translation of that advice. Again, it comes early for one simple reason, it is a crucial element that you must understand and appreciate. It is the foundation, it is how to skate in hockey, how to run in football and how to dribble a basketball. Until you learn and have a proper understanding of this concept, you will continue to waste your time and you will not make the progress you are after, regardless of your goals.

One of the challenges in learning the fundamentals in lifting is that they're tough to spot in all of the videos online and the pictures in the magazines. Enter one Kai Greene, our bodybuilder from Brooklyn. Kai and his sponsors created a contest where the winners were given the opportunity to train alongside one of the sport's best.

I strongly suggest you spend some time watching the videos of these sessions. You can find them by searching "Train with Kai". It won't take long for you to see why. Kai is known by his peers as "The Predator" but I see him as a professor, a philosopher, an artist and a preacher. In a world full of self-promotion, he educates with both reason and purpose. Kai does an amazing and unique job of explaining the fundamentals of lifting. At the core of all his lessons is the need to focus on contracting the muscle. The earlier you make the switch from just moving the weight to contracting your muscles, the sooner you will start heading down the path to becoming an experienced lifter. There are three main scenarios I can think of where people fall short on this task, I'm going to use these to help give you some practical advice that you can start using today.

1. Ego
2. Lack of Knowledge
3. Lack of Practice

Ego

There's a guy at my gym, goes the same time I do. He's very tall, well over 6 feet. He's thin, not a lot of muscle but he certainly is in good shape. Now this guy loves to move heavy weight, and I mean heavy. He does shrugs with 6 plates aside, calf raises with 8 plates stacked on top of the machine and he tries his best to squat almost 350 pounds. He is what those who lift call *a distraction*. Let's focus on the shrugs and calf raises to demonstrate my point.

Here's a test, if the majority of people your size or bigger are doing shrugs with anywhere from 200 to 400 pounds and you're using 600 pounds, there's a reason, and it's definitely not that you are stronger than everyone else.

Essentially what you are doing is powerlifting, and even the suggestion is an insult to powerlifters everywhere. The main difference between bodybuilding and powerlifting is in the objective, the first group is trying to build muscle mass, the second is trying to move as much weight as possible. We've all seen powerlifters competing in the Olympics, what they do is nothing short of amazing. Now imagine for a second a powerlifter doing calf raises in a competition. They would use their back, shoulders, traps and quads to move a massive amount of weight. When I train calves, I take all of those other muscles out of the equation and use JUST my calves...I focus on stretching the muscle at the bottom and flexing it at the top. The same thing goes for shrugs, sure you can load up the bar and use your whole body to get it moving but you aren't effectively working the trap muscles. There are so many downsides to this type of training and it is something you will never see an experienced lifter do, so why do it? Ego.

When you use too much weight, you lose the ability to focus on contracting the muscle, and therefore you lose the ability to PRACTICE focusing on contracting the muscle.

Does that make sense? How can your mind focus on stretching, contracting and pushing your traps to failure, when you're desperately trying to hang on to three times your bodyweight?

Lack of Knowledge

People wonder sometimes why they can swing a golf club as har-d as they can and the ball barely goes over two hundred yards. Yet even some female professionals can drive a ball over three hundred. What gives? Well, the difference is that the hackers are swinging with their arms, while the pros swing with their hips, legs and back. They use their "big" muscles to create lag and torque. The arms are just there to hang on and guide the club.

Guess what? The same thing applies to lifting. Have you ever worked on your back for an hour and the next day the only thing that is sore are your arms? Well, there's a reason, you're not engaging your big muscles. When you train chest, back or shoulders, your arms are simply there to hang on to the weight, and your hands are just hooks. This is by no means an easy thing to learn and it takes a great deal of practice.

One of the problems is that if you don't understand the mechanics, or how your muscles function, then you will have a really tough time engaging those big muscles while you train. That knowledge is essential. There are plenty of people with the opinion that bodybuilders are idiots, but just ask one about muscle mechanics and you'll think they have a degree in it.

Put simply, proper form isn't just for safety, it's all about putting your body in a position that forces your targeted muscles to carry the weight. Let's look at seated rows for your back, this is the one where you sit in front of a low pulley with your feet up against a platform. You extend forward before pulling the cable into your stomach. If you're just learning, chances are you're sitting up straight, gripping the bar with flexed forearms and pulling it in with your arms. I see this all the time, it's very easy to spot.

Until you learn that when you bring the weight in, you need to arch your back, stick out your chest and bring your shoulders down and back, you'll be missing out. That's just one small part of what you need to learn. Another one is the negative. If you look, you'll likely see those same people just extend their arms, letting them carry the weight. Again, they will eventually learn that the point of the negative is to ensure that the muscle continues to carry the weight in order to create a scenario at the bottom where your body has no choice but to engage the back muscles in order to bring the bar back in.

I will go through all of the proper mechanics in the next section, but for now, appreciate that it will take work to teach your body how to engage the different muscle groups. Let me give you some tips and get you on the right path.

Lack of Practice

So how do we learn? Same way we learn anything, we practice. It's a strange concept in the gym, one I very rarely see, but in every other sport, it's considered essential. Here's how to use seated rows to practice correct mechanics. Again, we're not lifting here, we're *learning how to lift*.

It all starts with the negative, you want to bend at the hips and let the weight pull you forward. Keep your chest out and your arms slightly bent, you don't want to roll your shoulders forward and extend your arms...that takes the weight off of your back. Do not focus on your hands here, using a grip with your thumbs over the bar helps. Now focus on stretching your back muscles. At the bottom, you should feel a pull along the sides of your lats, this is the key to a proper negative, it means you've engaged your muscles and they are now ready to fire. If you don't feel the pull then keep making adjustments until you do. Stay in that bottom position and focus on stretching your lats until you feel the pull.

Now, as you're ready to pull the bar back in, keep focusing on those lats. One trick is to imagine pulling with your elbows rather than your hands. Keep your forearms relaxed and squeeze those back muscles. As the bar comes in along the top of your quads, force your shoulders down while bringing them all the way back, this allows your lats to contract and you should feel that contraction.

This is an invaluable tip for any upper body movement. You have to purposely start that weight moving by contracting the targeted muscle rather than using your hands.

Once you get all of that right, one last tip. Don't forget to finish. By that I mean contract the muscle, forcefully. Don't just bring that bar in, squeeze those back muscles and hold that squeeze for a second or two. If you don't, your rep is not complete, and not as effective as it could be. Now remember, we're practicing, so do it over and over. As you get better at using your back, up the weight and use a little momentum. Stretch and squeeze those lats until you can feel them doing the work. Now, lower the weight and do it again, this time, completely relax your arms and try to pull the bar in using only your lats.

This should give you an idea of what each exercise should feel like from a sense of making the intended muscles do the work. It's a weird feeling to have your arms not involved and your chest or back doing all the work, to this day I still get a kick out of it.

Learning how to isolate the different muscle groups and engage them with forceful contractions is the fundamental core of bodybuilding. Once you learn how to train in a manner that revolves around these contractions, then you can start pushing yourself with the goal of reaching and eventually surpassing failure. Then you will begin to make significant progress.

Here are some other great exercises for practicing...

Back	– Close grip pulldowns to the front
Chest	– Seated machine press / machine flyes
Shoulders	– Seated machine press / Cable Laterals
Quads	– Leg Press

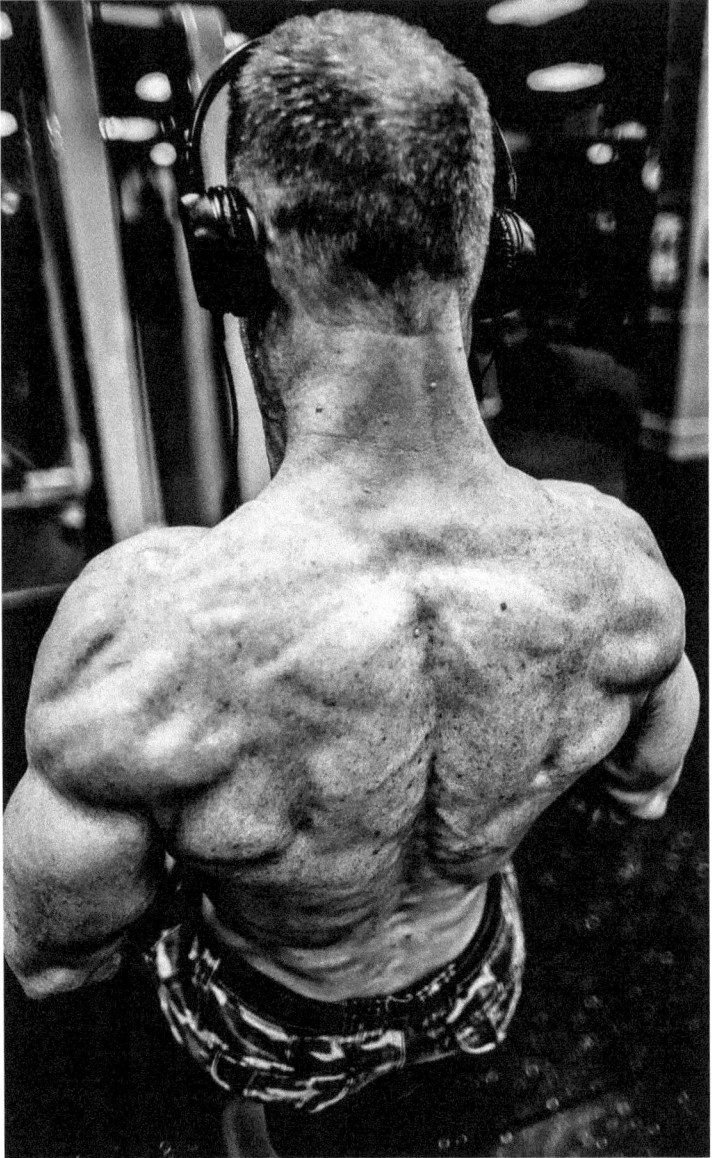

Seated rows – you can see how I'm upright at the finish with my shoulders down & back, every muscle is contracting. My lats, traps and shoulders are all working here because I'm pulling with my back, not my arms.

Chapter 12: The Warm-up

It's amazing how much of our lives becomes routine, day in and day out. The nice thing about writing or any other side project is that it forces you out of your routine, it gives you more of a sense of purpose. Sometimes an excuse not to watch TV at night sends you to bed feeling just a little more content with what you've accomplished that day.

What does this have to with warming up? It's the routine. The gym can be extremely repetitive, in every way. We all have our splits and rotations, our favorite exercises and even the same playlists...over and over. What's essential is that you recognize how important certain elements of that routine are. Elements that you might repeat hundreds or even thousands of times. It's all of the little things we do, or don't do, that determine the level of our progress or success.

This is where the warm-up comes into play. It's one area where I can say with confidence that most people could take another look at what it is they do. I'm going to run you through what I do to get ready for my chest workout. It's the easiest way to demonstrate the purpose and necessity, the cause and effect.

Here's my take on why your warm-up could likely be better.

1. The Pump
2. Focus

The Pump

One quick note...part of warming up is actually getting warm. Like I said before, wear whatever you want to wear but if it's cold outside, consider an extra layer, at least for the first bit of training. Then strip down to your cut-up tank top. Believe me, it helps.

Back to chest, I always start with the butterfly chest machine. It's the one where you sit and bring two handles together in front of you as if you were doing flyes. There are a few very key elements to selecting your first warm-up exercise.

1. First, it should always isolate the muscle, in other words, not involve any supporting muscle groups. This is important because our main goal here is to pump blood into the muscles we're working.
2. Second, the move should allow you to stretch the muscle and then hold the contracted position. The stretch allows you to incorporate as many muscle fibers as possible, thereby preparing as much of the muscle as possible. The contraction is what forces the blood in.
3. Third, the ability to very easily perform drop sets is a big bonus. Here you just adjust the pin on the stack and

bang out a few more light reps while focusing on that stretch and squeeze.

The majority of what I see is people going straight into their first 'big' move and doing a few light sets in order to get things going. Let's say we chose the bench press, I can't tell you how many articles have recommended this is where your chest workout should begin. How would that compare?

1. You won't be able to isolate the chest because your shoulders come into play.
2. You aren't able to stretch out the pecs here because your hands can only come down so far before the bar hits your chest.
3. You aren't able to hold a contracted position and squeeze at the end of a rep.
4. Finally, it's difficult to do drop sets here as you'll need a spot if you go to failure.

It's the same for squats & leg presses, deadlifts, bent rows, close-grip bench presses and shoulder presses.

So let's get back to our butterfly move and exactly what we're trying to accomplish here. One of the side effects of the repetitive nature of training is that people tend not to appreciate the toll it takes, the stress it places on your body and mind. Once you've learnt how to lift, your goal becomes pushing a muscle to the point of failure, to where it suffers physical damage. Preparing it for that stress is crucial. We need to get the blood flowing, the temperature up and get those fibers ready to work.

We've all heard of the mind-muscle connection. In practical terms, you want to be able to 'feel' the muscle working so that you can focus on pushing it. You won't feel anything until that muscle is warmed up and pumped with blood. It's a common belief that the 'pump' is something that builds through your workout and peaks at the end with an isolation move, again, hundreds of articles. What I am telling you is that the sooner you get that pump, the sooner the effectiveness of your workout jumps to that ideal level.

The warm-up is the creation of an environment where our minds can better connect with our muscles.

Having said all of that, once you appreciate the need to isolate and pump up a muscle, it's pretty easy from that point. Do five sets on the butterfly, stretch, focus on using only your chest to move the weight and holding that contracted position for a few seconds while squeezing the muscle. Finish with a drop set. When you feel that burning in your chest after those last sets, you know you're ready.

A quick word on your joints, you have to look after them. Specifically your knees and elbows. Consider riding the bike for 5 minutes before that leg workout and doing plenty of push-downs before those heavy tricep exercises. At my age, you'll be glad you did.

Focus

So apart from pumping up the pecs, what else should we be doing? Assuming you're not on your phone, here are some things to consider. When I perform these first few sets I'm thinking, I'm tackling a great deal of what I covered in the mental section, I'm preparing myself for battle. I have my music playing and I'm getting into that mindset. I'm forgetting about the other shit going on in my life, I'm clearing my head so that I can focus on the task at hand. I'm visualizing power, strength, and positive control of the weight. If you're just learning, you want to remind yourself of what specifically you want to practice or improve upon. It's no different than when I used to sit in the dressing room before a playoff game in hockey. You visualize winning, defeating the other players, in the gym, you want to defeat the weight. You need to be in a strong and positive place and you need to believe that you will have an effective workout and you will surpass everything you have previously accomplished in order to force your body to adapt and grow.

It may sound like a lot, but after a while the warm up
evolves into one simple task with one simple goal.
You need to prepare your muscles for battle,
you need to go to that place and become that person.

The Pump

Chapter 13: Stretch and Squeeze
The Anatomy of a Rep

"You never want to let the weight know you're scared, but this is some heavy-ass weight"

Jay Cutler

You should always have goals. Big goals that are broken down into little ones. I want to lose thirty pounds, I want to lose six this month, I want to eat well this week, I want to eat four healthy meals today. You should review these goals annually and throughout the year to make adjustments. I used to spend a great deal of time in airports. One company I worked for was based out of Montreal so I'd go there every few months, plus conferences, personal trips and family visits. For some strange reason, those airports became my favorite place to go over my goals. To see where I was at and where I wanted to go. You don't know anybody, you're not at work, or at home, you're in-between. You're stuck for a couple of hours with nothing to do, it's a good environment. It's good advice though, to find a neutral site and do your own strategic plan now and then.

Back when I first started lifting, we had no goals. Actually I'm lying, we had two. I'm sure most teenagers in the gym share the same two, I want to get big and strong.

The workouts we did starting out were all focused on strength. I remember them in great detail and I can look back now and know all the things we did wrong, which is pretty easy, we did everything wrong. We just wanted to lift heavy.

Lifting heavy is a skill, your goal should be to learn it, constantly improve upon it and always respect it.

Read that again. I think that it's a great way to summarize the mistakes that we all make in the first period of lifting. You need to respect how difficult it is to lift heavy, to push yourself and have your body and mind perform at their highest level. We all tend to dumb it down, how complicated can it be? Just lift as much as you can. Well it can be very complicated…think of those powerlifters and how many hours they spend learning how to lift, how to improve. Think of cyclists, sprinters, high jumpers. Millions are spent all in an attempt to shave seconds or gain inches.

The biggest mistake that my friends and I made, and that you're likely making, is rushing into too much weight before properly learning a lift. Once again, let's talk about the bench press. It is by far the best movement for this discussion. Ask most young lifters and they will tell you their goal is to bench a certain amount of weight. Their goal should be to learn how to bench.

There is a huge difference between those two paths. It's all about getting to a certain level before you start trying to push yourself.

Lifting heavy on any exercise before understanding and experiencing proper form and technique is not only unproductive, it's reckless.

I've already mentioned Dorian Yates and his 'Blood and Guts' video. I wrote about the impact it had on me, it gave me an overall sense of how powerful one human being can be and gave me the curiosity to find out exactly what it took to get there. This video was like a course of lifting. Dorian doesn't explain anything or hand out any tips, he just lifts, and that alone was extremely informative. I studied it over and over, to learn every-thing I could. It's something you should definitely watch. Here are the key points I took away from it and immediately started experimenting with at the gym.

1. Visualization
2. The Weight
3. The Negative
4. The Push
5. Feedback

Visualization

This was a huge lesson for me. I wrote about this in the 'build confidence' section but it certainly deserves another look from a 'physical' point of view. In every exercise, Dorian's first set is performed in the exact same manner as his last. What I mean by that is he didn't start out with one plate aside on the incline bench and bang out twenty quick reps. He brought the weight down slow, stretched at the bottom, paused and then powered it up to a full contraction. Keep in mind that one plate to Dorian is about twenty-five pounds for me. I thought about this a lot as my approach was to 'bang out twenty quick reps'. What do you think he was doing? Why such focus on so little weight?

I'm fairly certain that Dorian was imagining there were about four hundred pounds on that bar and that he was going through the exact same routine he would later. He was ensuring an exact range of motion with proper hand and body position. He was visualizing, and the next day, so was I, and I've been training that way ever since. It just makes sense.

Your first sets should be performed in the exact same manner as your heavy sets in order to give your body and mind confidence to take on what's ahead.

I always like to put on the belt and use the straps during those first couple of warm-up sets to help me visualize those upcoming heavy sets. By getting the same feeling, it's easier to pretend I'm using much heavier weight and in turn, convince my mind that I'm up to the challenge. Those early sets are always practice runs for what's to come, treat them that way.

If you watch Dorian, even on YouTube compilations, you'll see that he always powers the weight up with one big push. This is authoritative, forceful, this is the battle and this should be you convincing yourself you are unstoppable. This is deliberate lifting. Look at the quote at the start of the chapter, "never let the weight know you're scared". Back before we all wore headphones, I would get asked to spot people all the time and I would always hear them say "I'm going to try to get five but we'll see". That's not the attitude, I would much rather hear "I'm gonna throw this bar around like it's a toy so you might have to catch it". You might laugh at that but appreciate it, appreciate the difference it can make in how you lift. We all need confidence in the weight room, lifting forcefully, with intent and purpose will help give you that confidence

If you want the confidence you need to lift heavy on your last set, start building it on your first set.

The Weight

Once you do reach the heavy sets, you need to ensure that you aren't letting your ego creep in and take over. You still need to get your reps in. Remember what I wrote earlier, pros always perform the first five or six reps in perfect rhythm with full control, that's bodybuilding. This isn't about loading up the bar and squirming your way through three reps and getting your spotter to do another three for you. Lifting heavy is about getting eight reps when you should only be able to do six. It's taking a three second break at failure, tightening up, giving your head a shake and doing two more. This is your goal, don't ever forget that. Sure there are days when you decide to go really heavy just to see what you can do but that should be on very rare occasions, a lot of times it will do more bad than good.

In bodybuilding, heavy lifting is about pushing yourself through the seventh, eighth and ninth rep, not fighting to get two.

Imagine a chart with a bell curve. On one axis is the weight you are using and on the other is the effectiveness of the set. There will always be an ideal weight where you get the most benefit out of a set. The best rhythm, stretch, contraction, pump and push to failure. Once you exceed that weight, the benefits start to diminish. You start losing confidence, relying on other muscles and joints. You cut your range of motion short and do 'half' reps.

Squats are a great example of this. I see people all the time doing great reps in their warm-up. They keep it up for another couple of sets but then up goes the weight. They get sloppy, leaning over too far to keep the weight on their backs, not committing, with no full range and no benefit. You need to recognize at what point this happens, and have the sense to back off and lower the weight.

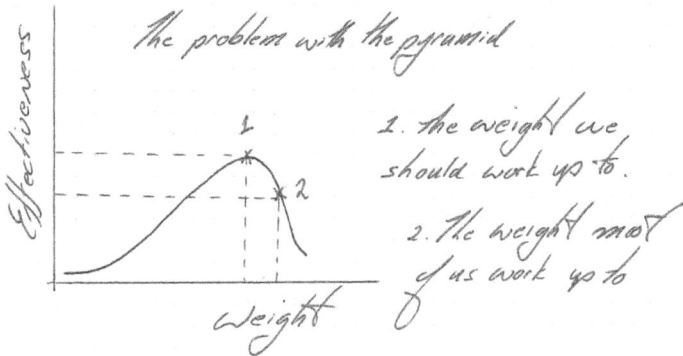

The problem with the pyramid

1. the weight we should work up to.

2. The weight most of us work up to

Effectiveness

Weight

This is what most experienced lifters are so good at. Even their heaviest sets are still performed with proper form and good technique. They know there is no point in sloppy training, and that usually comes from years of experience. You should start that practice today.

Most of us use a pyramid style of training, we start light and work our way up. We tend to take it easy on the first few sets in order to save up our energy and strength for that last 'heavy' set. We typically don't push ourselves to failure until the end. Here's the problem. If my peak weight on squats is 225, then that's what I should be using on my heaviest and most important sets. That's the weight I should be using to push my body as far as it can go with perfect technique. If my ego takes over and I decide to impress everyone with 275, I'll take it easy with the 225. The problem is that I'm into the right side of the graph, and as a result, I'm going to struggle, lose form, lose confidence, and fail to get any rhythm or good contractions.

Consistently lifting amounts greater than your peak weight is a very common mistake that can have a huge impact on your progress. It is ego driven and can be very costly.

Here's a test if you don't believe me, and you know you're too stubborn to stop using that big weight. Next time you do squats, after you complete that last heavy set with too much weight, have a seat and rest. Then, lower the weight down to what you know is reasonable, and complete another set. Focus on your form and pushing those quads, all the way down keeping it tight. Do as many reps as you can in good rhythm, when you're done, pause at the top and then do two more.

Once you're done, I want you to honestly compare that set to the previous one and ask yourself which one was better. Which set pushed your leg muscles more and which one allowed you to go further into that pain zone? Get away from the weight and focus on punishing your muscles, make the switch.

One more note, in all my years of lifting, I can probably count on one hand the number of times I've tested how much I can lift for one rep. I'm not a powerlifter by any stretch, so what's the point? It only serves to resolve your curiosity.

Failure in the gym is far more than 'as many as you can do', it is the practice of pushing your mind and body to the limit of their abilities within the context of proper lifting.

The Negative

Now let's talk about the first half of the rep, which by the way, is far more important than the second. Screw up the first and you might as well put the weight back.

Let's start with this, I was at my son's football practice one night and the kids were all doing push-ups. Every one of them was doing the same thing, flopping. They would get their bodies up and then drop to the ground and relax before the next attempt. I started telling them to firm up, to keep their bodies tight and go down slow. I showed them how to stay in control of their muscles and not rest at the bottom. Some of them got it, and they were quick to say how they could actually feel the chest muscles working.

The negative portion of the rep has a few key components that are all necessary to ensure that you have an opportunity to complete powerful reps in rhythm. Without incorporating them, you will not be able to push those muscle fibers anywhere near failure. You will hear Dorian say over and over in his video, 'STRETCH & SQUEEZE'. It simplifies a very complex practice into an easy repeatable saying, so repeat it! While you're doing that, let's dig deeper into the meaning.

Stretch refers to the negative but there is one key mistake made by many and it can have a very big effect. Let's take wide grip chin-ups for this example. Keep in mind I'm talking about bodybuilding chin-ups, not those crazy CrossFit ones where they swing all over the place.

The negative portion here is crucial. If you just drop your body down and hang each time you complete a rep, what's happening? The weight, in this case, your bodyweight, is always being carried by muscles and joints, and you need to know which ones. When you hang, you're taking the weight off of your back muscles and placing it on your shoulders and triceps. Before you come back up, you will either use your arms or have to switch the weight back onto your lats. This is inefficient and will make it that much harder to keep those arms out of the movement. Isolation now becomes almost impossible. Here's what you should be doing.

Avoid the Flop

Instead of hanging, which is just like flopping at football practice, you need to lower your body while maintaining the proper body position. For chins, that means chest out, back arched and head angled slightly upwards. When you maintain this position, you make it a great deal easier to keep the weight on your back. Go down slow to a point where your arms are still slightly bent, and don't flop. I'm asking you to lower your body using your lats, again, a very tricky thing to learn.

Here's a couple tricks that should help. The first is the elastic band. As you're lowering your body, I want you to imagine you are attached to a rubber band hanging from the ceiling. As you go down, you're stretching that band tighter and tighter. At the bottom, you imagine letting go and your body flies back up. It might help you visualize keeping your body tight and the weight on your back. It works really well with the bench press.

Lateral Force

This one is becoming quite popular and can work extremely well. As you are coming down on your chin-up, pull your hands apart as if you were trying to stretch out the bar. Again, this works great on pressing movements. That simple move does a wonderful job of keeping your arm muscles busy with something other than carrying the weight. If those muscles are busy pulling the bar apart, they're not lowering your body.

It is a great teaching aid that is easy to incorporate. Give it a try on any pressing movement, chins and pulldowns. You can see where it works best for you.

**By pulling the bar apart during the negative,
your hands and arms are given a task
that takes them away from trying to carry the weight.**

Control Your Stretch

Another common mistake is not knowing what you are stretching and when to stop. Back to chin-ups, as I said, you want to stop just before your arms straighten.

The key is simply focusing on stretching the muscles you are working, that's it. The mistake is thinking that stretching as far as you can is beneficial, the 'more is better' philosophy. With your arms still slightly bent, you can get a great stretch in your lats. By stopping at that point, you can keep your back engaged.

Keep going and you quickly approach the 'flop' position. It's like when people do dumbbell flyes for chest and they stretch their arms out as far as they can. Your goal is just to stretch your pecs, not your arms. When you keep going, your biceps take over.

Your range of motion should extend to a point where the working muscles are stretched without going to a point where the supporting muscles are forced to take-over and carry the weight. More is NOT better.

That's it, three simple points to ensure a good negative. I strongly suggest that you spend some time practicing. Cables are great for this, go slow and purposely keep the weight on the muscle, hold your position and then stretch the muscle, not your body. When I started training, this was an area where I had zero understanding, or appreciation for. As a result, I can remember the feeling of pushing on the bench press with nothing but my arms. I see people doing it every time I go to train.

You either keep the weight on your working muscles or you lose it, and when you lose it your set is shot. Once you fully understand what role the negative plays and you practice it, you will feel a world of difference, the benefits will amaze you.

A strong isolated and forceful contraction can only occur as the result of a properly executed negative.

The Push

Hopefully, if you take my advice and practice the negative, you'll be able to put yourself in the right position to now focus on completing your reps. I can't emphasize enough how important it is for you to work on these elements. Forget the weight and develop the fundamentals you will rely on for years to come. This topic needs practice as well, it may continue to seem simple or idiot-proof but believe me, it isn't. Moving the weight requires a great deal of focus and while we covered that in the mental section, the physical element must now be matched to your thoughts. The big mistake? Simple, not pushing with your chest or shoulders and not pulling with your back. It sounds pretty basic but people lift for years without getting it right.

Here's a great way to practice: hop on the floor and start doing those push-ups. If you're like most, you focused on your hands and pushing with your arms. If you did, try this, lower your body slowly using my advice on the negative. Keep your chest slightly out and your hands at your sides with your elbows pointed back. Lift your head up just enough to look forward along the floor. If done correctly, you should now be able to focus on lowering your body with your chest. Now, I want you to keep it going and using only your pecs, lift your body. Keep practicing until you can take your arms out of the movement. Then, keep doing sets, do ten reps keeping the weight on your chest the whole time, get a stretch at the bottom and a good contraction at the top. Try lateral force and pull your hands apart on the negative, it might help.

You should not be thinking of your hands, just your chest. Feel the difference? This is by far the biggest stumbling block in the gym and it is just a matter of focus. It is a thought process that must be incorporated into every set you do. While you're learning, it's not a bad idea to do those push-ups throughout your workout as a reminder.

You don't need to get down on the ground. Just lean into a railing or machine and do forty-five degree push-ups. I guarantee that if you ask any pro bodybuilder, they will recount the day they stopped using their arms, and started using their 'big' muscles. They will then tell you that's the day they started growing. For many it can take years and for some, it will never happen. Make it happen with your training today.

Focusing on your hands during any exercise is a mistake. Until you start focusing on moving weight with the muscles you're training, you will not learn how to lift.

The Finish

Just one easy tip here for when you're trying to take a set as far as you can. Don't get sloppy. If you watch people they do this all the time. They start out great, get some rhythm going but as they approach failure, it all falls apart. What happens? A few things can happen. Some people panic that they won't be able to lift the weight, others just forget everything they should be doing and switch their mind to doing whatever they can to finish the rep. They lose their form, lose their rhythm and start swinging the weight or adjusting their bodies into a 'cheating' position.

Most of the advice in this book centers around a basic principle of working the muscle rather than moving the weight. Physically, a proper set should mean maintaining the position and technique that will directly punish the muscle right through to the last rep. Try this:

Once you are getting close to the end, exaggerate the form. Focus on maintaining that arch in your back, that tight core or a strong balanced stance. Force yourself to make that set as hard as you can for the muscle you're working. Then, if you can't do any more reps, your set is done. If the weight is too heavy to keep your form for a good number of reps, it's too much.

Now I know there is cheating involved with heavy lifting. What that means is that you always maintain your form but use a little momentum to get the weight moving. That's all. If I'm doing standing barbell curls I can certainly get the bar going with a little hip action but I still avoid leaning back too far at the top. I'm ensuring all of the weight is on my biceps through the range of motion. Keep in mind too that you can only cheat on certain exercises, presses, rows and squats should not be included.

When you assess your training to gauge how well you're doing, remember that sloppy reps don't count, only the good ones do.

Feedback

How do you know if what you are doing is right? Most of us don't have coaches and trainers when we lift, and even if we do, they don't know what our muscles are doing or feeling. So how do you know? Our bodies give us feedback after every set, clues to what's happening, and you need to learn how to interpret that information in order to know how effective your training is.

When you're learning how to lift, it is crucial that you listen to your body and adjust what you're doing according to that feedback.

Bad Feedback

Let's say you're doing squats. Right away you feel stress in your knees, or your lower back. This is bad and is usually the result of either poor set-up, technique, lack of warm-up or going up in weight too quickly.

At the start of every rep, the weight should be 'on' the quads and off your knees and back. We all have a tendency when learning how to squat to keep the weight on our knees because we don't yet have the confidence to commit to the move. We hesitate to place it all on our quads and squat down to parallel in case we can't bring it back up, It's a natural tendency. That's why it is so important to practice form with light weight. In this case, and with most moves, bad feedback means not feeling that burn in the right place, or feeling pain or stress in your joints or lower back.

Another example would be your wrists or forearms hurting. This can be quite common and again, don't assume it's normal. On a lot of wide grip or close grip moves we place a great deal of stress on the wrists. This points to bad form and that pain or stress should act as a warning that you aren't doing the move correctly. A friend of mine was doing wide grip bench press for a while and eventually, with all that stress, he injured one of his wrists. As soon as an exercise doesn't feel right or is causing pain, stop, adjust or switch to something else. Hack squats are famous for this, depending on the machine you can very quickly place a whole bunch of weight directly on your knees. If you can't get that weight on your intended muslces, find something else to do.

Good Feedback

Let's move onto the incline bench press. I've been doing these for years. Here is the feedback you should be looking for, and you can make adjustments until you find it: no pain in the joints and no stress on supporting muscles. You should feel a stretch in your pecs followed by a conscious feeling of your chest moving the weight. It's a little hard to explain and can actually feel weird. When you manage to take your arms and shoulders out of it, it's like someone else is pulling the bar up. As the set continues, you should start to feel your chest muscles burn on the negative. When you're done, you're done, no cheating here.

As soon as you rack the weight, you should feel this burning continue in your chest and only your chest. That is what you're looking for. If you can achieve that, you have done your homework, you've practiced and *now* you're nailing it. It's actually a great feeling. If you warm-up properly, you should feel this burn fairly early on in your session.

When you listen to your feedback and help it guide you to a great workout, you should finish with a great pump in your chest or back with hardly any in your arms. That's a great gauge.

Devote a month to mastering the negative and the push, to finding the peak weight and to finishing sets off with good feedback. I guarantee you will see better results, experience more progress and feel a greater satisfaction. Progress is what motivates us to keep going, progress will get your ass back in the gym.

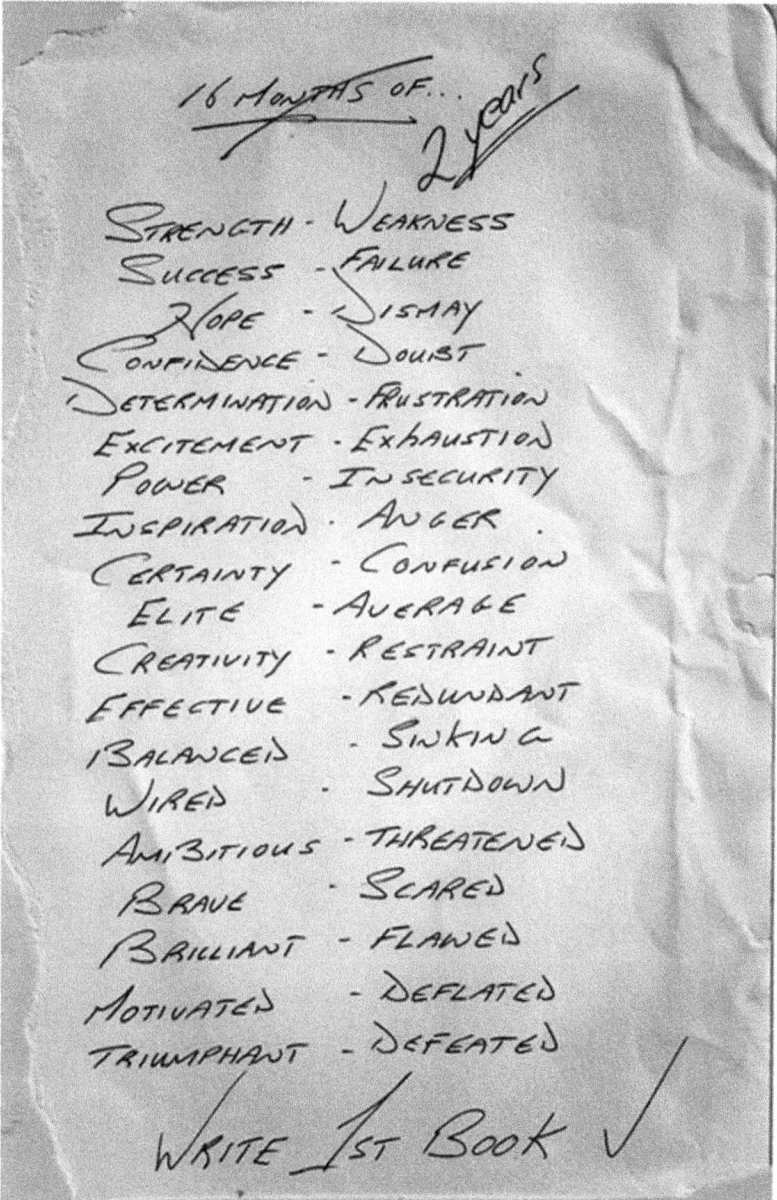

16 MONTHS OF...
2 years

STRENGTH - WEAKNESS
SUCCESS - FAILURE
HOPE - DISMAY
CONFIDENCE - DOUBT
DETERMINATION - FRUSTRATION
EXCITEMENT - EXHAUSTION
POWER - INSECURITY
INSPIRATION - ANGER
CERTAINTY - CONFUSION
ELITE - AVERAGE
CREATIVITY - RESTRAINT
EFFECTIVE - REDUNDANT
BALANCED - SINKING
WIRED - SHUTDOWN
AMBITIOUS - THREATENED
BRAVE - SCARED
BRILLIANT - FLAWED
MOTIVATED - DEFLATED
TRIUMPHANT - DEFEATED

WRITE 1ST BOOK ✓

A piece of scrap paper from a recycling bin, a borrowed pen and a half hour to kill during football practice.
As with many things, writing can become addictive.

Steve Foxall

Chapter 14: The Pros and Cons of Machines

I hate sleep, I hate that we have to sleep. I've always struggled with it, and it frustrates me like nothing else in my world. I was thinking about it the other day and the reason it frustrates me to the extent that it does is that I can't seem to learn how to sleep. I've tried everything, I've read the articles, done all the routines. I even read a book on meditation that said I need to step outside of myself and watch myself fall asleep...what?

Sure I have pills that I can take but I'm very much against any type of reliance on a drug. I only started drinking coffee out of desperation a couple years ago. My routine involves staying up at night until I'm so exhausted that it's a struggle to get up the stairs, and then I'll sleep for a few hours because I'm too tired to think. Every now and then I'll take a drug and pass out for ten hours just to get my brain functioning again. It wouldn't be a problem except for the fact that I'm tired. When you don't sleep, you never accomplish what you planned for that day, you procrastinate. Most of the time, what you do accomplish is far from your best work.

The funny thing is that on my days off from the gym, every-thing else in my routine is the same except for one difference, I feel like shit. I don't get out of bed right away, I take my time with breakfast and getting to work, and for the rest of the day I just want to go back to bed. On days I do work out, I get my ass out of bed, head outside and hit the gym, and I feel great all day. It's a pretty common excuse for skipping workouts, I'm too tired, I didn't sleep well, I'm really busy at work. It's the first thing most people tend to give up, that one hour of lifting, running, cycling, swimming, bootcamp or even CrossFit.

Now, let's think about this. We don't sleep because we're stressed. When we don't sleep, we skip our workouts. We skip our workouts, we miss that opportunity to clear our heads and de-stress. We keep skipping workouts and our stress builds up, then we have an even harder time sleeping. Get the point? You want to feel better and have more energy regardless of your abil-ity to sleep? Get your ass out of bed and get after it.

Now while I can't seem to learn how to sleep, I'm fairly con-vinced I can learn pretty much anything else. Here's what I do.

1. Find Sources - Who will be your teacher? Your coach? Can you learn from the internet, books, video, an actual person or a combination of several sources?

2. Go to School - As I've repeated over and over, lifting has to be learned and so does pretty much anything else you want to do. Accept that fact and become a student, take in all the information you can and study it.

3. Graduate - Ensure that once you've finished learning that you are ready to move on. Ask an expert to grade you, watch you, have them confirm you're on the right track.

4. Become that expert – Once you have the confidence that you are doing something right, repeat it, over and over until you have total control of your ability.

5. Get Creative - Once you've mastered your new talent, take it in new direction, think outside the box and make it even better, be an innovator.

The problem here is that most people skip the learning process all together. You want to lift, just go to the gym and lift. You want to play basketball, just start shooting hoops. You want to be a runner, grab your shoes and go. That is not a recipe for success. If you've played team sports then you know what a good coach can do. They teach you the fundamentals, make sure you're doing them right and then make you repeat them over and over again.

Just Starting Out

When it comes to learning the fundamentals in the gym, machines can be a problem. They're everywhere in the gym now and because I'm forty-two, I can remember when they first started taking over. Don't get me wrong, I use machines a fair bit and I'm not going to preach to you about being 'hardcore' and sticking to free weights. I'm talking about learning, and teaching your body how to lift.

The biggest problem with machines is that they can force you to go through a fixed range of motion. Now I'm not talking about cables here, they're fine because you still have control. I'm talking about all the Hammer Strength stuff and the other ones like it. At the beginning, lifting can be very awkward, it's new and your muscles aren't used to it, especially with dumbbells. I can still remember trying flyes for the first time or presses and feeling completely uncoordinated. This can make machines quite appealing.

Let me break this down. Lifting is all about putting your body in a position that allows you to isolate and contract your muscles in order to move the weight. By isolate, I mean that you are able to 'place' the weight on the desired muscle and not your joints or supporting muscle groups. Remember when I talked about push-ups and moving your body with your chest? What free weights allow you to do is adjust your body, the angles, the stretch, all in an attempt to find that perfect position. When you do find it, and all you feel is that muscle contracting, chances are you're doing the move correctly. Machines limit your options, they limit the amount of adjusting you can do and therefore reduce the probability of learning how to perform the exercises correctly.

We all come in different sizes, height, weight, reach etc. I'm five foot ten, which is average, and even I have a hard time getting into a correct position on most machines. I'm almost always adding a plate onto the bench or adjusting it to its max height in order to get a good contraction, I even sit backwards on a lot of them. One size does not fit all and this can also be a big disadvantage for women who are petite. I see personal trainers all the time putting their clients into machines that don't 'fit' and their range of motion is totally off.

Also, a great many dumbbell exercises benefit from a range of motion that involves a slight turn of the hands or involve an arc rather than a straight path. This allows for a better stretch and a stronger squeeze. The machines do not give you that ability.

Let's go through an example. Take the incline dumbbell presses for chest, an extremely popular exercise that almost everyone does. The key is all in your body position: shoulders down and back, chest out. You bring the weights down enough to stretch the chest, but not the shoulders. As is the case with most exercises, it's all in the negative—when you bring the weight down you have to get into the correct position at the bottom in order to allow your chest to do all the work on the way up. With the arch in your back and your chest out, you push the weight up by contracting your chest muscles. At the top, some like to keep the dumbbells apart and some like to bring them in and even turn them in a little as they squeeze the chest.

Now let's say you're on a machine. First of all you have to adjust the seat. It shocks me how many times I see people just sit down and never adjust the machine for their body. Most machines just don't allow you to get in to the right position. You can't scrunch down and get your chest out because you have to keep your body up to try and hold the bar at the right level. Do the handles come down far enough? For safety reasons a lot of them won't, and this doesn't allow for a good stretch and a proper negative. Next you push, and what you'll usually find is that you're incorporating a lot of your shoulders to do so, it will be very hard not to.

With free weights, the range of motion is determined by your muscles contracting. Machines force you to follow a determined path, and how your muscles contract is restricted by that path.

Learning to lift is all about getting the 'feel' of the weights, the feel of using your intended muscle groups and making those small necessary adjustments. It's literally a game of inches and the only way to find those perfect positions for YOUR body is by finding and experiencing that feeling.

Machines are designed to copy a free weight movement. In order for them to be an effective part of your workout, you need to first know what the free weight version feels like.

When you're just starting out, you aren't quite certain of the feeling you should be getting from each exercise, therefore, you aren't able to effectively mimic that feeling with a machine.

Getting the hang of it

That doesn't mean there's no place for machines. If you've been lifting for a while, your body should be quite accustomed to the proper ranges of motion. You should know what it feels like to isolate a muscle and have it, and it alone, move the weight. In that case machines can be a great tool in your arsenal.

A few tips:

1. Don't ever feel like you 'have' to use a machine just be-
    cause everyone else uses it. Every machine you
    incorporate has to pass the test, it has to allow you to
    get that feeling. You can adjust it, play with it, sit, stand,
    turn around but if you can't make it work, leave it out.

2. Machines should still allow you to go heavy and push
    yourself, and some don't. One of the major benefits of
    machines is that you don't have to worry as much about
    your balance or getting the dumbbells up or having a
    spotter. This allows you to focus more on pushing the
    muscle and squeezing out those few extra reps. I wrote
    earlier in the mental section about just closing your eyes
    at the end of a set and banging out six or seven reps. I
    tend to find the ability to do that on machines more than
    free weights for that exact reason. Some machines will
    do the opposite and restrict you from pushing yourself,
    so weed out the bad ones and stick to the good ones.

3. I almost always finish off my workouts with machines for
    a couple of reasons. First, it helps me alleviate my tired
    secondary muscles and allows me to focus on harness-
    ing whatever is left in the tank to completely exhaust my
    working muscles. Also, I find machines less tiring. It
    doesn't seem to take as much mental effort to sit there
    and bang off a few sets vs. having to keep racking
    weight or looking for dumbbells. This is especially true
    of machines with stacks and pins for weight. I find I can

sit there and focus even though my mind is fried at that point.

4. Another benefit of machines is that they allow you to really focus on the negative. With a fixed range of motion it's easier to make sure that once you've found that perfect path, you keep it. By bringing the weight through the negative slowly while flexing the muscle, you are truly able to maximize the pump and to some degree, better stress those muscle fibers.

5. Having to only adjust a pin instead of moving plates makes it very easy to do drop sets. These are also great at the end of a workout. I'll rep out and then move the pin, immediately rep out again and then go again for a third time. It's fast and very effective.

Overall, machines can either hurt you or help you. Using them properly should get you going in the right direction.

Chapter 15: My Principles

"Strive for excellence, exceed yourself, love your friend, speak the truth, practice fidelity and honor your father and mother. These principles will help you to master yourself, make you strong, give you hope and put you on the path to greatness."

Joe Weider

Joe Weider will always be remembered as the father of bodybuilding. Born and raised in Montreal, Quebec, he published his first magazine at age 14. He went on to create an entire sport, a lifestyle, a world of extremes. Together with his wife and brother, they created the IFBB, the International Federation of Bodybuilding, and with it, the Mr. & Mrs. Olympia competitions were born. This event is now massive.

Joe was a constant educator, always teaching. If anyone would have backed my passionate belief that you need to learn how to lift properly, it would have been Joe. Throughout his years of writing, he communicated a great deal of his advice through principles.

What are principles with regard to lifting? They are your tools, a repertoire of means to push your mind and muscles to and beyond failure. Principles are the reason we don't just blindly do three sets of ten. They are the tricks of the trade and they are not used nearly enough. If performed correctly, they will make all the difference in the world. Some will have a negative effect, others will take your training to a new level.

Let's take a closer look at these principles, at the pros and cons of each, so you can progress even further with your own lifting:

1. Forced Reps
2. Pyramiding
3. Muscle Confusion
4. Drop Sets
5. Partial Reps
6. High Rep Sets
7. Pause Sets
8. Supersets
9. 100 Rep Workouts
10. Flex Sets

1. **Forced Reps**

The idea here is that you take a set to failure, and then with the help of a spotter, continue with a few more reps essentially going past failure. It's a very advanced technique that is used a great deal more than it should be. It's a principle that is almost standard, and for some, a part of every workout.

The problem is that people need to understand the difference between using a spotter, and performing forced reps.

The Cons

a	The biggest problem with this principle is that people automatically associate it with using a spotter. A spotter is there for safety, to help you if you get stuck. Many people assume that since they are there, they should also help you struggle through a few extra reps after failure. Forced reps is a technique that should only be used by experienced lifters in certain situations. Safety is a constant concern.
b	Your job is to learn how to lift and how to take your muscles to failure. Forced reps are only beneficial when they actually take you past failure, not help you get around it. How can you experience and practice reaching failure on the tenth rep when the person spotting you starts helping on the 7th?
c	It's hard to spot, even for experienced lifters, because you don't know what's going on in the other person's mind. When I spot someone, I try to do just enough to help them through the sticking point so they can finish the rep, because that's effective. When they keep going

with forced reps, I then have to work harder to keep the bar moving. Some exercises also put the spotter in an awkward position where they have to lean over. This makes it difficult for them to control how much they help you. This all makes for some ineffective sets and ineffective training.

d	Having a spotter and using forced reps can encourage you to use more weight than you should. You grab 70 pound dumbbells instead of 60s because you have a spotter and you know you'll get help. Together you struggle through five reps when on your own, you would only get two. I preach throughout this book about how you need to use manageable weights in order to learn and this principle will lead you away from that practice.
e	Forced reps can be dangerous, especially when you are new to the sport. When you haven't yet developed the necessary muscle memory on the basic exercises, it's easy to fall out of the range of motion. This is something you might have experienced with dumbbell presses. As you're trying to get the dumbbells up at the top, you lose one and it falls back to your chest. What happened is that the weight came off of your pecs and straight onto your arm which isn't strong enough to hold the

	weight. Once you become more accustomed to the move, this shouldn't happen. If at this point, you're using a spotter to push past what you're capable of, you're asking for an injury, and it could be a bad one.
f	Having someone spot you can be distracting, it gets in the way of your focus and your mental routine. You will tend to worry about how many reps you can do and most often, fail sooner than you otherwise would. I train alone and I very rarely ask for a spotter. I used to and then realized that I was never experiencing good sets, it would always be disappointing. To me, reaching failure on my own is what lifting is all about. As for safety, I don't do exercises or use weights that force me to give up control. Remember, in most cases, if you lose the weight, there isn't much a spotter can do to help you. You're squatting two hundred pounds and you lose your balance, then what? Is that person going to hold you up? Train smart.

The Pros

a	There is a specific benefit you can realize here and it has nothing to do with lifting heavier weight. The idea is that when you get to failure, your other supporting muscle groups want

to come in and help and this usually means that your form goes out the window. With a spotter, you can maintain perfect form and get just enough help to allow your targeted muscle to complete two or three more reps while leaving the other muscles out of it.

This can be very beneficial in both isolating and pushing a muscle through failure. **If done correctly**, it can also help teach you how to control a muscle through failure.

b | When you're learning, certain exercises will challenge you with a 'sticking point'. This tends to disappear as your muscles become more accustomed to lifting. Until then it can be quite frustrating. Using this principal can help in allowing you to complete sets with good rhythm and solid contractions. Again, this only works if the spotter gives you just enough help through that sticking point and no more.

It's pretty clear that I'm against the whole practice. I structure my workouts so that I purposely don't need a spotter for safety or for forced reps. If you are going to give it a shot, make sure that when the spotter says "how many you going for" that you don't just say "I'll try for six." It's important that you explain exactly what you want them to do and what you're trying to do with the set. Communication is always a good thing. Also, make sure whoever is spotting you knows how to lift and can handle what you're asking of them. All in all, I think the principal does a lot more harm than good as it prevents learning and makes for ineffective practice.

2. **Pyramiding (3 sets of 10)**

The idea here is to start with a relatively light weight and high reps on your first set and work your way up to a heavy set for lower reps.

I've read countless articles on training and in every one there's this little chart that shows the feature bodybuilder's routine and it goes something like this.

Chest Workout

Bench Press	3 sets of 10-12*
Incline Dumbbell Press	3 sets of 10-12*
Incline Dumbbell Flyes	3 sets of 10-12*
Dips	3 sets of 20-25*

*Pyramid with increased weight in each set

Over and over you would see something like this or a very close variation. This was by no means the intention of Joe Weider's principal but that's the norm that's been created. Joe also believed and preached Holistic training which recommends mixing up your reps and sets in order to push your muscles and even though realistically, that's what the pros do...it didn't get much press.

The Cons

a	The idea of each set is to target a muscle from a certain angle, to recruit as many fibers as possible and push those fibers to the limit. For some core exercises like squats, deadlifts and bench presses, that can be quite a task. It can easily take up to six sets or even more before you're comfortable pushing yourself to the limit.
b	The idea of starting out with around 12 reps and working your way down to 8 is nonsense. I've already talked about how I don't agree with counting reps. Maybe I'm a simple guy who can only focus on a couple things at once but I think you need to be concentrating on isolating and contracting your muscles, not how many reps you think you can do. It's the quality of the reps performed, not the quantity.
c	The principal has drilled it into our heads that you're finished after your heaviest set. It tells us to only go up the one side of the pyramid. One of the main goals of your workout should not only be to push the muscle, but to maximize the amount of blood you can force into it. One of the best ways to do that is to lower the weight back down after that heavy set and continue. Do a couple of sets in a slow and strict manner and you will definitely benefit.

d	This principal can rush you. If you know you're only going to do three sets then you will add weight each set in order to get to your heaviest weight on the third go. A good strategy is to always add very little weight between sets so your mind still believes 100% that you're capable of completing the task. I add ten pound plates all the time and work my way up. This keeps my confidence up and helps me avoid poor form. By moving up slowly, sometimes I need five sets to get to my maximum weight and sometimes I need eight: the quality of my sets comes first. The volume becomes the result of how strong I am that day and how hard I can push it.
e	Certain moves like squats and rows need a great deal of practice. Therefore, some workouts will mean hanging out in the squat rack trying to master the move and get the feel of it. On other days, there will be times when the exercise you're doing just feels right. You've got the proper form down pat, you feel strong and you just want to stay there and do set after set. Maybe the gym is really busy and you want to stay in the corner and do your thing because you know getting an incline bench by the dumbbells just ain't happening. My point is that your job in the gym is to get a good workout and improve and if that means

> doing twenty sets of squats or six different cable exercises for your back, then you do it. Don't fall into that trap of 3-4 exercises, 3 sets of 10, pyramid the weight, it lacks creativity, it's boring, and will limit you.

The Pros

> a   As I just mentioned, I'm a huge fan of moving up slowly from set to set. With that, I can definitely say that the premise behind this principal is essential. Confidence is everything in the gym and you have work your way up to staying 100% positive while you lift. Small increases will help you learn how to keep those negative thoughts out of your head. This newfound skill will come in handy outside of the gym and reinforce your need to be positive in order to achieve what you want in other areas of your life.

While pyramiding is a solid premise, what it has turned into isn't. I'm sure if you trained alongside any pro for a week you'd see that the little chart in their article doesn't come close to describing their actual typical workout.

3. **Muscle Confusion**

It's always been accepted that by mixing things up in the gym, you are better able to shock your muscles and therefore cause more damage. By constantly altering your workouts, your muscles never know what they're in for. By changing the angles, you get different muscle fibers involved and therefore ignite further growth. Oddly enough, if you look at the top bodybuilders in the world, they tend to stick to same routine for years, here's why.

The Cons

a	We're all different, and when we learn to lift, we also discover what works for us. Some people are built to bench press and others aren't. Some machines are great while others just don't fit. My point is that for any given muscle, we all have our favorites, those exercises that allow us to push ourselves to the limit, the ones that work. While mixing it up is great, forcing other exercises into your routine just for the sake of confusing your muscles might not be truly effective.
b	Lately, it seems that I'm the only one doing the basic exercises in the gym. Everyone is getting creative and finding all sorts of ways to lift. I see people standing on one leg doing bicep curls or swinging 45 pound plates over their head to work either shoulders or triceps, not

	sure which one. They're mixing it up, trying to get results. The problem is that when you lift, you have to ensure that the targeted muscle is carrying the weight throughout the entire range of motion. That's hard enough to learn with the basic exercises but when you start getting too creative, it becomes extremely difficult. The majority of times, what happens is that your forearms take over. There's a reason any top bodybuilder will tell you to stick to the basics, because it works. Save the creativity for that posing routine.
c	Muscle memory takes years to develop. Once you have it, there is a huge benefit in that you don't have to 'think' about your technique anymore while you lift. This allows your mind to focus 100% on contracting the muscle and taking it as far as it will go. Mixing up your exercises all of the time will increase the time it takes you to acquire good muscle memory.

The Pros

a	Once you've decided on the core exercises that really work for you, a more effective strategy might be to focus more on the 'shocking' part of the principal, rather than the 'confusing' part. You should try and shock your muscles all of the time while still sticking to the

	basics and the few machines that you enjoy using. Many of the other principles that will be covered allow you to do just that.
b	Shocking a muscle is a principal that is essential in the gym. The general idea is to push the fibers farther, to add more stress. While the end of a set is usually dictated by that first failure, there are many different ways to keep things going, to continue the punishment. This type of training can be far more effective than standard sets, even if you're a believer in low volume, high intensity training.
c	This type of training is actually very safe. While performing very heavy low rep sets can be dangerous, using these techniques can allow you to take your muscles farther while maintaining full control.

The Muscle Confusion Principal to me needs some interpretation. While many will argue that constantly adding different exercises is beneficial, I simply disagree. I do believe strongly in mixing things up in order to shock the muscles and the next few principals will help you do just that.

4. **Drop Sets**

Here we go, one of my favorites. Drop sets are performed by finishing a set to failure, and then lowering the weight for another set, and so on. It's an essential tool that I don't see being used nearly enough of in the gym.

The Cons

a	If you are NOT yet performing an exercise correctly, this principle will simply reinforce a negative behavior. It should not be used on moves that you haven't yet become accustomed to. If you don't know how to squat, then keep the weight light and practice until you get it right first.

The Pros

a	We all want to see progress in the gym—that's why we're there. The standard mindset is that you have to lift heavy to get big and that is true, however, lifting big is a technique that needs a lot of practice. It's not something we can do on every visit and if not done correctly, it can be counterproductive. Progress comes from pushing yourself, forcing blood into the muscle and getting good strong contractions, and that's exactly what drop sets allow you to do.

b	Probably the biggest challenge in lifting heavy is maintaining your form, not letting those secondary muscles take over. Drop sets give you the opportunity to get your form back and push those targeted muscles.
c	Drop sets are safe. You don't need a spot to push yourself right to the limit and there's very little chance of injury because the lower weight allows you to maintain complete control.
d	While you learn to lift, you are also learning how to think and how to block out those negative thoughts. Drop sets take those negative thoughts out of the equation. It's not about "Can I do five reps?" or "Can I bench this much weight?" I hat all goes away. All you need to focus on is contracting the muscle and not stopping. You will find this to be of great value.
e	This is a great technique for searching out those exercises that work for you. If you complete three drop sets on a certain machine and you don't get that burning feeling in the targeted muscle then you know your set up, or the machine in general just doesn't work for you. It's the perfect gauge to let you know exactly which muscles are doing the work. If you do an Incline Bench Press machine and after those sets your shoulders are burning, you know what you're doing is ineffective. You

		might not get that burn from struggling through five reps, but you will from doing thirty.
	f	While this isn't a principle that should be used on every exercise, it should be used on one, maybe two times at the most in order to push yourself.

5. **Partial Reps**

This concept is fairly simple but also fairly easy to mess up. The idea is that once you reach failure in a set, you should still be able to get a few "half" reps in. The theory here is that we usually hit a sticking point somewhere on our way to completing a rep so why not just keep going with the first half and take the muscle as far as we can?

The Cons

	a	From a learning point of view, there are a few issues to consider here. The major one is that anytime you continue after failure with the same weight, you have to ensure that your form is correct and that you're keeping your body tight. In other words, people tend to get sloppy at this point and start using their whole body to find a way to keep the bar moving. This is both unproductive and dangerous.
	b	Another danger: make sure you are not putting significant stress on any of your joints. Once

	your targeted muscles have essentially failed, it is natural for the joints to hop in and carry some or even the majority of the weight, and this is not a time to continue pushing.
c	On most pressing movements with free weights, you will need a spotter when doing partials. You could fail at any time and lose control of the bar or dumbbells. This is especially dangerous when the weight is over your head as with shoulder presses.

The Pros

a	Just as drop sets do, this principle enables you to take your muscles past failure. **The key here is that you do not attempt these with your heaviest weight**, because the risk of injury is too high. With a moderate weight, you can remain in full control and manage to keep the weight on the targeted muscle. One tip is to exaggerate your form just prior to beginning the partial reps. For example, stick your chest out more on presses, and tighten your core right up, this will help keep the weight on the muscle.
b	This principle also enables you to focus on the bottom half of the rep or 'the stretch'. When you don't have to focus on actually completing

	the rep, you can focus more on getting that complete stretch, recruiting as many fibers as possible and making the muscle move the weight up to that sticking point. Standing calf raises are a good example.
c	Many top bodybuilders are accused of doing partials throughout their workouts and in their videos. They aren't, and the difference is all in the sticking point. Partial reps involve the range of motion up to the sticking point. What these pros are doing is stopping after passing the sticking point. Many of them believe that in some exercises, further movement doesn't push the fibers and therefore doesn't benefit the muscle. For example, with dumbbell presses, once you get three quarters of the way up, you've done enough. Again, they prefer to focus on the stretch and getting all of the weight on that targeted muscle. Opinions differ. Ronnie Coleman used this technique all of the time and Dorian Yates insisted on squeezing out every rep. Both did quite well.

5. **High Rep Sets**

The idea here is to shock the muscle. We tend to get caught in a trap of constantly being in the 8-12 rep range and while that's certainly effective, it can 'dull' your mind and its ability to push you beyond what you're capable of. Here, an occasional all out set to 100 can have a great effect, convincing your mind that you need some muscle growth. The reps don't have to get done in one set, which is fine, it's the total you're after.

The Cons

a	This is definitely for experienced lifters only. To effectively accomplish this daunting task, the muscle memory absolutely has to be there. If you have to worry about form then you won't get far with high reps.
b	Experience is also required on the mental side. If you are still getting the hang of blocking out those negative thoughts, your set will end up short due to simple doubt.
c	This is tough if you're working out with a friend because of the time it takes to complete these sets.

The Pros

a	These will push you, both physically and mentally. It's not just a few sets, it's an all-out challenge, a test to see what you are capable of. I was never one to test my strength with one rep max sets, I always left that practice to the powerlifters. When I wanted to gauge my ability, this principle was all I needed.

Steve Foxall

b	I'm a big believer in convincing the mind it needs to provide you with more muscle and these sets will do just that.
c	This, and similar techniques, have long been hailed as a cure for plateaus. When you're stuck on a weight with any major exercise, sometimes the best thing to do is to break your routine and push the muscle in a different manner, attack it from a different point of view.
d	This is excellent practice for advanced lifters looking to improve their ability to control their thoughts. It is a lesson in blocking out pain and maintaining focus under extreme stress.

6. Pause Sets

This is another great technique for shocking the muscle and mixing things up. You simply pause in the stretched position for a couple of seconds before powering through the contraction.

The Cons

a	None

The Pros

a	This is a great technique to stop you from using momentum or 'bouncing' the weight.
b	If done correctly, this will help you learn how to start the contraction with the targeted muscle, instead of the supporting muscle groups or your arms, when you aren't training arms.
c	This is a great way to ensure you are in a good stretched position which will help recruit as many muscle fibers as possible.
d	A further trick is to pause and then let the weight drop just an inch or two before contracting, this will place even further stress on the fibers. An example would be shrugs.
e	This is another principle that will help take the emphasis off the amount of weight you are lifting, and help you focus on technique, form and using the muscle. Less weight on the bench press while pausing at the bottom is a great way to practice and push those pecs.

7. **Supersets**

A simple technique that involves taking on two different movements at once by alternating sets. This can be done while working one muscle group, or two. The most common example for two groups would be biceps and triceps.

The Cons

a	The major problem with working more than one exercise at once is the simple fact that gyms are busy. That's not a problem if you're doing bent over rows and then jumping up for the some chins in the same rack, but moving from machine to machine is tough. We've all started on a machine or a cable only to have someone come up a few minutes later and tell you they're doing three exercises at once. Train like that all the time and you won't be too popular with your fellow lifters.
b	If you consider the benefit here with regards to muscle growth, supersets don't really add a lot of value. The first exercise certainly doesn't put you in a better position to push yourself on the second. Very often, you're too tired to benefit.

The Pros

a	Supersets do serve a couple of purposes. The first is cardio. Doing squats and then grabbing a bar for lunges right away isn't easy and the more you train in that fashion, the better your cardio and the more calories you will burn. Bodybuilders tend to incorporate this principle more when preparing for a show.

> b | If you're in a hurry, this technique can save time. Two or three different supersets for arms will give your bis and tris a crazy pump and an effective workout in a good half hour.

8. **100 Rep Workouts**

This is another advanced technique that is commonly used for squats. I find it extremely useful when I'm tired or just not feeling the usual mental excitement about training. It also works well if the gym is really busy because you don't have to worry about moving around. The idea is to pick one basic exercise like squats or deadlifts or a Smith machine press for chest or shoulders and perform 100 reps in as many sets as it takes. You want to use a weight that will allow for sets of around 12 at the start. For legs, I'll warm up with extensions and hamstring curls and then hit the squat rack. I'll work my way up starting with the bar and then one plate and once I reach 225 pounds, I'll start working towards 100 reps with that weight. It might sound easy but believe me, you'll be walking funny the next day.

The Cons

> A | I say it's advanced because what it does is exhaust your muscles and then demand more, and with that comes the need to have at least some muscle memory. If you aren't 100% comfortable with a certain movement, and you're not yet performing it correctly, you may be putting yourself at risk of an injury.

The Pros

a	By sticking to the one exercise with only one goal, it creates a simple scenario that should allow you to focus all of your mental and physical energy on performing only that task, 100 reps.
b	While this principle requires muscle memory, it also helps further build what you already have. By removing the need to add weight and see how much you can lift, it forces you to pay close attention to form rather than power. If you lose form, you will not reach your target.
c	This technique forces you to practice. What have I kept repeating over and over? Use lighter weight and perform good solid reps in rhythm. This principle requires just that. It will also teach you how to maintain focus and form when your muscles are screaming for you to stop.
d	It's quick, and efficient. We're all busy and if you only have 40 minutes or so to train, this principle is perfect.

9. **Flex Sets**

I'm not sure if this one's been put out there yet and if it hasn't, then I'm declaring it mine. I discovered this principle during the photo shoot for the book. The photographer, was getting his equipment ready and the first shot was of my calves. While he was adjusting his camera settings, I held a flexed position on the standing calf raise machine for a good minute. I wanted the pictures to look as good as possible so of course I was flexing as hard as I could. That's all I did before moving on to the next shot and the next day, my calves were killing me. Since then, I've been incorporating it and I believe it's been a very effective addition. I know there's the Peak Contraction principle but this takes that to a whole new level. Give it a shot, pretend you're being photographed and you'll see what I'm talking about.

The Cons

A	Difficult to do with quads and back.

The Pros

a	It's very safe. The beauty of these is that it won't work with very heavy weight, it doesn't place any stress on your joints and you'll never need a spot.
b	It will help teach you how to focus the weight directly on the muscle you're working and get accustomed to what that 'feels' like.
c	It's great when you don't have a lot of time.
d	If you plan on competing either in fitness or bodybuilding, this is a great tool to teach you how to control your individual muscles, flex

> them and hold that position. Trust me, it's a lot harder than it sounds.

Some final points:

1. Stop worrying about forced reps. Pretend they don't even exist, because they are by far the most unproductive practice you can incorporate into your workouts **while you are still learning.**

2. Everyone talks about how you need to change your workout constantly in order to shock your muscles. As I've mentioned before, I believe you should stick to the exercises and machines that work for you, and mix things up by using the principles. You will find that some work best for certain muscle groups, and for certain exercises. I'll use partial reps on shoulder presses and calf raises, pause sets for chest, 100 reps for squats and drop sets in almost every workout. If you know them all, then they become tools you take to the jobsite, and having the right tool for the job makes all the difference.

    Remember when I wrote about keeping a journal? I told you not to worry about sets and reps but to focus on taking notes. Write out the principles you want to incorporate. Design a workout ahead of time that includes them and then *after* you're done, write about it. This is homework, this is what you need to study and a notebook always helps.

3. There are three things I like to accomplish with every workout and I choose my exercises and principles to do just that. Here's my list.

    a. Do one or two power exercises that focus on a shorter, but *correct* range of motion and reaching pure failure. What I mean by pure is that I don't cheat, I get in the proper position, I isolate the muscle and I take that muscle as far as it can go. (Incline bench press)

    b. Do a stretch exercise where I get a full range of motion. Here I want to really stretch the fibers and get a strong contraction. (heavy dumbbell flyes)

    c. Do a pump/flex set. Maximizing the pump is an essential part of convincing your body to grow, machines & cables are great for this (cable crossovers)

Given those objectives, I use the principles to push myself and mix up what would normally be a very repetitive routine. Try tackling those three objectives in your next workout and plan to use a couple of principles each time, then take notes. I'll give you plenty of examples of how to incorporate them when I tackle the individual muscle groups. This will help make your workouts more challenging and a little less boring. I guarantee the effectiveness of your training will only improve, and for many, dramatically.

One last note to this very important section. A big mistake, and a major reason a lot of us struggle to develop our secondary muscle groups is that we don't incorporate the majority of what

I just wrote about. One reason is that we only do one, maybe two movements. It's very important to put as much effort and creativity into one exercise for a small muscle group as you would for chest or back. Let's say you're doing a few sets of barbell shrugs for traps at the end of a back workout. There is no reason you can't accomplish the three objectives listed above by incorporating several principles into that one movement. Do three heavy normal 'overload' sets, do three pause sets empha-sizing the stretch, and finish with a couple drop sets. The same thing applies to calf raises or hamstring curls.

Simply put, that's what it takes to grow. It took me years of trial and error to figure that out and I'm hoping you will get there a lot sooner.

Rather than just tell you not to do something, I've tried to jus-tify it with reasons to ensure you appreciate my direction. Again, this book isn't meant to be read in a week and thrown in a draw-er, it's meant to be your textbook, your manual, and this section is a perfect example of why you should keep referring to it.

Chapter 16: Recovery

"Exercise to stimulate, not to annihilate."

Lee Haney

It wouldn't be a stretch to say that serious lifting is probably one of the most demanding hobbies out there. It can quickly take over and become a huge part of your life. That's why I preach that you have to be able to turn it off and on. Be a meathead in the gym and go back to being normal when you leave. Arnold writes about this one competency he always maintained and it's something I drill into to my children's minds. In today's environment of constant distraction it is that much more relevant.

Arnold is a master at focusing his mind, when he was in the gym, he was 100% focused on the workout, to the point where everyone else had to be quiet as not to distract him. When he left the gym, it left his mind. Away from the weights, he focused on his career. Whatever he was doing, from reading a script to working on his English, the task at hand always received 100%

focus. That commitment ensured that he was doing the best and most efficient work possible.

It's good advice. In other words, turn your damn phone off and focus on something. You see it everywhere now, whatever people are doing, it can always be interrupted with that sound of a text. That text derails your thinking, it takes your mind off what you're doing.

What I tell my teenagers can easily be drilled into the heads of adults. Allocate time and focus on the task. What does this have to do with recovery? Simply put, it is often ignored. Look at all the ads for supplements right now. They all market 'the workout', everything points to these crazy sessions in the gym fueled by 'insane' pre-workout formulas. But in reality, if you don't appreciate the need to recover, learn what has to be done and give it the focus it needs, everything else becomes a waste of time.

Recovery is by far the most overlooked aspect of lifting, it is an essential piece of the puzzle that can easily determine success or failure. It demands your respect, your appreciation, your willingness to learn and above all, your discipline.

Let's look at all the different ways you can help your muscles and your mind keep up with those grueling workouts.

1. Volume
2. Food
3. Rest Days
4. Injuries
5. Massage
6. Water
7. Positive Thinking
8. Supplements
9. Preventing illness

Volume

We all train too much, even the pros. We do it because we love to lift, we love being in the gym, because it's our escape. We see videos and pics of men and women on social media and we want to follow their lead. The bottom line is that we damage our muscles when we train and the fibers need time to recover, rebuild and then, given the right environment, grow. Spend too much time tearing down that muscle and it will catch up to you, not only will you not grow, you will bring into play a number consequences such as injury and illness.

One of the challenges here is that there's no formula, no set of guidelines and no way of knowing if a muscle group has completely recovered and is ready for another attack. What makes it even more complicated is the effect training one muscle group has on the rest of your body. What I mean by that is if you do back one day and legs the next, you don't know the impact all of those squats will have on your back's recovery.

When you stop and think about how important it is to give your muscles a chance to recover and grow, you begin to appreciate the need to put a great deal of thought into your training schedule. I can guarantee you that most don't. Here's a typical week for most people:

Monday – Chest	Saturday – Shoulders/Arms
Tuesday – Arms	Sunday - Legs
Wednesday – Back	Monday - Chest
Thursday – Chest	and so on…
Friday – Off	

Without even getting into all of the other aspects of recovery, a schedule like this simply doesn't make recovery possible. To make things even more challenging, consider this…you know why very few people in the gym have big hamstrings? For one, very few do stiff legged deadlifts properly. But that's for an-other chapter. The main problem is that it's become almost standard to add three or four sets of leg curls to the end of a workout and that's it. Same with calves and even traps. Three sets of shrugs and I should be fine. That's what we've read in the magazines for years. The thing is, there's no difference between chest muscle fibers and hamstring muscle fibers and three sets of anything isn't going to have an impact on a muscle. If it did we'd all be huge.

This was my hamstring workout yesterday morning.

Five sets of Lying Leg Curls (finish with a drop-set)
Four sets of Wide Stance Stiff Legged Deadlifts
Four sets of seated leg curls (finish with a drop-set)

That's what it takes to create a scenario for growth, and it's the same for any muscle group. If people consistently incorporated this workout, or something similar, they'd have hamstrings that matched the rest of their physique, rather than being stuck with a weak body part. Problem is it's hard enough to incorporate all of the major muscle groups, let alone full workouts on the minor ones. So here's one of your biggest challenges, and it's one that most don't even consider or put thought into.

How do we incorporate full 15-20 set workouts
for each muscle group in a given rotation
while allowing for adequate periods of recovery?

I know nobody likes to work on those secondary muscle groups. We all like to work chest and arms and shoulders. We like to do squats with our buddies on Sunday morning so we can go collapse on the couch and watch football. I was no different back when I started.

But for many years now, I've trained every muscle group with the same level of intensity. I train calves as hard as I train chest, if not harder. I have weak points of course, we all have our stubborn areas, but my focus is always on a balanced approach. This allows me to create an illusion of size. On every visit to the gym I see individuals who don't, the ones I never see train legs. People with massive chests and no calves, giant arms and no back. It all depends on what you want out of the gym. Maybe you just want big arms and that's it, but keep in mind that when you're young, if you train properly, your body will respond and grow. This is the time to maintain discipline or things can get way out of whack in a hurry.

There are ten different muscle groups that you can train.

Chest	Abs
Back	Traps
Shoulders	Quads
Biceps/Brachialis/Forearms	Hamstrings/Glutes
Triceps	Calves

Many of us take the time to write down a set schedule or training split with great intentions. The problem is that certain traps always seem to pop up and get in the way.

Trap 1	One trap is starting the week with a chest workout (which is brilliant because everyone else in the gym is training chest). Then we continue the week training our favorite muscle groups, or the ones that we want grow the most. By the end of the week, a good portion of your muscle groups have been left out. Rather than train the leftovers, we start all over again with chest on Monday. This cycle continues and down the road, you're left with several weak points. The answer is to add that one leftover workout where you hit several minor body parts that were missed in one session. Train hams, calves, traps & rear delts. It may not be as fun but you chose this hobby, so you might as well do it right. Maintain that habit and your physique will benefit. If you need motivation, just look at 'that guy' in the gym with the massive chest and no legs.

Trap 2	We all want big arms, plain and simple. Guys want to stretch out those t-shirt sleeves and girls want that nice shape muscle provides. I'll detail how to train arms but the point I want to make here is that one of the biggest challenges when you're learning how to lift is taking your arms out of the equation. Pulling with your back and pushing with your chest isn't easy and it takes time. The result is that you will use your arms when you train chest and back and even shoulders. And so your arm workouts should be short, efficient and at the bottom of your priority list. This is especially true for biceps, try spending ten to fifteen minutes after your back workout, it should be plenty.
Trap 3	On any given day, we only have so much time and energy. If your schedule has you working chest and shoulders on a day when you're rushed or feeling tired, then you need to adjust. The mistake is doing your usual chest workout and then running out of time or not having enough left in the tank to hit the delts. What you should do is select two exercises for each body part and complete more sets while incorporating some of the principals to really push the muscles. You are far better off hitting both with less than skipping one.

Here are some strategies to help you avoid the traps and train all of your muscle groups while incorporating the need for recovery.

1. The Push-Pull System
2. Cycling
3. HIT (High Intensity Training

The Push - Pull System

The idea here is to split your workouts into three different groups.

The pushing muscles (Chest, Shoulders, Triceps)
The pulling muscles (Back, Traps, Biceps)
Legs (Quads, Hamstrings, Calves)

Benefits	This is a great system when you are learning how to lift. When you're new, you will have trouble isolating muscle groups while your body continues to become accustomed to the movements. Therefore, you will be working all of your 'pushing' muscles when you train chest. Grouping them this way should allow you to work all of the involved muscle groups in one session and give them time to rest on the days you work other muscle groups. This also lets you work all ten areas in three workouts which is very efficient. This will also let you work three different muscle groups that effectively share a 'pump'. If you work chest, and then work legs, it takes a while to get rid of the pump in your chest and then transfer it to your legs. Here, when you do chest, your triceps and shoulders will 'share' the pump.

Cycling Muscle Groups

Once you've been training for some time and you know what you're doing, you'll know which muscle groups are growing at a faster rate than the rest. Mr. Olympia title holder Phil Heath's arms exploded with growth when he started training. Now he barely trains them to keep in balance. Others have legs that grow faster and overpower everything else. That's just the way we're made, pure genetics.

How do we fix this? Easy. Let's say you had a weak back because you never really focused on it or learned how to train it properly. Now you decide to train nothing but back for three months. You train it three times a week and then just go home, rest and eat. Would your back grow? Of course it would. Does anyone ever do that? Of course not.

The idea is to incorporate that into what you do. What that means is that while you're still training all of the other groups, you don't expect the same results. You certainly won't lose any muscle, you're just looking to bring up weak points.

Try this:

- Ensure these groups get trained no matter what
- Ensure you have ample time to complete a full workout
- Ensure you've eaten well and have lots of stored energy
- Pay attention to detail when you train, the warm-up the focus etc.
- Use your principles to push yourself and force growth
- Ensure you follow the workout with the necessary protein and carbs to help with recovery

- Take your days off after these sessions to help with recovery
- Train your other areas around this process

Benefits	It's not possible to follow the above steps for all muscle groups all of the time, even for the pros whose job it is to train.
	Even if you don't have major weaknesses in your physique, focusing on a couple areas this way will incur growth. If you keep rotating different areas, you will continue to build your overall physique.
	This will help you become better at training the areas of focus and more confident in the major lifts. (If you focus on quads, you will become better at squatting)
	With only a portion of your workouts being full on high intensity, you will be creating a scenario that is better for recovery and less stress will be placed on your nervous system

HIT - High Intensity Training

These is a constant debate in bodybuilding, HIT vs. high volume training. Dorian Yates followed the advice of Mike Mentzer and trained for short periods of time typically using a two day on, one off schedule. The idea being to pyramid up to one very high intensity set to complete failure. Do around three or four exercises for major muscle groups and two to three for minor. The goal is to use that one last set to damage the muscle fibers. Once you've accomplished that, what's the point in continuing? You only make it more difficult for your body to recover. Less is more, if done properly.

On the other side of the coin, Jay Cutler used high volume. Lots and lots of sets with little rest in between. Pump the muscle with as much blood as possible and force it to keep contracting again and again. Obviously each one works, both Dorian and Jay were multiple Mr. O winners. You can argue each approach all you want and take sides, as most do. It all depends on what you like to do and for me, it's both.

HIT is a very valuable tool that you should consider. However, it is definitely one for experienced lifters and should be used sparingly, if at all by beginners.

The whole concept revolves around taking a set to absolute failure and using principles to do it. You won't be able to do that unless you're accustomed to the movement and confident enough to take it that far.

Benefit	I don't know about you but I don't have that much time to lift, usually an hour max. When you're trying to get in two or even three muscle groups to keep up with the schedule, HIT makes a lot of sense. It's extremely efficient.
	I also tend to agree with the whole 'less is more' theory, simply because it makes sense. I think the key here is in the warm-up. You need to make

> sure you get a good pump and that you thorough-
> ly warm the joints.
>
> The fewer all-out sets to failure you complete, the
> less stress on your body and your nervous sys-
> tem. That can only make it easier to recover.
>
> The emphasis here is not on weight, it's about
> pushing that one set as far as you can go. It's
> about stressing the muscle and not stroking the
> ego. That's always a good thing.

I want to encourage you to appreciate how much your progress relies on your body's recovery between training sessions.
We all fall into traps that make it very difficult to train our whole
body. If you find that you're not getting all of the muscle groups
in there, or you are but you're not able to take the necessary
days off to rest, then give these strategies a shot.

You should always have an idea of what it is you're trying to
accomplish in the gym. Goals vary, some want to get stronger
for their sport, build bigger arms and abs to impress or model,
bodybuild, recover from an injury or just be fit. A balanced approach in the gym is always the best answer. Give those
strategies a shot and see how you make out. Trust me when I
tell you, it's a big challenge. If you're this far into the book, you're
likely up for it.

Food

There's a saying in bodybuilding, I remember reading it in one
of the magazines years ago. It was an article by Achim Albrecht,

this massive and somewhat crazy German man, crazy in the gym that is, and in the wrestling ring.

"There's no such thing as overtraining, just under-eating."

There's a reason this section is called "Recovery" and not "Overtraining." If there's one complaint I have about the hundreds (if not thousands) of articles I've read, it's the lack of focus on recovery. There was always mention of overtraining and the debate among lifters as to how many days you should or shouldn't take off.

Here's the thing, overtraining is like over-studying for exams. You work to the point of exhaustion and pass out in bed. You can only push your body so hard in the gym until your muscles stop firing. What we all need to learn, and the sooner the better, is that everything we do outside of the gym determines how our bodies cope with all of that training.

To be successful, make progress and reach your goals, you need knowledge, time, money, desire and a big ass bucket full of discipline and work ethic. I'm here to help you with the knowledge part.

The saying should read...There's no such thing as overtraining, just under recovering.

This book doesn't really address diet or get into what you 'should' be eating. While I consider myself to be quite knowledgeable when it comes to nutrition, this is a book on how to lift, not how to eat. What I *am* going to focus on is what you need to get out of your diet, and give you some tips on how to go about it. These are just tips. If you're truly serious about lifting, just getting in shape or sports then you shouldn't just research nutrition, you should become an expert.

1. Purpose
2. Preparation is everything
3. Enjoy what you eat
4. Quality over quantity

Purpose

When it comes to nutrition, a good place to start is with the basics. What do you need from your diet, what purpose does it need to serve? Regardless of whether you're bulking or cutting, for me, there are only two needs.

1. Fuel you workouts

Regardless of anything you read, your muscles use carbohydrates as fuel. I'm not getting into any of the science behind it but that's just the way we're built. Even if you're trying to lose fat, you can't effectively lift without fuel.

2. Be Anabolic

Outside of the gym, which is by far the majority of the time, your diet should focus on maintaining an anabolic state. More specifically, you need to maintain a positive nitrogen balance. Our bodies are always either breaking down muscle, or building muscle or doing some combination of both. What you eat and drink can allow you to control that balance and make it possible for your body to add the muscle it wants to in order to cope with the workouts you're putting it through. One of the biggest mistakes people make when dieting is not understanding or respecting this aspect. The result is losing a significant amount of muscle along with some fat. If you ever compete in a bodybuilding contest, you'll soon realize that losing fat is easy, losing fat and keeping muscle is where the challenge lies. This is something you need to research and become an expert on.

Preparation is everything

Learn how to cook: You can ask any athlete, any bodybuilder or fitness competitor and they will all tell you about when they came to realize how important nutrition is. They will recount that day when they made the switch to planning their diet and preparing their own food. They will then tell you how much of a difference it made.

Preparing your own food means learning how to cook. I say that because you're going to want to enjoy the food you eat and throwing everything in the microwave or burning it half the time won't help that cause. Learn how to cook meat so it's tender and easy to eat, how to make really good rice, homemade fries, sweet potato, healthy pancakes or muffins. If you're living at home then encourage your family to try some healthy meals (if they don't already). Add what you need to the grocery list and start experimenting. Knowledge is everything so start learning.

Food prep is your job and the kitchen is your office, and just like any other office you need your tools and that means a good quality blender, lots of cutting boards, non-stick pans and Tupperware. A rice cooker is a great addition and so is a vegetable steamer.

Be efficient. I always get a laugh out of the recipes in the health magazines, lots of ingredients and lots of work. That's great if you have all day to cook but like me, you probably don't. The key is to come up with a menu of meals that are quick, easy and suitable for leftovers.

Always be prepared and avoid situations where you go hungry. If I'm going somewhere and I'm not sure how long I'll be, I always bring something to eat just in case. Even if it's a protein shake and a peanut butter and jam sandwich, it does the job. I don't know about you, but I turn in to one grumpy-ass sumbitch when I have to go without food.

Enjoy what you eat

Ask anyone who's been lifting a long time and they'll tell you stories of some of the crazy shit they used to eat. I remember making tuna milkshakes in University. Today, that would definitely make me throw up. It's an image that goes side by side with bodybuilding, eating a bowl of oatmeal and a plate of egg whites or plain fish with green beans. It's an outdated image that's made to create an illusion of sacrifice, devotion and doing whatever it takes.

Today, things are a little different. Unless you're one month out from a show, there's no reason you can't enjoy every meal you eat and still achieve your goals. The key is knowledge, and understanding food. Experiment with the base foods that you like and get creative. I never eat egg whites without at least one yolk. I can't stand tuna and I will never put anything resembling kale in my protein shakes. A diet that is far too boring and dull will only temp you to give in and order that pizza.

Quality over Quantity

Another big "image" issue is the amount of food you have to eat. Once again, bodybuilders are associated with eating eggs by the dozen, steaks by the pound and whole chickens for snacks. You can give that route a try but the only thing you will accomplish is wasting a whole bunch of money.

Never compare yourself to someone who has over a hundred pounds more muscle than you. What Dallas McCarver says he's eating, is not what you should be eating.

You need to spread out your food consumption throughout the day. Eating three chicken breasts in one sitting is simply a waste. Instead, have one at dinner, one before bed and one for lunch the next day.

Appreciate the need to look after your digestive system. If you're not eating any vegetables or oatmeal then you should probably take a fiber supplement...or better yet, just eat your damn vegetables!

If you're full, don't force feed. There are days when I can eat 8 meals and still be hungry, and there are days when all I want is protein shakes and some pancakes.

Don't get hooked on protein bars. They might be great for emergencies or when food isn't available but don't have one every day for a snack. You are way better off having a shake. The protein bars can be very hard on your digestive system.

If someone says you need to eat at Wendy's every day to get big, they're wrong. Once a week should be just fine. When it comes to cheating, a lot of times it's not what you're eating, it's what you're not eating.

Here's a look at what I'm eating now. Keep in mind my food and supplement budget is pretty small but I want to show you how to get creative so you can enjoy your food while keeping prep time down.

Breakfast Options

Scrambled eggs: a cup of egg whites with one or two yolks, mushrooms and salsa
Ezekiel English muffin with natural peanut butter and jam
Pancakes with blueberries and a protein shake
Two fried eggs with some leftover steak & potatoes
Turkey bacon with an Ezekiel English muffin

Lunch/Dinner Options

Rice stir-fry with chicken or steak, vegetables and almonds
Teriyaki flank steak with homemade fries and veggies
Trout with sweet potato
Tilapia with salsa and veggies (when dieting)
Ground turkey burgers with black olives, tomatoes and onions
Thin crust pizza with sliced chicken breast and hot sauce
Pasta with chicken breast and/or turkey sausage
Rice with ground turkey and pasta sauce

Treat Meals

All-you-can-eat sushi
Fajitas
Homemade hamburgers with fries

<u>Dessert Options</u>

Frozen yogurt
Melon
Dark Chocolate

<u>My favorite shake...</u>

Chocolate protein powder
1 tbsp of natural peanut butter
Skim milk
Espresso (optional)
Ice

Rest days

It's those 6 a.m. workouts in the middle of the winter that make you shake your head sometimes and wonder why you didn't take up softball. You sit in car shivering, waiting for the engine to warm up and some mornings you just laugh at your-self. It all reaffirms just how addicted you can become to lifting, or running, or yoga or whatever it is you do before most people get out of bed.

As addicted as I am, it can become increasingly tempting to spend way too much time in the gym. But as I said before, I don't so much believe in overtraining as I do in under-recovering. So I want to talk about all of the times and reasons you need to respect how essential rest days are in your overall progress.

✓ **Injured** - Don't be stupid.

✓ **Too sore** - If your legs are still crazy sore, don't train them again, it's a waste of time.

✓ **No food** - A good day of eating beats a good day of training…always!!!

✓ **No sleep** - If your nervous system isn't ready, then you're not ready.

✓ **Headache** – Lifting increases the blood pressure in your head…not a good mix.

✓ **Had two great intense workouts in a row** - Time to take advantage, stay home and eat.

✓ **Sick** - Go to bed.

✓ **Too rushed** - If you don't have enough time then don't rush, make more time tomorrow.

As for the training split, I typically do a two on one off split, but life can always get in the way. I've always tried to follow this rule…don't work out more than three days in a row, and don't take more than two days off in a row. With that approach, it's tough to go wrong.

Injuries

How to avoid injuries:

Understand that the gym weakens you, it weakens your muscles, joints and tendons. The majority of injuries occur outside of the gym, resulting from careless activities. Here are some tips.

1. Take your time in the gym when moving weights around. Don't carry a 45 pound plate in each hand and then try swinging one up to the bar. Put one down and use two hands.

2. If you're lifting a heavy dumbbell, again, take your time, make sure you're square to it and not reaching. Lift with your back.

3. When you're doing a movement, keep your head straight. If you suddenly turn to look in the side mirror half-way through your set, you can easily wrench your neck.

4. Always be cautious of your rotator cuffs, both in and out of the gym. Mess one up and you could spend months trying to fix it.

5. When a set is too heavy, it's just that, too heavy. Don't squirm or panic and get out of position. Losing your form with heavy weight is the easiest way to get injured.

6. Don't squat or deadlift with too much weight. Giving up form for weight on these exercises can not only lead to injury but be extremely dangerous. Mess up your lower back and you just might regret it for the rest of your life!

7. Don't ever think that because someone is spotting you, it's OK to use more weight or get sloppy. There's very little he or she can do if things go wrong.

8. Don't go too heavy before your body gets accustomed to the movements. I see guys struggling to get dumbbells up for shoulder presses, and then awkwardly squeezing out reps. That's a rotator cuff injury waiting to happen.

9. If you feel something 'tweak', stop! Don't be a tough guy and keep going. If you want to keep training then work another un-related body part. Best to get home and ice it.

10. Watch out for your wrists. Taking too wide or narrow a grip can put a great deal of pressure on the joint. The close grip bench press is a good example: if your hands are almost touching, it creates a crazy angle for your wrists.

11. I've been very fortunate to never suffer a major injury in the gym after years of heavy training. Take your time, maintain your form, and be careful moving the weight around. If something does happen, let it heal.

If you have a bad pull in your upper body, then take it as an opportunity to train your legs more. Training something that's damaged will only delay the recovery.

Massage

My day job comes with some pretty good benefits, and they include massage. While a lot of you might not have that luxury, there are a number of less expensive franchises opening up. A one hour massage runs about seventy-five bucks and when your budget is tight, that's a lot of money. You can try negotiating with someone and tell them you don't have benefits, even a 30 minute session on your back is well worth it. I think of the hundreds of dollars some kids spend on supplements when there are much better 'recovery' related items that should attract some of that coin.

Again, I'm not going to get into the scientific details of massage but if you've ever had a professional athletic massage, you already know, it helps in a huge way. I'm not talking about a dark room with candles and sappy music, I'm talking about pain.

My usual request on a visit is pretty simple, "tear my back to shreds". Deep tissue massage usually includes grinding the muscle fibers against your bones and that's not fun. I'll take a couple of Advil, drink a shitload of water, and tough it out. You'll feel like crap after, like when you have a couple pints at lunch and it just doesn't sit right. But as soon as you get out of bed the next morning, you'll feel it. It's like someone gave you a new back.

I relay this message to so many people that sit at a desk all day, or spend hours in traffic commuting, or even lie on a cheap couch most nights. Go get yourself a deep tissue massage from someone who knows what they're doing. I laugh when I hear people say they're covered at work but feel guilty going. The company covers massage to help keep you healthy and work-ing!

From a bodybuilding point of view, you'll see that all of the pros now do it. When you train several times a week, especially if you train heavy, your muscles become tight and full of knots and that certainly doesn't make it any easier for the fibers to re-cover, rebuild and grow.

Water

I used to work with this lady, her desk was right across from my office. After a couple of weeks I noticed that her morning ritual always included two Tylenol. I became curious and wanted to know what the issue was, and it wasn't that hard. Other than a coffee every few hours, I never saw her drink water. You don't want to pry into people's business, and especially their health, but things can get pretty boring in the office world. One Monday morning I asked her about the pain killers and she told me they were for headaches, which she got every morning. I then asked her how much water she drank and she confirmed what I sus-pected: barely any.

Rather than get into the science of why we need water, I simply told her that if she started every morning with a big glass of water, and kept drinking water throughout each day, I would take her out for lunch on Friday.

It was Wednesday morning when I saw her take out the bottle before even turning on her computer, she looked at it, paused, and then threw it back in her drawer. Later that day, she sat down in my office with a smile on her face and all she said was "Thank you...but you still owe me lunch."

If you want to know more about the many benefits of drinking water, Google it. We spend money on supplements every week, we eat what we can and we get up in the morning and we train. To ignore one of the most important ingredients in the recipe for success, when it's free and available everywhere doesn't make a lot of sense, now does it?

Make a habit of drinking a large glass of water every morning as soon as you wake up. This is especially important in the summer when you sweat more at night. Take a water bottle with you in the car, to a meeting, to a friend's house... *wherever* you go. I'm not saying you need to drink ten gallons of water a day, just be hydrated, and it will help you with everything from concentration to your sex life, and of course, with your training.

Being Positive

There was a DJ on one of my favorite radio stations, he went by the name Iron Mike Benson. One morning, they reported that he had passed away after battling cancer for months. Listeners called in all day and recanted stories and spoke about the impact Iron Mike had on their lives. Listening to it all day really got me thinking. I wanted to write something about it. I wanted to write about the effect this man had on so many people, even without ever meeting them.

One caller said, "Iron Mike didn't know me, none of you do, but I know all of you, and I want you to know that more than anyone in my life, you've gotten me through all of the lows, and there were plenty of 'em, and I want to thank you for that...".

The DJ's fought off tears all day, and every caller had a tough time doing the same. Why is that? DJ's come and go, some last, some don't, some are funnier than others, why did this one have such a huge presence? If you listened to all of the stories, a certain quality stood out, and that's that Mike was positive. All of the time, he was happy. He made people smile every day and he made people feel good about themselves.

In today's world, social media has created an avenue for hate, and it's growing. It fuels bullying and racism. A place kicker misses a field goal in a playoff game and he's afraid to go home because of the death threats on Twitter. A black hockey player scores a game winning goal and the racist remarks start before he sits down in the dressing room. I'd like to see one person say any of it to that player's face, or confront the place kicker. It's a horrible side effect of growing technology. Just the other night I was telling my son how I never want to hear the word 'hate', that it's one of the worst words in the English language, even worse than swearing.

Then I decided to tell the kids about Iron Mike. I tried to make the point that if you're a positive person, and a happy person, you will have a great impact on others. I explained that you should seek out positive people and out of all your friends, avoid the ones that seem angry all of the time, that pick apart others or bully or put people down. While they're too young to have much to complain about now, I assured them the time would come. Always focus on the positives, smile and make others smile. That's the road to happiness.

You may not realize how deeply negativity affects your mind and body. I've lost count of how many jobs I've had but the one thing that always made me leave was extreme negativity in the work environment. Staff would complain all day, managers would take their frustrations out on them. I could never accept that type of atmosphere. I left my first marriage because I couldn't take living in a home that was always negative. I think that's why so many do get divorced. Not being happy at home will slowly drive you crazy, literally.

Sometimes, for many, both work and home are bad, or maybe school and home, either scenario can be very dangerous. I wrote earlier about how the gym was always my escape, it's what prevented me from losing it. I recommended that you use the gym to help deal with problems, to release your anger so you can better deal with your life and resolve issues. I don't want you to skip that last step. You can't live in negative environments and while it can be extremely difficult to change them, you have to protect yourself. We see so many teenage suicides and even adult suicides, we see drug use on the rise across the board. I can only give you the advice that you shouldn't accept it. Find another job so you can get away from that boss, change or get out of that horrible relationship, and don't wait too long to act. Find someone to talk to about what's going on at school. Find positive people, positive environments and positive relationships. The difference will astound you, not only with your health and your ability to recover both physically and mentally from training but in all of your weekly activities.

For many, Iron Mike was one of the few positive things in the listeners' lives, when so much of everything else was negative, and that's why he had the impact he did. I guarantee you that he saved people's lives, people he'd never even met for reasons he never even knew about. He saved that one caller's life, you could hear it in his voice. Iron Mike will be missed every day by thousands for some time to come.

Supplements

Every six months or so, the store where I usually buy our supps has a big sale. The first 50 customers get a big bag full of samples and a t-shirt. I rarely miss it, the price of this stuff has skyrocketed, so it's worth the 30 minute wait. Lately, I've come to enjoy standing in line more and more for the discussions I get to listen in on. Last time I think it went something like... "Bro, I'm grabbing this pre-workout shit man...heard it was sick! Jack you right up man" or "Called the trainer...said to stack the weight gainer with this sick-ass test booster, packing on another ten by Christmas" to which his friend replies "Fuck-ya...be lifting some sick fuckin weight man!"

Now I'm not trying to make fun of today's youth but if you happen to talk this way, please understand that it's very im-portant that you maintain the ability to go back to your 'intelligent' voice. And if you don't have an intelligent voice, maybe you should read more and watch a little less reality TV. Once in the store, I load up on what I need and while waiting in line to pay, I continue to watch. I always see the same thing, the guys who lift spend a fortune, hundreds of dollars.

Let's face it, there's no shortage of products. There used to be protein powder, vitamins, creatine, and a few other sketchy products making crazy promises. Now there's a pre-workout, intra-workout, post workout, NO boosters, test boosters, GH boosters, dozens of fat burners, all kinds of creatine, glutamine, ZMA, amino acids, and of course, every kind of protein powder in all kinds of flavors.

Here's a few things to think about.

Supplement companies pay bodybuilding magazines and websites millions in advertising dollars that in effect, make it possible for those businesses to exist. How many articles do you ever see written in those magazine about how ineffective some of those supplements might be?

If I were to say that the fitness industry is full of crap, which I do on a regular basis, supplements would certainly be part of my justification. Basically we are made to believe that supplements will either shred all of our body fat exposing very well developed abs, or provide a safe alternative to steroids allowing us to pack on significant muscle. Neither statement is even remotely true.

While this might seriously lower my chances of ever being sponsored by a supplement company, you need to be smart when it comes to advertising. As soon as possible, develop the ability to see through the bullshit when it comes to spending your money, not just on supplements but on any product or service. I could give you so many other examples, but this isn't the place for it. Read a book on marketing, get educated about the tricks they all pull and you will likely save yourself a substantial amount of money.

So what do you do? There are certainly some good products out there that can make a big difference. Let's start with the last thing you should do, and that's to walk into a store and tell the person at the desk that you want to lose a bunch of weight or gain a bunch of muscle. Doing that puts you at a serious disadvantage, and merely opens the door nice and wide for a good salesperson.

First, have a look at Layne Norton's material on the internet, he is a PhD and someone you should definitely take notice of.

All I can give you is the best set of tips I can think of that are based on my hard-won experience.

First and foremost, and this is extremely important, food comes first. If you aren't eating the way you need to in order to achieve your goals, then every dollar you spend on products will be wasted. Supplements do just that, they *supplement* a good solid diet. Now assuming you are in agreement and your diet is looked after, here's what you should be asking yourself.

- ✓ What is my need
- ✓ What am I looking for the supplement to do
- ✓ What ingredients are actually proven to help with that need
- ✓ Am I better off just buying that ingredient by itself
- ✓ Where does it rank in priority with my other needs
- ✓ Is the amount it will help worth the price
- ✓ Does it fit into my budget

Let's run through some standard examples of needs.

- ✓ I need energy & focus when I train
- ✓ I need a meal replacement for when I can't cook
- ✓ I need help recovering between workouts
- ✓ I need to maximize muscle growth
- ✓ I need to lose fat
- ✓ I need to preserve muscle while I'm dieting

By going through this process, your trip to the store should be about getting a good deal on what you know you want, rather than being sold something you don't need.

You might be wondering why this is all in the recovery section of the book. While most of the new supplements out there are aimed at the actual workout, you should be spending your money on the ones that will help you recover and grow between workouts.

1. The best pre-workout formula is having eaten solid meals the day before and the day of and being properly hydrated with a good night's sleep. I use a stimulant-free pre-workout product because I suck at sleeping and I'm older. If you're young and full of energy, there's little benefit, just a load of caffeine and other products that may or may not be good for your system.

2. Protein powder is essential, I can't imagine lifting without it. But what you need to understand is that some powders digest quickly for post workout and some digest much slower for meal replacement and before bed. The top isolate blends are very expensive, so consider the benefits vs. the cost.

3. Research doesn't mean reading the ads in the magazines that are written by the very same people that are trying to sell you their product! Look around and find good sources of non-biased reviews of the studies on the ingredients. Do not rely on some kid's review on a forum.

4. Learn about vitamins and minerals. Zinc and Magnesium for example are key to recovery and hugely popular with professional athletes.

5. Fat burners work if you're dieting correctly, if not, might as well just take your cash out and burn it.

6. Amino acids, specifically Leucine, are great for recovery and maintaining/building muscle.

Just keep in mind that significant muscle growth comes from working hard in the gym, spending hours in the kitchen, paying attention to detail and above all, patience. It does not come from taking some supplement promising staggering results in a matter of weeks, but the right products can definitely help you train and recover.

Preventing Illness

I've done it, and so have you, or if you haven't yet, you will. For me it was always a sore throat that led to a cough that took forever to finally go away. I'd be in the gym hacking up a lung and I'm sure, annoying everyone around me. It seemed like every winter I would get it and back then, I *had* to lift, there was just no staying home.

One year, I'd finally had enough, there was no way I getting sick again and spending another winter coughing all over everyone. That was about ten years ago and I've been cough free since. The thing about lifting is that it wears you down, it weakens you, more than most other forms of exercise. Once you finish your workout, you're susceptible because your immune system is also weak. Combine that with the fact that you're in a room full of other people who are potentially sick and sweating all over everything and the odds are stacked against you.

Here's what I do. How far you take it is up to you and how easily you seem to get sick.

1. First of all, when it's cold, bundle up before you leave the gym. Wear a hoodie with the hood on and the zipper all the way up. Keep a toque in your bag. Track pants and socks are also a must, no shorts! Keep it all on until the car warms right up. Sweating out in the cold is never a good idea.

2. Before you leave, wash your hands and face thoroughly. Costco sells giant packs of facial wipes in little dispensers, throw one in your bag and you're set. This is a very important habit, and it's always a good idea to wash the sweat off your face, especially if you get acne.

3. I'm not crazy when it comes to cleaning the equipment before I use it unless I notice someone was coughing all over it. Nowadays, people spend half their workout time in the gym cleaning so that's usually pretty safe. It's a good idea to avoid touching your face while training, and to bring a towel.

4. Another good habit is to bring your water bottle with you so you don't have to keep going to the fountain. If someone has a sore throat they'll be grabbing a

drink between every set and that means plenty of germs.

5. If you're coughing or have a sore throat, take the day off. Being stuffed up or just having a cold is fine but it's that chest cough with phlegm that you don't want, that can last for weeks. As soon as I feel a sore throat coming I grab a bottle of anti-bacterial mouth-wash and gargle with it every hour. It will help kill all those germs in your throat. You can buy anti-bacterial lozenges but the mouthwash is a hell of a lot cheaper.

Doing those few little things has made a huge difference for me and I certainly don't miss getting sick. I do chuckle when it's February, minus twenty with the wind-chill and a couple of guys are walking out in their shorts and sleeveless shirts sweating up a storm, mostly because I was stupid enough to do it for years.

Remember: the majority of your time is spent outside of the gym. Appreciate how much stress you put your body and mind through when you train and how crucial it is that you do what you need to do in order to recover. This is definitely a chapter worth reading a few times or even jotting down notes to summarize and to remind yourself. You won`t get big if all you do is tear your body down and exhaust your mind. And remember: stay positive.

Part Three

How We Lift

Steve Foxall

Chapter 17: Back

Now it's time to learn how to get huge. I'm going to go through each body part for you. I think the best way to teach you is to detail what you need to avoid. Strip away the bad and you're left with the good. All the books and magazine articles I've read all tell you what you should be doing while very few discuss those common mistakes people make every day in the gym. You need to eliminate your mistakes before you can focus on taking your training to the next level. By structuring these sections like a text book, my intention is that you will be able to read it over whenever you seem to be struggling with a body part. Give it a quick read now and again before you train, it should help.

The back comes first because it is by far my favorite body part to train. In a bodybuilding competition it is what wins shows. All of the top contenders always have amazing backs. It's the body part I find the most impressive on the human physique. I remember the first time I watched that scene in Pumping Iron where Arnold does a rear double bicep pose in the gym and his partner says "it looks like a road map...with fingers all over it," I was amazed. Even in the magazines, I've always favored the back pictures, especially the training ones. There are some amazing black and white pictures of Dorian Yates working his back at Temple Gym.

If I had to sum up the way I've learnt to train my back, I would use the term "controlled aggression." It's primal in nature, the exercises are unique in that the pulling motion deamands that you summon all of your strength. Think of the events in the world's strongest man competitions where they lift the big round stones or even the cars—it's their immensely strong backs that are doing the work. The ability to harness all of that power and use it in a controlled fashion is something well worth learning. It's the ability to pull with everything you have while maintaining the required form and focusing on getting those shoulders back and contracting those big back muscles.

That's controlled aggression. Once you learn how to do it, the workouts become so much more rewarding. You get a feeling of having conquered, of having overcome. I have consistently trained my back as a priority and I enjoy doing it.

This is a body part that I see so many people train incorrectly, and this includes some pretty experienced lifters. It can be difficult to learn, but not if you practice until you get it right. Think about it: you can practice for a month, or mess it up for years. Your choice, here's where you should start.

1. Pulling with Your Hands
2. Flat Wrists
3. Eliminating the Shoulders
4. Rhythm
5. Stretch and Squeeze
6. Visualization and Feel
7. Straps

Pulling With Your hands

When you start working on your back, you might notice something. The next day after you train, your biceps are killing you and your back isn't. The cause? You're pulling with your hands. Everyone does it, grab the handles, squeeze hard and pull. The problem is that when you pull with your hands, you aren't doing much else. In other words, you aren't using your back. I mentioned this tip already, imagine pulling with your elbows. It's a very simple technique and the best way I know to start focusing on your lats. Lower the weight and practice.

Once you learn how to pull without using your arms you will get used to that feeling of your back doing the work. Then you will always know if you're doing a move correctly.

Flat Wrists

I hand out a lot of back training tips in the gym. The most common one has to do with the wrists. It's such a simple fix but without it, you will not be able to contract your back properly. Whenever you pull, in any exercise, you have to keep the top of your wrist flat. Most people 'break' their wrist when they pull the bar close into their bodies, as if they're revving a motorcycle. Why is that bad?

- ✓ Anytime you break your wrist, you transfer most of the weight on to your wrist and the muscles along the top of your forearms.

- ✓ This will make it difficult to contract your back muscles.

- ✓ This can lead to injury as your wrist and forearm muscles are not as strong and you are suddenly forcing them to carry a lot of weight.

- ✓ Whenever you rely on weaker muscles, it will limit how much weight you can use. In other words, you'll think you are at your max, but you're only at your wrist/forearm max.

Eliminating the Shoulders

I see this all the time. I've already written about how you need to understand the mechanics of how your muscles work, and to know what they are designed to do. It is so important that you learn this, and the sooner the better.

Try this. Stand up, and with your arms hanging down at your sides, try to touch your elbows behind your back. This should engage your lats and you should feel them contract. Now, lift your elbows up high, so they're parallel to your shoulders, keep them that high and try and again, touch them behind your back. Notice the difference? Now your shoulders and traps are forced to contract. That's half the battle right there. When you train your back, the position of your elbows, and in turn, your upper arm, will determine which muscles are working. When they're low and at your sides, the lats work; the more they flare out and up, the more your rear delts will kick in. This is a lesson that you can use with almost every back exercise you will do. If in doubt, do thirty reps with lighter weight and see which muscles start to burn.

The mechanics of what your muscles are meant to do, what their role is on the human body is not that complicated. Learn them, and you will be miles ahead of most lifters.

Rhythm

If you watch some videos online of bodybuilders training, you will notice a whole group of things they do that most people in the gym don't. It all comes from years of practice. One big difference is rhythm, and it's especially important with back work. I'll see people in the gym doing bent over rows or seated rows and they are moving slowly and even stopping at the stretched position before pulling the weight back. While this can be great for other areas of the body it's a problem with the back. The main reason is that your lats are one of your biggest and strongest muscle groups. Given their size, you need to use a fair bit of weight and get aggressive. When you stop the momentum of all that weight, it can be very difficult to get it going again without relying on your arms to start that pull. Think of a big train and how powerful it is. From a stopped position, a train takes a long time to get going. So don't stop the train. This is not cheating by any means, because you are not swinging the weight, you're just maintaining momentum. You will find it makes it a lot easier to keep the weight on your back muscles.

Also, with these exercises, you don't want to slowly pull the bar into your stomach or chest either, you want to bring it in hard which will help you to really squeeze your lats. Just watch a video of a pro doing seated rows and you will immediately see what I'm talking about. Remember, controlled aggression.

Stretch & Squeeze

Dorian Yates had one of the best backs in the game and I'd credit his stretch and squeeze mentality. It wasn't about how much weight he could lift, it was all about the contraction. In order to get that contraction, you have to properly stretch out the lats, without extending the shoulders. It's all about getting into that perfect position at the end of the negative, powering that weight in using your lats and then forcefully squeezing them. I always think of it as a trigger. Say you're doing pulldowns behind your neck, from a contracted position you allow the bar go back up with full control as always. When you get near the top you go up just enough to stretch the back and then that trigger goes off and you deliberately and forcefully pull that weight down and contract. Stretch & squeeze, always in rhythm.

Visualization & Feel

A big reason why working your back is a challenge has to do with the fact that you can't see it. When you work your chest, you can look in the mirror and watch your muscles contract, same with legs, shoulders and arms. As a result, with the back, you need two things: feel and visualization. To help me focus completely on everything I just described to you, I will either close my eyes or, if I'm in front of a mirror, I'll watch my shoulders and upper arms.

The other thing I do is visualize. I know which part of my back each exercise works so I focus on that area and what I'm feeling, I imagine that area contracting and I picture it in my mind. When I do this, it's not my back I'm picturing, it's Dorian's.

I used to think visualization meant lying in bed at night, closing your eyes and imagining what you wanted to look like, then I figured out how to use it in the gym. It's an extremely powerful tool that will help you lift correctly, and as a result, grow.

Straps

Lifting straps are an absolute necessity for your back, and I don't mean down the road when you're using too much weight to hold with your hands. Straps let you turn your hands into hooks, which is all we need them for. They let you stop focusing on your hands and better allow you to pull with your big back muscles. They help you to concentrate on learning how to contract the muscles. I use straps even with light weight simply because mentally I'm preparing to use big weight and I want to mimic those sets, just without the weight.

If anyone says you shouldn't use them, ignore them, unless you're training to be a power lifter. Here are some tips.

✓   Buy a good pair that has a little padding around the wrist area.

✓ Wash them once or twice when they're new just to soften them up a little, because they need to be worked in.

✓ It's a good idea to wear a long-sleeve shirt of hoodie so the material can go under the strap to protect your skin, especially for heavy back work.

✓ Write your name on them with a sharpie. If you leave them behind people are more reluctant to grab them.

✓ If they're awkward at first don't worry, you'll get used to them.

Let's look at some basic back exercises, in no particular order. Please use them as a reference guide and revisit often to ensure consistent effectiveness and progress.

1. Deadlifts
2. Bent Over Rows
3. T-Bar Rows
4. Seated Pulldowns
5. Seated Rows
6. One Arm Dumbbell Rows
7. Chin-ups
8. Pullovers
9. Extensions

Deadlifts

This is one of my favorite exercises, always has been. You can't help but judge a workout by how sore that muscle group is the next day and nothing will give you that soreness in your lats like deadlifts.

This exercise is very basic. Some people like to start with the bar on the ground like the powerlifters do, others like it up on the rack so they can start from a standing position. Either way works, but I find it's easier to load and unload weight from the rack.

What makes this move difficult to learn is that you are using your back for the top portion and your quads for the bottom. Errors in form occur mainly when people rely too much on one or the other. Just last week I was watching someone and they kept their back at the same angle throughout the entire rep. It was like some crazy awkward squat.

Let's assume you're starting from the floor. You want a shoulder-width stance. You can grip the bar with one overhand and one underhand like the powerlifters tend to do or just use overhand. (Never use two underhands!)

The width of your grip is very important. In order to minimize the stress on your wrists, arms and shoulders, you want your arms to hang down in a fairly straight position. I will be repeating this again and again: you have to learn the impact that the angles you use have on your muscles. People make the mistake of "mixing things up" by throwing in wide grips here and there and it can only be done on certain exercises, very rarely can it be used on moves where you use large amounts of weight.

In addition to stance and grip, you need to appreciate that your back has to remain arched throughout the entire movement. If you 'round' you back, you are putting yourself in a very dangerous position. Your back is a big strong muscle, your lower back *(spinal erectors)* are not nearly as big or as strong. Rounding your back means that you can very suddenly place a great deal of weight right onto your lower back and that can lead to a very serious injury.

Throughout this move, it is absolutely essential that you use a weight that allows you to maintain an arch in your back.

One way to think of this is to always have your chest out and shoulders back. As you work your way up in weight, it's just discipline. As soon as you can't maintain this position either on the negative or the positive, stop and lower that weight. This is no place for ego or trying to match your training partner.

As for the eyes, your body will react to where you look so to help you do this, always look forward, or slightly up. As is the case for squats, you shouldn't look too far up as it can tense up your neck and place your spine in an awkward position. It also impedes your ability to focus on your technique. Try doing anything at home while looking at the ceiling. It just throws you off.

From the side, the starting position should look like the bottom of a squat, your legs should be parallel to the ground with your butt sticking out behind you. Your knees should be just ahead of the bar.

As you continue to learn this movement, the tendency might be to pull the bar with your hands, arms and shoulders and 'shrug' the weight. It's just natural. You have to remember that your arms are just long hooks that hang down. Watch the serious lifters in the gym deadlift four or five hundred pounds—there's no way their arms could lift that much weight. Their legs and back do all the work and their arms simply connect them to the bar.

To help you avoid this tendency, start out by pushing your heels down against the floor, this will engage your leg muscles and they will start the bar moving. From there it isn't long before your back muscles take over, usually when the bar is just below the knees. From that point, it is extremely important that you maintain focus on your back muscles. You have to think them through this exercise, mentally force them to pull the weight up and contract. I always imagine I'm a machine when I deadlift, a giant unbreakable piston. Everything is tight, nothing moves but my hips and quads. I imagine I'm extremely powerful and solid. I stare straight ahead focusing on my eyes and nothing can distract me.

Once you get to the top, one common mistake is leaning too far back. Some people do this quite aggressively, swinging their whole upper body backwards. There is no benefit to doing this as it will not further contract your lats, it can however be very dangerous as you may again be placing all of that weight directly on your lower back. All you need to do is stand up and bring your shoulders back and squeeze, this will force that contraction, and if done correctly, you will feel it. Keep your arms stretched and focus on your back.

For the version where you start from a standing position, it is very important to keep the weight on your lats and not transfer it to your arms or your knees. As you stand, do not lock out your legs, this is key, keep a slight bend in them. When you completely lock out you can place a great deal of stress on your knees and you take the weight off of your back muscles. That lock out does not further help you contract your back muscles and that is the main goal of any exercise. Better to keep all of the weight on the muscles and focus, focus, focus! Do not stop thinking of your back muscles.

Going back down with the negative portion of the deadlift can be a little tricky. Trying to slow the move right down can make this even more challenging. Keep a reasonable pace as it will tend to "flow" more. As you stick your butt out behind you, commit to the exercise, lean forward with your back and lower the weight. When the bar passes your knees, your quads have to again squat down.

One mistake I see quite often here is starting the move by bending your knees as if you were going to squat. This completely disrupts the move. You need a slight bend in your knees but they shouldn't move anymore until the weight is below your knees. The whole negative move has to feel natural, like one motion without a top or a bottom. This can take time to learn, as it's not easy and will feel awkward at first. Keep at it with reasonable weight until you get it. Don't be afraid to ask an experienced lifter to watch you and give advice, it can save you hours of trial and error. Even have someone video you with your phone so you can see exactly what you are doing.

Avoid the tendency to start adding 45 pound plates, add 10's or 25's. When you are learning any move, it takes time. Until you learn it, impressing yourself and others with the weights you use is a quick path to failure. I use a belt and straps as I work my way up, I could certainly do these sets without them but it helps me mentally, it helps me feel like everything is tight, it helps me feel like that machine.

Finally, if you remember what I've said about 'deliberate lifting', it definitely comes into play on these powerlifting moves. You can't casually deadlift. For me, I try and keep my body as tight as possible on the negative and as the plates hit the ground I explode up. I imagine the piston firing and nothing being able to stop it. That's what I like about this exercise, the way you need to harness so much power from your legs and back. Always keep in mind that your mental focus is essential on these moves. You can't perform deadlifts and be looking at the person next to you. Nothing can break your concentration and you need to learn that as much as you need to learn the mechanics.

Top of the deadlift

Bent Over Rows

This is a fantastic exercise for building thickness in your back muscles, however, it is also a difficult one to master. You have the choice of an overhand or underhand grip and the technique for each is quite similar. The challenge is all about putting your body in a position where you have the ability to engage those powerful lats and then do your best to take them to failure.

The mistakes I always see with this move fall into three categories, and they all have to do with stance. First, let's go over how it's done right and then we'll look at those creative variations.

Again, shoulder-width stance and grip, that's right, shoulder-width grip. Don't start arguing that you should use a wide grip on these, you don't. I'll explain why in a moment. Now, setting up for these is all in the way you go from a standing position to the starting position. I've been doing these for years and I still take my time to make sure I get that set-up just right.

Step 1: Get the weight on your lats. There is no set way to do this, it's just a conscious practice of holding the weight up with your back instead of your arms. I'll probably mention it a few dozen times in the book, just practice it until you get it.

Step 2: Stick your ass way out. Your stance is a balancing act. You can't lean over while carrying two hundred pounds without counter balancing that weight, otherwise you fall over. By sticking your butt out, you move your center of gravity. It sounds simple, but most of the mistakes start with that move, or the lack of it.

Step 3: As you continue to lower yourself, you bend your knees and stick out your chest. This should ensure a good arch in the back. Keep lowering that weight while maintaining your balance. When set, your back angle should be between 45 and 90 degrees.

Step 4: Once there, make sure the bar is close to your body. It should travel along your thighs. Bringing it away from your body will engage the hamstring muscles and rear delts. That's it, all of that is just to get into the right position to start the exercise, that's why I always take it slow.

Here's the true test: if you do those four steps correctly, you will be able to get your back down low enough to put you in a very powerful position while still maintaining your balance. You should be ready to pull that weight right up into your gut. It should 'feel' like your back is doing the pulling. If not, focus on bringing those elbows in closer to your sides and bringing the bar up closer to your hips.

Now let's look at some of those creative variations.

The Shrug – When you don't stick your butt out, you can't lower yourself down into the right position. This leaves you in a very upright position and as you try to row, you're essentially shrugging the weight up with your shoulders and traps. This couldn't be more wrong.

The T-Rex – Again, when you don't get into the proper position and remain too upright, there is a popular tendency to pull the bar in to your chest rather than your waist. The result is that you have to use your hands rather than your back. Throughout the range of motion, your forearms should always be hanging straight up and down in order for there to be a direct connection between the weight and your back muscles. When you bring the bar up high you are forced to break that angle. This puts all of the weight on your forearm and will quickly limit how much weight you can use. Picture T-Rex's arms from the side.

Rows for Rear Delts – This one is actually right, it just works a different set of muscles. When people exaggerate the move and bend right over at the waist they create a ninety degree angle with their body. They tend to use a very wide grip, have the bar far away from their thighs and then pull it up to their chest. Back to mechanics, when your elbows go out and up you engage the rear delts instead of the lats. A great exercise for shoulders, not so much for back. I say this because if you see someone doing it and they know what they're doing, you need to understand it's for delts,

If you watch people train in the gym, you will find they do one of the four lifts I just described. I hope very much that reading this book will not only elevate your training, but enable you to identify the mistakes others are making. Those mistakes you see should act as a constant lesson, they should make you want to focus on the proper form and keep the weight manageable. With rows, go with the first one I described, the right one, and practice until it becomes automatic.

T-Bar Rows

This is one of my favorite exercises, ever since I saw Arnold doing them in 'Pumping Iron.' It's just all-out lifting, no holding back. The mechanics are very similar to bent-over rows. You're looking for the same position in order to activate the lats.

There is one common mistake that people tend to make that's specific to this movement. With the bar being fixed at the back, people tend to use it to their advantage. They will stand almost straight up and pull the bar in towards their chest. There isn't much benefit here for a couple of reasons. First, the more you stand up, the less weight you are actually carrying. You can hold a thousand pound bar straight up with one end on the floor and you won't be carrying any weight, the floor's doing the work. Second, that position makes it very difficult to focus on your lats, you will find that your arms and shoulders are moving the weight.

Follow my recommendations for the bent rows and make sure you adjust your feet so that your hands come up as close to your hips as possible. Keep those elbows tight and you won't have to break your wrists. Make sure your keep and arch in your back by sticking out your chest.

On the negative, remember not to let your arms extend too far, your elbows should always maintain a slight bend at the bottom. Again, you need to keep a good pace with forceful reps, you can't do 'slow' T-bar rows.

When you get really good, you'll find that at the bottom, you're able to 'catch' the weight with your lats before contracting them to reverse the weight and ram that handle into your gut.

Once you get it right, this is an excellent choice for building thickness in your back. Try using drop sets, it's very easy to lean forward once you reach failure and take a plate off. With your back, drop sets are very safe. Forced reps are out and it can be dangerous to keep going if you aren't able to maintain proper form. As the weight gets lower, focus on using your back and squeezing at the top. That's how you'll really push those muscle fibers.

One quick safety tip…when you move up in weight, you want to make sure you don't lift with your lower back. Use your legs and back to get the weight off the ground and then let your back take over. It's a good habit.

Seated Pulldowns

This is a pretty easy one, as in pretty easy to perform once you fully understand the mechanics of your back muscles. We'll cover wide-grip pulldowns to the front, behind the neck pulldowns and the reverse close-grip version with an underhand grip or with your palms facing each other.

The key to each of these is to keep in mind that the upper arm has to undertake a certain range of motion that forces your back muscles to contract. The consistent challenge with training your back is to learn how to avoid pulling with your arms and these movements are a great training aid.

Always sit with your knees under the pads and adjust those pads so they are tight enough to stop your legs from sliding around too much. You'll need that stability.

The golden rule for all pulldowns:
You should always be able to draw a straight line from your elbow, through the handle and up to the pulley. When you have that line, there is a direct connection from the muscle you are working to the weight you are moving.
Break that line…lose the connection.

Wide Grip Pulldowns to the Front

This is an extremely popular exercise, There is one very common mistake that I see on almost every trip to the gym. I think it comes down to that 'more is better' mentality that can lead to so many errors in form. The funny thing is, when it comes to lifting, nothing could be farther from the truth.

Think of this movement as mimicking a wide grip chin-up, with those, you pull yourself straight up until the bar comes to the top of your chest With pulldowns, you need to bring that bar down to the top of your chest. The mistake many people make is that they don't stop there. They keep the bar going down in front of them, their elbows go back behind them, and their forearms end up being almost flat.

You probably recognize what I'm talking about. If not, you'll soon see it in the gym. Why is this bad? Let's look at the mechanics and that golden rule above. As soon as you break that straight line and create a bend at the wrist, your lats can no longer carry the weight and they get disconnected. Now all the muscles along the top of your forearms are doing the work. This is bad for a few reasons, first, your forearms aren't nearly as strong as your back and this will lower the weight you can use. Second, you give up that finishing squeeze that's so important, that forceful contraction.

Focus on leaning back just enough, look up at the pulley and contract your lats. Pull with your elbows and let the bar go where it naturally wants to. If I were watching you from the side, I'd want to see the bar hitting the top of your chest with that straight line from the elbows to the pulley. That's all you need to focus on. Again, go with drop sets, don't start swinging your body back farther in order to get more reps.

Behind the Neck Pulldowns

Same idea here, only this one should be easier. The only mistake you are likely to make is leaning over at the finish. It happens when you're trying to pull too much weight. This movement doesn't put you in a very powerful position as it focuses on the upper back muscles. Start light and work your way up. If you aren't able to sit straight up with a slight arch in your back then lower the weight. You shouldn't feel your arms doing anything here, just the lats contracting. It's an isolation exercise, like concentration curls, so treat it that way.

Close Grip Pulldowns to the Front

This is by far my favorite pulldown, and I start every back workout with them. Almost the opposite of the behind-the-neck version, this puts you in a very powerful position. It focuses on the lower lats, a weak point in a great many physiques. Since incorporating this move and prioritizing it, I've seen some significant improvement in my lower back.

Two options here: you can grab a long bar and use an underhand shoulder width grip. Or, you can use a handle like you would on seated rows or T-bar rows. The secret is not to lean back, you should remain almost upright during the whole move with your chest sticking out and your back arched.

Out of the three pulldowns, it's the one I see performed the least, My advice is to learn it, include it and put everything you have into it. When you get it right, you'll find that it's very easy to keep the weight on your lats as long as you keep that slight bend in the elbows at the top. Aside from that, just keep your arms in tight to your body and pull straight down. You should feel your lower lats contracting. Use your straps here to help keep the hands out of it.

For comparison's sake, on the stack at my gym, I'll use 75 pounds for behind the neck, 150 for front pulldowns and 210 for close grip. Some people make the mistake of assuming the weight should be the same for all three.

Seated Rows

Just a quick little rant about the new equipment that's popping up in gyms everywhere: it sucks. The cables are like pulling on an elastic, you add weight and you can't even feel the difference. I can use the stack and feel nothing. Not sure who designed these machines but they definitely don't lift. Thankfully, there's one old school cable station at my gym and it does the trick. You might find the same thing. Not sure what I'll do if they upgrade but it will mean less cable moves, and it would be a shame to have to give this one up.

Seated rows are great when done correctly and it's tough to match the way they allow you to squeeze those lats. That's if you do it right, of course, and that requires proper technique and a good smooth rhythm. Above all, once you get it right, it takes some aggression. I prefer a little madness on top of that but it's your call.

Just this afternoon I saw a girl caving in her whole upper body around the bar when it hit her stomach. I was right beside her so I leaned in and quickly explained that she should be doing the exact opposite. As the weight comes in you need to exaggerate sticking out your chest as you bring your shoulders back as far as they can go while keeping them down. This forces your back to contract. This move is all about the finish and I see so few get those shoulders back far enough, it's why instruction needs to be detailed. It's literally a game of inches.

You lean forward at the hips just enough to stretch the lats, but not so much that you're extending your shoulders. As you lean back just past 90 degrees, forcefully bring the bar into your gut right along the top of your thighs, not into your lower chest! Your elbows come in tight to the body and your chest comes out. From the side, there should be a 90 degree angle at the elbow in the contracted position. Hold that contraction for a second and squeeze those lats before releasing forward for another rep. As I said, you need aggression when you train back and this move puts you in a very powerful yet safe position to pull…so pull!

With all back exercises, it's a balancing act with the amount of weight you use. Not enough and you aren't challenging your back, too much weight and won't be able to bring those shoulders back enough to get a good contraction. I see very few people get it right, and I see very few people with well-developed backs.

One Arm Dumbbell Rows

Not a great deal to say on these. It's pretty similar to the seated rows only you have one knee up on a bench or one hand on the dumbbell rack. Everything I wrote about seated rows applies and the mistakes are basically the same. People actually tend to pull with their arms more on this move than the seated version. A few tips:

- ✓ You absolutely *have* to pull the dumbbell back and into your waist. People tend to grab the weight and pull it straight up into their armpit, again, this will work your arms and shoulders.

- ✓ On the negative, bring the dumbbell down and forward in an arc before bringing it back along that arc into your waist

- ✓ Always look straight ahead. When you look down you will tend to lose the arch in your back.

- ✓ Don't try and stop the weight at the bottom, stopping it will force you to flex your forearm to get it going and that takes the weight off your back.

- ✓ You don't need to keep your hand parallel to your body. It can help to turn it in a bit, as if you were trying to peek at your watch. It just places the arm in a more natural position.

- ✓ Finally, get aggressive! I know I keep saying it but your back is big, put some effort into it, get angry, challenge yourself to ram that weight up into your waist.

- ✓ Women in particular tend to do this exercise a lot and they use perfect form but they use ten pound dumb-bells. Probably the same weight they use for dumbbell curls. Your back is made up of big strong muscles, see what you can do...push yourself!

- ✓ One tip for pushing it a little more is to put the weight down once you can't do anymore, wait a few seconds. Then try and do a few more.

Chin-ups

These are one of the best back exercises and for some reason the only people I see doing them weigh about a buck-twenty and do sets of twenty-five. If you're strong enough to do at least six good reps, then you should be on these and working your way up from there. The reason they're so great is that with all the cables used, it's nice to just go up against gravity. Again, be aggressive and go a little "Rocky" on this one. It's important to keep your head still so pick a spot on the wall and stare at it. The key is to find the groove, the range of motion that puts your body at that perfect angle where your lats are doing the work and you feel nothing in your arms. Once you find that groove then keep your body in that position and move only what you have to. When you come close to failure, DO NOT take a break and hang at the bottom, your set will likely end there. In order to get those

extra two or three reps in just keep going, block out those negative thoughts and squeeze the back. Even if you only get up
around three quarters of the way, don't stop.

As for technique, I wouldn't recommend any cheating on these, no swinging or using the legs, there really is no point. Save
those for the CrossFit crowd. You don't have to go all the way up
either, as long as your elbows get to that 90 degree angle. Just
don't 'hang' at the bottom.

It's quite common to see this exercise being used as a warm-
up, which I think is a great idea. It stretches out the arms and
back, it gets the blood flowing to the whole back area and at the
start of your workout you should have the strength to do a few
sets. If you can bang out three or four sets of chins at the end of
your back workout then it's a sign that you need to be working
much harder. At that point, your lats should be fried.

If you aren't yet strong enough to do these then don't, work
your way up with the front pulldowns until you get there. It really
all depends on what you weigh.

Pullovers

There are two versions of this exercise. First is the machine
pullover which I use and love. Obviously your gym needs to
have one of these in order for you to do them so look around, it
might be off in some corner somewhere. You grab a bar over
your head while sitting straight up. You pull the bar in an arc
from over your head down to your waist. It's pretty tough not to
contract your lats on this one because of the range of motion
you're forced to take. You hold the bar at the bottom and
squeeze your back for a second or two before slowly letting it
come back up. You get a great stretch at the top and then bring

it back down for the next rep. This is an exercise I usually do either first as a warm-up or last as a "pump" exercise. If you watch Dorian Yates' video, he always starts his back workout with these. The key is to make sure the machine fits and you can place yourself in a position where the bar comes into your belt allowing you to keep your shoulders down.

Second, there's the version where you stand in front of the high pulley and using a wide grip you pull the bar down to your waist while keeping your arms extended. I prefer the machine version a lot more, you're able to stretch significantly more at the top and you can use more weight which increases the intensity of the contraction. In order to do the standing version, you really have to practice the move and keep the weight down. You'll see ten people doing it wrong for every one you see doing it right. Done correctly, the upper arms come down and in while your chest comes out. This is where you get the contraction.

Most will use too much weight and focus on pulling the bar down while forgetting the crucial move at the end. As soon as you try to use too much weight, you will engage your tricep muscles, which takes the weight off your lats. Just keep the weight low enough to allow your back to do the work and always bring your upper arms back while you squeeze your back muscles. This is not a mass building exercise and it will not cause a lot of damage to your muscle fibers. Again, it is commonly used as a warm-up or finishing move. I would use it only for a warm-up as it doesn't challenge your muscles enough to finish off a workout. When doing so, focus on contracting your lats, and remember to keep contracting them for the rest of your workout. Check out Jose Raymond, the Boston Mass, he's a master at these.

Extensions

Extensions focus on the lower back muscles, or spinal erectors. Your gym will likely have several machines or stands for this one. There's not a lot to explain here and it's usually done correctly. One key here is to keep it slow. Your lower back is not a muscle group you want to get sloppy with or too aggressive. Just a nice stretch and a slow controlled contraction with a two second hold. You can use weight with these but don't go crazy. Your lower back gets all kinds of work from your other back exercises and I don't do these just for that reason. I think it's a good idea to include them if you're learning, as it will build up strength in that area and teach you how to contract and feel that muscle.

Stretching

I love to stretch my lats after a good workout. One reason is that it's an easy muscle group to stretch. You simply bend at the waist, grab on to something and pull while turning your hips slightly away from the side you're pulling with. Get into a position that gives you that pulling feeling all along your side, then stretch it and hold.

Some gyms will have the "rocker." It's a small unit that lets you grab on to a handle and then rock your whole body back and hold it.

So that's it for your back. Once you get it right, I guarantee you will enjoy working on your back as much as I do. You will make progress and the results will be impressive. A well-built back is an impressive accomplishment.

Steve Foxall

Chapter 18: Quads

I did end up competing. The Henderson Thorne Natural Clas-
sic was held in Ancaster, my home town. It was put on by the
OPA (Ontario Physique Association). It made for a really long
day. Melissa brought the kids to the pre-judging which was
great. They made a sign for the old man and cheered like crazy.
At night it was just me, the girls had plans.

I ended up winning the middleweight class and after the
show, I grabbed my trophy and headed home. It was just after
midnight and the girls weren't back yet. There was a congratula-
tions card and a plate of brownies on the table, I grabbed one
and headed up for a much needed shower.

The next day Melissa asked me if I was going to do another
show and I said no, what for?   "Because you won, you're good
at this, and you love doing it." (Remember the chapter on support?) I told her that if I could manage to build a career around
fitness, then I would try and get a sponsor and do the provincial
show, the next level up. At the same time, I knew that competing
again would require one major improvement. I would have to
build what the overall winner at the show had: bigger quads.

There are quite a few challenges that come along with natural bodybuilding, both physical and mental. One of those challenges is building your quads. Watch any natural show and you'll see what I'm talking about. I used to think that there was little I could do about it but I was wrong. Like anything you want in life, commit to it fully, work your ass off, then work harder, and you'll get there, you'll achieve your goal.

Now I don't have skinny legs by any means. I can go through an entire mall and not find jeans wide enough. What I don't have are the big sweeping outer quads and those thick defined teardrop muscles. So how can I write about building quads if I'm not satisfied with my own results?

In my opinion, ineffective and inconsistent training is the reason people fall short. Starting with the latter, training legs isn't fun, it's hard work, very hard work. If we ever miss a couple workouts, we don't go to the gym and catch up on legs, it's usually chest or maybe back. If we're tired, we'll skip legs and work shoulders.

We don't think it's a big deal but after years of training, our physique represents the sum of all the little things we did, or didn't do, it's the attention to detail.
The result of inconsistent leg training is a weak body part.

Let's look at ineffective training. I can say with 100% certainty that when it comes to technique, the most consistent mistake made in the gym is performing squats incorrectly. I'm sure the more experienced readers will agree with me. People butcher this exercise week after week. I certainly fell into that group for my first few years of training. Sometimes I see people squat really well in their warm-up sets but then after loading on too much weight, they lose their form for those important heavy sets. Other times, it's wrong from the get-go. The mistakes aren't limited to squats, plenty more are made on the leg press, Smith machine and hacks. I'm going to try and solve all of your squat issues.

Squats

We never stop learning in life, and you should never stop wanting to learn and wanting to improve. You should want to be good at what it is you do for a living, and what you do outside of work. If you lift, you should want to excel at it, not just go to the gym to kill time and impress your buddies. One of my goals is to help you do just that, excel. I don't want this to be a good read over the weekend, I want it to be your textbook, your reference and guide, I want it to have an impact. I want to give you a degree in lifting. If I succeed, and you're willing to sign up, then squats will be your final exam, your thesis, and it will be by far your toughest course.

As I mentioned, this exercise is very rarely done correctly, and if it is, the person doing it knows what they're doing and it's very evident in all of the other exercises they do. Here's what I want to cover.

1. Not taking the time to learn how to squat using proper form

2. Continuing to shorten the range of motion in order to use more weight

3. Squatting on a Smith machine prior to mastering the free weight version

Let's start at the beginning: why squat? Growth comes from convincing the mind that more muscle is required to handle the workload that the body is continually being asked to manage. There are two exercises that are known for having a very strong effect on the mind, in other words, having a very strong anabolic effect. They are the deadlift and the squat. It's pretty easy to see why. Both movements involve the entire body and require several muscle groups to work together (compound movements).

While there are plenty of machines and alternatives, the free weight version will always maximize this effect. That in itself should be enough reason for you to keep reading with interest.

As I've repeated over and over, you have to learn how to lift weights before you can expect results. That statement is crucial when talking about squats. The reason you see so many people wasting their time in the rack is that they don't respect that statement.

If you've been squatting for some time but not getting the results you were hoping for, I urge you to go back to the start and re-learn it. As with any movement, you should start with very little weight, just enough to offer some resistance while you get accustomed to the range of motion and the feel of the muscles contracting. Then slowly add weight until you can't maintain that form.

Many just refuse to squat with less than a 45 pound plate on each side, again, trying to impress a whole bunch of people they don't even know.

Let's dive into the lesson here and now.

1. *The Bar and the Takeaway*
2. *Stance and Balance*
3. *Before you Start*
4. *Going Down*
5. *Powering Up*
6. *Increasing the Weight*
7. *The Smith Machine*
8. *Using a Bench*

The Bar & the Takeaway

A couple of points you might not even think about but both are very important: Where does the bar sit on your back? How do you lift the bar off the rack?

First, the bar needs to sit where it is comfortable and well balanced for a range of motion that will ensure the weight is placed on the quads. For most that means sitting it just below the top of the cervical spine and resting on the trap muscles. The top of the spine is where that one bone sticks out at the base of your neck. Powerlifters will tend to hold the bar much lower across the top of their backs to help involve additional muscle groups. If you look up pictures of bodybuilders and powerlifters squatting you will see what I'm talking about. Our goal is to work the quads and save our back muscles for another day. Always keep in mind that if your goal is to bodybuild, don't watch the powerlifters and try and copy them because you're impressed by how much weight they are using, the two are total-ly different.

Some like to use a pad or a towel to help with comfort, **but** I wouldn't. As I've mentioned, feedback is always so important and eliminating that feedback will make it harder to understand what your body is doing. If done correctly, the bar should not hurt you.

When it comes to the takeaway, you should learn to always lift the bar with your legs and hips, not your shoulders and traps. The bar should be at a level on the rack where your knees have to bend to get under it. You can have one leg out in front and one back, lift the weight and then bring that front foot back in line with your other one. You can stand under the bar with both feet parallel and then walk it back. The key is that you're lifting the bar with your legs.

Stance & Balance

Balance is everything when squatting. Throughout the entire range of motion, it gives you confidence, stability and therefore, safety. Without it, you won't have much success. It is the reason so many lifters fail to lower the weight enough to properly engage the quads. As you practice with very little weight, maintaining balance should be your focus, and it should be maintained as the weight builds.

Stance for the basic back squat is fairly straightforward. Your feet should be slightly wider than shoulder-width. Some prefer a wider stance, some narrow. Some use both in order to change the focus from the outer quads to the tear-drop muscle just above the knee. When learning, keep it simple, and ensure that you give yourself a solid base allowing for good balance.

Where you grip the bar isn't as important, but keep comfort in mind. As your hands come in your will tend to flex your upper back and traps more. Some like to have their traps flexed and some keep their hands wide which will relax the neck more. Whichever works best is best.

Before You Start

This is a very important point that should help you focus on your quads and commit. Remember, as soon as you take the weight off the rack, or the dumbbells, or engage the machine, your body is holding that weight somewhere. It is being supported by muscles and joints. You have to know what's holding it and ensure that the right muscles are involved. The big mistake with squats is holding the weight with your back and your knees right before starting the negative. So many people squat with their backs and knees and it's pointless! Please do not fall into that trap. Once you have the weight off the rack and you have your feet set, I want you to bend your knees slightly. It's something golfers do before they start their backswing; basketball players do it before the take a free throw. They "sit" in their stance and the purpose is to engage those big leg muscles.

Your goal here is to "place" the weight on your quads and get it off of your back. You will feel what I'm talking about.

Going Down

Continuing from the starting position we want to ensure that we keep using our quads to control the weight on the way down. The first move is always to stick your ass way out, as if we're going to sit. Women in particular seem to be very good at this, probably because they use a weight that allows them to have confidence. Getting your ass out helps tackle another priority for the negative portion and that's keeping your balance.

The rest of the negative is fairly simple. If you're in balance and you've managed to place the weight on your quads, then keep going until you reach a spot at or just below parallel. Don't start thinking about squatting to the basement or ass to the grass, your job is to elongate the quad muscles and then contract them, that's it.

Keep in mind that as you lower the weight, your head should remain level, with your eyes looking straight ahead. It's common to see people look way up when they squat and that's not a good idea. This position will make it harder to focus on your technique and your balance. I think people usually feel the need to do it in order to avoid that "falling forward" feeling. You are far better off learning how to lower the bar in complete balance rather than trying to compensate with your head back.

It takes time to get accustomed to how far back you have to sit in order to keep that balance, and you will purposely fight that from fear of falling. Force yourself to master the technique and you will be well rewarded.

A great habit to get into to help with balance is to pause at the bottom. If you can slowly lower the weight and hold that parallel position at the bottom while looking straight forward with your feet flat on the ground, then you are squatting properly. In order to do this you have to be confident in your ability to move the weight. In other words, too much weight and you're wasting your time. When you have too much weight, the 'half-rep' creeps in. This is when people are unwilling to commit, unable to place all of the weight on the quads and incapable of reaching parallel.

This isn't something that you should expect to master right away. It may take a few weeks. The key again is to keep the weight down, there is absolutely no rush to pack on plates. Do it right, and repeat it over and over again.

The squat requires a mental commitment. You have to place the entire weight on your quads and then lower that weight to a point just below where your hips are parallel with your knees. If you are not able to complete that full range of motion and be comfortable at the bottom, then you need to immediately drop the weight and keep practicing.

One more note. You might see people place a couple ten pound plates under their heels. Know that this should never be done to help with balance. People who are very good at squat-ting will do it in order to place more of the weight on their quads, and in turn, take it off their hips. Perfect the squat before getting into variations.

Powering Up

Everything to this point should have you in a position where you can isolate the quads and contract them. One trick to doing this is to incorporate lateral force and push your feet out as you begin the positive portion. Your feet don't move of course but by pushing out you might find that you engage those quads and not the rest of your body.

I've mentioned a couple of times about going just below parallel. This is something that you need to experiment with that light weight to see what works best for you. For me, going that little bit farther creates a more fluid turnaround, it feels more natural.

In golf, many will tell you that if you get the backswing right, then the rest just falls into place. The same goes here, get the negative right, and all you have to do is squeeze those quads. So please practice the negative! Set after set, spend hours on it if you have to.

When you do get to the top, do not lock out your knees, this is a no brainer. When you lock out you risk placing all of that weight on the knee joint. There is little benefit to this. Squeeze your quads while keeping a slight bend and you will keep the tension where you want it.

Increasing the Weight

At this point you should have done the practice and can now comfortably get into the bottom position, pause and power the weight up while isolating your quads. Now and only now should you start adding weight and pushing yourself. You're ready to start punishing those legs and demanding growth.

Remember what I wrote about in the principles section? This is not the time for three sets of ten. When I squat I find myself a bench and a rack and I go to work for a good half hour. I don't attempt it at 6 p.m. on a Monday when the gym is packed—it's always best really early or late at night. I've already done a few sets of leg extensions and hamstring curls to warm up and this is so important. Your quads are big and your knees are vulnerable. You need to get that blood flowing and warm up the whole area. After the extensions, I still start with no weight on the bar and you should too. This is where you remember everything you practiced.

Now start working your way up with some easy sets. There is absolutely nothing wrong with putting on 25's or 35's here depending on your level of strength. Do not feel like you have to put on a full plate!

You might be wondering how to tell if you're using your back. Here's how. For years I did squats and on the heavy sets I'd get all the way down, struggle getting the weight up from the bottom and then around half way up I would just stand up with no effort at all. With the position I was in, I was allowing my back to get involved and when it took over, I had no problem with the top half. This is what powerlifters do, the legs get the weight moving and the back takes over.

Now, my stance is more erect through the whole range and I can feel the weight on my quads the whole time. As a result, I struggle through the entire range of motion. One of your goals should be to get to this point.

Do a set, rack the weight and sit on that bench, don't go talking or texting, just focus on the task at hand, focus on the next set. I even make sure I bring a water bottle so I don't have to walk to the fountain between sets. Keep adding weight as long as you can reach that bottom position and get at least ten reps. I say ten because most bodybuilders agree that with legs, you should be doing ten to twelve reps, it's just more effective. Don't expect any miracles here, squatting is a very demanding exercise mentally and physically so it will take time. The key is to be able to control that negative and keep your balance. That should always be your focus.

I've been training for twenty-five years and a recent example of my squat workout is below. As you will see, it's not about how much weight I have on the bar, it's about how far can I push my quads, and how hard can I punish those muscle fibers.

Bar x 25   225 x 13
135 x 20   245 x 10
185 x 15   265 x 8
205 x 15   225 x 12 (twice)

The Smith Machine

Without a doubt, I see more people squat with the Smith machine than with a free bar, by a long-shot. There's a simple reason for this: it's easier. It's easier because it shortens the list of what you need to worry about. It's far less demanding mentally and allows for a much greater margin of error.

The biggest mistake you can make with this move is switching to it without first mastering the free squat. Let me explain why. Free weights teach you a great deal. High on the list is feel. With a free bar, you have to teach yourself how to keep the weight on your quads and how to maintain your balance. You learn by listening to your body and making adjustments. The squat is a precise movement. If you move out of the necessary range of motion, even by an inch, you can start to lose your balance.

When you use the Smith machine, a lot of the usual concerns disappear. Balance is not an issue because the bar is locked-in and you can lean back against it. Range of motion becomes less of an issue because the bar is on a track.

You might be thinking that's great, it's safer and easier and I can just focus on my quads. While it is safer and definitely easier, you're at the gym to train and bust your ass, not save it. By having a fixed range of motion you are not able to adjust and you are forced to squat in a way that allows the bar to remain on that straight path. You might think you're isolating the quads but people tend to always use significantly more weight on the Smith machine and that should tell you that you're using your back, glutes and hips too much.

In order to really isolate the quads you need to know the squat, and you have to be used to squatting. Remember: there should be some muscle memory.

Believe me, if you can master the squat, then you'll know what to do on the Smith machine, plain and simple.

Using a bench

One tip if you're trying to get used to exactly how far you have to stick your butt out or how low you have to go to reach parallel, you can incorporate a bench. The goal here is to go down until you can just feel your butt hitting the bench, then you power back up. If you're tall and the bench isn't high enough, just stack some plates on top of it.

When it comes to squats, I can't emphasize enough how important it is that you practice. If at any time you aren't able to get right down while staying erect and looking forward, then you need to lower the weight. If your goal is to squat four or five plates then go be a powerlifter, and if you want big legs, focus on form. I've read several articles by pros sporting some of the best quads in the game and they all tell the same story.

The day I learned how to squat using only my quads was the day my legs started to grow.

Leg Press

There really isn't a great deal of technique to talk about here because it's pretty tough to go wrong. That doesn't mean we can't have a good chat about it. 'The sled' is a pretty useful tool and a very versatile one at that. It can be used to isolate the quads, the hamstrings/glutes and it also makes a pretty good calf raise machine. Most of all, when I think of the sled, I think of punishment. When it comes to legs, the stability you have in this machines gives you the opportunity to safely push your quads. The biggest mistake I see is people not pushing themselves and not using principles to increase the effectiveness of the movement.

People will tell you to isolate the outer or inner quads by adjusting your foot position but don't listen to them. Everyone is different and you need to experiment to find out what works for you. What is far more important than forcing a foot position is determining where you need to place your feet in order to take the weight off of your knees so that you are moving that weight with your quads. Remember that the sled is a machine and all machines fit differently, so if you see a video of Dennis Wolf and his feet are low on the plate, remember that the machine at your gym is probably different than the one he is using. Use a relatively light weight and do plenty of slow reps and see if you can move the weight with your quads. If you can feel a good burn and your knees don't feel any stress, then you should be in a pretty good position and ready to start adding weight.

Most leg presses have an adjustable back rest, so play with it and see what works. What you want is to avoid your upper body sliding up the pad as you push. If this happens when you go heavy, you need to shorten the angle of the seat by raising the back. If you raise it too far, you will struggle to bring the weight down far enough. It all depends on your frame. If your gym has more than one press and they're different brands, try them all and see which one fits you best.

Before you start, grab the handles at your sides and pull, this will scrunch your butt down into the seat. As with many exercises, the key to success is all in the negative. You want to bring the weight down slow and focus on the quads, you want to create tension, and you want to engage the muscle. Keep going until your knees are fairly close to your chest, enough to recruit the majority of the muscle fibers but not so much that you lose that smooth turnaround and rhythm. People might tell you to bring the weight down as far as possible but again, don't listen. When you do that, your risk bringing your hamstrings and glutes into play and losing your position, and that's not what you're after.

As you switch over to the positive move, you should not be focusing on your feet or 'pushing' the plate. All of your focus should be on contracting those quads. I don't recommend locking out your knees as this will place an awful lot of weight on them. We want to keep those quads engaged. If you want to contract them without locking out, try bringing your toes off the plate so only your heels have contact. When bodybuilders flex their quads on stage they do the same thing, they lift their toes slightly.

This is important: You should not feel pain in your knees. If you do, then either you need to adjust your foot position or you need to better warm up your legs and get more blood into those big quads. What you should feel is a burn down the outside of your thigh, a burn in the muscle. The burn might not show up until the fourth or fifth set but when it does, you know you're on the right track. Anytime you finish any set and you feel an intense burn in the muscle you're working and nowhere else, take note. That's your feedback. It means you're doing everything right and you shouldn't change a thing! Write it down in your journal, remember it and repeat it!

Here's a great tip for the sled. Remember all of your principles? Most of them don't work here---but one in particular works wonders. After your last set, start dropping the weight, and start punishing. Drop sets on the sled will destroy your legs, simply because you don't have to worry about balance like on squats. You can scrunch down in the seat, stare at the wall and just keep on contracting. Get a good song playing, turn it up and do your thing. Two sets will do it, just keep going. You will have to ignore a whole bunch of pain from the lactic acid but I promise you, it will be worth it. This is great if you're in a hurry or all the racks are full. I'll warm up on extension and then spend half an hour on the sled and by the end I'll struggle to get back to the car. I told you building legs isn't easy, it's hard physically and mentally, but that's what it takes.

One Legged Leg Press

There are many days when I rely on this variation to get me through my workout, and there's a very simple reason. With one leg, I'll go up to three plates a side. With two legs, I need about ten or eleven. Loading all of those plates on and off after already doing squats can sometimes be a pretty big deterrent. However, I'm not just being lazy, the one legged version has one big advantage: isolation.

I find it helpful here to turn my body in a little. If I'm using my right leg, I'll place my right forearm against my knee. It's not there to help out, it's just for counterbalancing the weight. You have to go a little slower with these to ensure you're engaging the quads. You might find more of a burn in the teardrop muscle vs. the outer quad, which is fine. When you get to the end of the set, you can use that forearm to help you squeeze out a few extra reps, even if they're partial ones. When I wrote about muscle confusion I detailed how you should stick to the exercises you like and mix them up rather than trying new movements all the time, and this is a great way to do that. Give them a try and see what you think. Just be careful going too heavy, you can wrench your lower back.

Hack Squats

This is a tricky one. I've worked out in a dozen gyms and I've yet to find a hack squat machine that doesn't hurt my knees. As a result, I usually stuck to squats and presses. Nowadays though, there is the Hammer Strength version and other machines like it. These are much better as they bring you down in a more natural path. The only problem with using the machine is the ability to use your back. This is why you'll see people using hundreds of pounds.

If you can manage to keep your back out of it and make it as hard as you can for your quads, you will get a great burn and be able to push them in a safe environment. If you ever get stuck at the bottom you just put your hands on your knees and your back will get you up.

Again, there's usually a big plate at the bottom for your feet. Play around with different positions and find what works for you, what helps you isolate those quads.

I prefer this exercise near the end of the session when my legs already have a crazy pump, that way I don't need a ton of weight, I can focus on making them do the work and getting a great contraction.

To push yourself, rest at the top when you've done what you can do, catch your breath and keep going. Don't cheat, make it difficult, go right down just past parallel, pause and move the weight with those quads. When you get to the top, squeeze. This is a great exercise for contracting the legs. Just stand there with your knees slightly bent and squeeze the hell out of them. Remember what I said about pretending you're in a photo shoot, a tip that works great here. Imagine that you are Evan Centopani on the cover of MD. Visualize.

Extensions

This is simply a great exercise that pretty much everyone does. Here are some basic tips.

1. Find the machine in the gym that works for you and make the necessary adjustment.

2. There's a debate over the position of the back rest. Some say it's better to have the seat farther back so you can bring your legs up and easily contract. Some prefer to have it forward so you're sitting straight up, that way your quads have to do all of the work. Personal preference.

3. Work your way up slowly. You don't need a great deal of rest between sets so do plenty of them.

4. As for your feet, you shouldn't have them pointing up. They should be relaxed. I don't think pointing them to either side will make much of a difference here but others will argue.

5. If you're using these to warm-up, which you should, then keep the weight moderate and focus on the squeeze at the top in order to force blood into the muscle. Do lots of sets, because it takes a while to warm-up the quads.

6. If you're finishing off your workout with these then it's all about finding your rhythm and banging out as many reps as you can. There should be plenty of 'good' pain involved and if there isn't, you're doing it wrong.

7. Finish off with a drop set and a few partial reps on top of that. Legs need pushing, It's not easy to make them grow and it takes a little 'crazy' to get the job done.

8. I typically do this exercise twice, I use it both for warming up and finishing off. Give it a shot.

Wraps

I tried wrapping my knees for about a month or so in an attempt to squat more. I remember adding about fifty pounds more than usual and ending up with nothing more than a couple sore knee joints. Now I'm not going to tell you what's right or wrong here, just that I chose not to use them. I find that if you can effectively isolate and contract the quads, then the knee joint should not be carrying the weight.

The point I want to make here is that you should not assume that wrapping is essential. It isn't. I'm very comfortable in recommending that you learn to squat without them as you continue to work your way up. I would certainly not use them as I once did, to see if it helps you lift more weight. Learn from my mistakes and save yourself time.

If at a later point you feel it will help, by all means give them a shot but listen to your body, pay attention to where the pain is and ask yourself if they are really helping.

If you're serious about training legs, you'll be there. Early in the morning or late at night you'll be banging out squats in the rack and reps on the sled. You push, and then you keep pushing. You get into that zone where you're a little out of it. You get that feeling in your stomach so you look over to make sure the garbage can is where it should be. When everything is telling you to stop and go home, you convince yourself to keep going, to finish what you started. When you're done, you slowly make your way out of the gym hoping your legs don't give out. We all sacrifice, we get our asses out of bed and we lift. That's why it's so important to get it right, to learn and to practice.

You should strive to become proficient at your trade, to justify your sacrifice, to validate your commitment.

Chapter 19: Chest

I've talked a lot about pushing yourself, just closing your eyes and doing five more. I've talked about finding exercises and using the exact weight that lets you do just that. Funny thing is, I rarely see it. I do it all the time: I do dips at the end of my chest workout, I have my song on, I'm focused, in the zone and I just keep pushing. I don't count, I just listen to the music, make sure I go low enough to get that stretch and I keep going, 25, 30 reps. I finish and there's always some guy next to me giving me this weird look.

Look at it this way, the only people I ever see doing it are the ones that look like either bodybuilders or fitness competitors, men and women who have made significant progress. So my point is, if you're at the gym to try and make progress, why aren't you?

I think a lot of it has to do with that same old advice, 3 sets of 10, pyramid up in weight, big compound moves followed by isolation moves. Over and over and over again. I'm hoping by this point, I've taught you enough that you realize that it's all crap. Your job in the gym is to efficiently beat the shit out of those fibers so your mind gets convinced you need more muscle to keep up. Yes, that does involve lifting some heavy weight on the basic exercises (once you learn how of course) but that's just the first half, and I think that's the difference. Success comes to the people that do the second half, lowering the weight and doing those drop sets, pushing through that lactic acid pain and demanding that their bodies keep going. It is just as important, and I need you to hop on board.

I bring this up here because your typical chest workout is the perfect example of what I'm talking about. It's working your way up to that heavy bench, the incline dumbbells and seeing how many plates you can stack on the Hammer press. I even see people struggle to get the weight going on cable crossovers or machine flyes—they use their shoulders more than their chest. It's nonsense. I talked about making the switch and starting with your next chest workout, I really want you to do it. Forget about weight and start focusing on working your chest muscles so that when you leave the gym, they have nothing left. I want you to go home thinking that after that workout, your mind will have no choice but to repair and rebuild more than what you had going in.

Butterfly Machine

This move comes first for a very good reason, the warm-up. It is essential that you do not warm up your chest on the bench, or the incline bench. The reason is that those moves don't allow you to stretch and squeeze the muscles while forcing blood into them. Unless they are all taken, I always turn to this machine. It's the one where you sit and bring the handles together in an arc, like a fly motion. It's a safe and easy way to get a great pump in the chest and warm up the whole area including the shoulder joint. Do sets of around 15-20 reps focusing on stretching and squeezing. Once your pecs start to burn after 4-5 sets, then you're ready for that bench.

The mistake people make here is bringing their elbows up and their shoulders forward. This takes the chest completely out of it. This isn't a shoulder exercise, you have to keep your elbows down and force your chest to do the work.

This is also a great finishing move along with dips. Sometimes I'll superset the two. End with a drop set or two and your chest will be begging for mercy. Remember, as with any of the moves you want to take to failure, near the end you want to accentuate the form rather than give it up and let other muscles take over. In this case, force those shoulders down and stick that chest out even further, force your chest to do the work. Those reps are the ones that count, so make them count.

The Bench Press

This is the biggest 'love it or hate it' exercise. There are plenty who will say it's dangerous and that you don't need it. Then there are those who swear by it and list it along with deadlifts and squats as the must-have basic moves. The simple reason for it is mechanics, and the difficulty many people have in safely isolating the chest muscles while minimizing the involvement of the shoulders. The ones who swear by it are usually the ones who can bench a lot of weight. To them, it's just a natural movement. These are the people who were born to bench.

Now of course, there are those who simply don't take the time to learn *how* to bench. Maybe they can't yet block out those negative thoughts or they're simply trying to push too much weight to keep up with their buddies. When I was starting out it was all of the above, and it was frustrating. Remember my advice about leaving the basic exercises alone until you've spent time learning the other moves? That's why.

Assuming you are ready to learn, there are definitely a few things I can help you with.

I will say I'm no fan of the decline benches in the gym so I won't cover those. I don't like how steep the angle is and the awkward climb into the bench while you try and hook your feet in. I definitely don't like the crazy head rush you get from what is an almost upside down press. What would be ideal is a bench with just a slight decline, enough to help alleviate the shoulders, but I've never seen one. It remains a move people do simply because the bench is there; if it weren't, I doubt it would be missed.

Back to the flat bench. I think a big problem with people mastering this move is that the bench is just so basic, bring the bar down and lift it back up. How much 'learning' can there be? Well, it's not what it seems. The press is a complicated task that involves a great deal of practice to get right. That practice needs to be taken seriously and each time, performed with a manageable weight. Here's what you need to know to bench with success:

1. Setup
2. Negative
3. Positive
4. Lockout
5. Breathing
6. Focus

Setup

1. Feet on the floor, and to the side, always. You might occasionally see someone pressing with their feet up on the bench, but please don't copy them. Your core is definitely involved in this movement and raising up your feet will eliminate that key component.

2. Shoulder-width grip, or a slight variation that allows you to 'feel' the weight on your chest more. Going too wide can put too much stress on your wrists and again, while giving you a great stretch, it will bring your front delts into play. If you want to go wide, use flyes or cables that allow you to turn your wrists in. Too narrow a grip will bring your triceps into play.

3. Keep your head still. This is so important. I see people all the time pushing like crazy and their heads are moving from side to side. This is never an option as it could lead to jarring a muscle in your neck or even worse, losing control of the weight.

4. Your back should be arched and your shoulders need to be down and back. This is the key to isolating the chest muscles and slowly developing power with this exercise.

Negative

The basic range is to bring the bar down somewhere around the bottom half of your chest. Again, it is up to you to experiment with a manageable weight to find the best path that allows you to isolate your chest when you push the bar back up. As the weight comes down, you always want to bring your chest out to meet the bar while keeping your shoulders down and 'pinching' them behind you. This might sound tricky but it can quickly become routine. It's not a bad idea to watch a few videos online by people who know what they're talking about, again, bodybuilders, not powerlifters.

The negative portion of the bench will determine how effective this exercise is and I think many people struggle because they don't focus on it enough. For me, I always bring the bar down slowly on the first rep, making sure the shoulders are staying out of it. Then I maintain that position throughout the whole set. One trick is to use lateral force on the way down, it's a simple way to help alleviate those delts. As I lower the bar, I stick my chest out, shove my shoulders back and imagine pulling the bar apart. During the last few reps, this allows me to get this crazy stretch in my pecs where I can feel all of the fibers working. The weight for me doesn't mean anything. What's important is that stretch, and the pain that comes with it. My goal with the negative is to punish the pecs, to make them suffer while incorporating every muscle fiber possible.

Positive

As with many exercises, if you perform the negative correctly, the positive becomes a simple contraction of the target muscle group. With presses, a proper negative should result in this smooth and powerful push of the weight that you can feel in your chest, and not in your shoulders. This is the problem with the flat press, it makes it very difficult to experience that feeling and get that strong contraction. After the heavier sets are finished, can you feel a burning sensation in your pecs? If yes, then you know you're working the muscle.

Try pushing your feet into the floor while moving the bar up. This helps involve the hips and the core for a powerful move. It's a good idea in that it can help you maintain your form, and makes sure that you rely on the lower body to get through those final reps, rather than bringing the shoulders and arms into play.

When it comes to 'bouncing' the weight off your chest in order to squeeze out some extra reps, you do have to be very careful. A slight bounce off your chest is fine, and I mean slight. Bringing the bar down quickly and using your body as a trampoline is a terrible idea. You should always lower the bar in full control, trying to keep the weight on your chest. You need to maintain 100% focus with presses. It is far too easy for your shoulders to take on the weight and lowering the bar quickly only increases the likelihood. That will eliminate the effectiveness of the move and could result in injury.

Lockout

This is where many lifters struggle to keep their form. It isn't enough to say you shouldn't lockout your elbows in order to save your joints. You have to keep your shoulders back. The mistake here is letting them come forward and flattening your back at the top. Once you do that, you'll be using your arms and shoulders and that will bring any set to an early end. Focus on getting a good strong push with your chest and let that push determine how far the bar goes, that's it. There are plenty of chest exercises that allow you to get that strong squeeze at the end, this isn't one of them. Your goal here is to incorporate as many muscle fibers as you can at the bottom and then overload the muscle while you push against gravity.

Breathing

This is a big one with bench as people will tend to hold their breath more. You have to consciously remember to breathe out at the top and take a breath. Start doing this early on and it will become a very good habit. It's definitely something I wish I worked on more when I was younger. Another tip is that if you ever get a little lightheaded and you're using a belt, ditch the belt. You don't really need it and the pressure can make it harder to get the oxygen in.

Focus

I spoke of this in the mental section and discussed how the bench press is one of the most mentally challenging moves you will perform. When doubt creeps in, your set is basically over. Keep in mind as you practice pressing, one of your goals should always be to remain positive and convinced you can move the weight. Headphones are also a big help as it's easy to get distracted, breaking your concentration.

This is where the weight comes in and being able to get into a rhythm.

With presses, you should always be 100% certain you can complete at least five reps, your job is not to find out how much you can bench, it is to learn how to punish your chest.

Incline Press

I find this move far easier than the flat version simply because it is easier to isolate the chest. There are only a few differences and the majority of the information above still applies. The big difference is where you bring the bar down. With the incline version, you want to bring the bar down higher up, in line with the top of your chest. This will enable you to get a better stretch in the pecs while keeping your forearms pointing straight up. Everything else should mirror the flat version.

It's a move that will feel very awkward at first and it takes time to get used to it. Don't let that discourage you, keep the weight down and let your muscle memory build. It is, in my opinion, the best chest exercise available.

One tip though, when your set is done, it's done. Don't try and force reps or get a spotter to do them for you. When you're able to stay positive and your chest just can't push the weight up, re-rack the bar.

Smith Machine Incline

This is a very popular move, it gives you the benefit of not needing a spotter. I've used it a great deal in the past. However, looking back I wish I'd stuck with the free weight version as you just can't compare the two.

Here are some tips:

1. As with all Smith machine movements, there is one problem, the new Smith machines. My gym pass gets me access to five local locations, one of those spots has

an old school Smith and it's great, I love it. Unfortunately, they're being phased out with new counterbalanced units that in my blunt professional opinion...suck. They just don't feel natural and they don't allow for a smooth transition from negative to positive. If that's the only option, I won't use it.

2. If you are going to do the exercise, there are some key mistakes that will quickly diminish your results. The biggest common mistake is in the set up, and it is very easy to fix. During the range of motion, your forearms have to stay completely horizontal. In other words, your elbows need to be directly under your hands. Typically, during the negative portion, people tend to let their elbows move backwards. Now your forearms are pointing towards the mirror in front of you and not the ceiling. Remember the last physics course you took? The force you are now generating is pushing the weight towards the mirror, while at the same time, the bar is moving up the Smith machine track. Only a portion of the force you are generating is moving the bar, which means the remainder is being wasted. What this does is prevent those nice smooth reps and strong contractions that are essential.

3. The key to avoiding the elbow problem is to purposely keep them forward with your shoulders down and back. Bringing the elbows back also makes it very difficult to keep the shoulders from taking over. It makes it very difficult to keep the weight on your chest.

4. Again, this is simply something you need to practice with light weight until you get it right. Don't be afraid to ask someone in the area to check if your forearms are straight, it only takes a second. Once you do get it right, you will immediately notice that there is less stress in your arms and shoulders, and that is always a good thing as it confirms that the weight is on your chest muscles.

5. In addition to solving the setup issue, you should always try and exaggerate bringing your chest out to meet the bar while pinching your shoulders back and down. This will aid in the overall goal of isolating the chest.

6. A major benefit to using the Smith machine is that you can incorporate more principles. Partial reps at the end of your set that focus on the bottom portion of the range are great, as is pausing at the bottom. Drop sets are also great as you can go right to failure and then just push the bar up enough to reach the first set of hooks. These are all quite challenging with a free weight bar, even when you do have a spotter available. You don't want to take up their time while you do five second pause sets.

7. As with all the press movement, always bring the bar right down. I see so many people press and only perform the top half of the rep. Bringing the bar right down allows you to incorporate as many muscle fibers as you can. If it means using less weight, then so be it. If

you're going to do something, then you might as well do it right!

Dumbbell Presses

I consider this to be the king of the forced rep exercises. I see people all the time struggling through reps with their buddy's hands on their elbows doing half the work.

- ✓ Forget grabbing the biggest dumbbells you can and forget about forced reps. Treat this like every other chest exercise.
- ✓ Chest out, shoulders back, bring the weight down while keeping it on your chest.
- ✓ I find it helpful to turn your hands in slightly, it helps me keep my shoulders out of it.
- ✓ Make sure you keep that 90 degree angle at the elbow. People often have the dumbbells either too close, which will focus the weight on the arms, or too far apart, which will force the shoulders to hold the weight in. Your forearms should always be straight up and down.
- ✓ At the bottom, don't ever relax, keep your chest stretched and just squeeze. It helps to imagine that you're pushing your chest apart while keeping that 90 degree angle at the elbows.
- ✓ You might have experienced this: on the way up, one arm will give out on you. That's because the weight is coming off the chest and it doesn't have anywhere else to go, so the dumbbell just drops. This is usually a result of letting your chest flatten against the bench. You always have to keep it out with an arch in your back.

Always remember that as a set goes on and gets tougher, you need to keep your body tight and hold your position to avoid frustration and a possible injury. Control the weight, don't let it control you!

✓ To make it harder and to push your chest farther, go down slow, then pause at the bottom for a few seconds before powering up, even if it's a partial rep.

✓ Change the incline from time to time in order to mix things up, but not too high or the delts will take over.

Machine Presses

While I'm not a huge fan of machines, this is one area where you can certainly benefit.

✓ All the gyms now have them, some form of flat and incline press machine.

✓ I'm not a fan of the incline versions for two reasons. First, they just don't feel right to me which means I have trouble pushing my muscles to failure. Second, I feel strongly that barbell or dumbbell presses are essential and shouldn't be replaced by machines.

✓ On the other hand, flat press machines can feel better than the free weight version. Without the need for a spotter, you can really punish those pecs safely with the drop sets, pause sets and partials. Always make sure you're fully warmed up though.

✓ Make sure to position yourself so that you can isolate the chest. In other words, the machine has to fit. If you can't push yourself, go to failure and get that intense burn, then don't waste your time. People tend to use some machines simply because they're there. The Hammer press is a perfect example. There are more benefits if you push yourself, don't just use it because it's easier than free weights. Doing anything that is not effective comes at the cost of doing something that is!

Dumbell Flyes

Probably one of the top 'wasted' exercises, and by that I mean it is such an extremely effective tool that is rarely done correctly. Let's go through it.

- ✓ I can't emphasize how important it is to exaggerate the chest forward, the shoulders down and back position I keep talking about.
- ✓ These can be done flat or on an incline. I always recommend a slight to medium incline as it puts you in a better position to keep the shoulders out of it.
- ✓ Start with moderate weight, too light and you'll just use your arms.
- ✓ Once the dumbbells are up, bend your arms slightly, stick out your chest and scrunch those shoulders down and back.
- ✓ Bring the weight down while keeping that slight bend at the elbow.
- ✓ At the bottom, you should be looking to stretch the pecs. A big mistake is to lower your arms and then straighten them, I see this quite often. Straightening the arms at the bottom will place the weight on your

elbow joint and bicep, and that's both ineffective and dangerous. Keep those elbows bent and you will keep the weight on your chest.

✓ I always pause at the bottom when doing flyes. The pause is so that I can ensure the weight is on my chest before powering it up.

✓ When you're in the correct position at the bottom, your chest will pull the dumbbells up and you will feel it. Get it wrong and your arms will be doing the work.

✓ At the top, squeeze the pecs and keep your chest out, don't ever relax and bring it in.

✓ For me, a set of flyes takes quite a while to finish because I always bring the weight down slow and squeeze at the top.

✓ As you move up in weight, you need to keep that slow pace and focus on keeping your body position tight while making sure your chest is carrying the weight at the bottom.

✓ This move will feel pretty awkward if you're just learning. Use a moderate weight and don't go heavy until it feels natural, even if it takes a few weeks.

Cable Crossovers

Probably one of the most overused exercises. While everyone seems to love doing crossovers, they would be much better off sticking to the free weights.

✓ By far the biggest mistake everyone makes with cables is using too much weight.

- ✓ It's easy to spot poor form with this one. Leaning over, their elbows are up high and their arms and shoulders to do all the work.
- ✓ This is a pump movement. The goal is to isolate the chest and force it to contract when it's tired and doesn't want to. Weight is irrelevant.
- ✓ In order to isolate, you have to keep your shoulders down and back. Your hands should be low which will keep your elbows from flaring up high.
- ✓ Here's the test: when you bring the handles back, do you feel your chest stretch, or are you flexing your shoulders? The latter means you are following a track that's too high. Bring it down. Watch a video of Dorian Yates doing them, you'll see what I mean.
- ✓ When you feel the chest stretch, then the positive move should only involve squeezing the pecs.
- ✓ As you get close to failure, don't let those elbows come up, keep your form and focus on punishing your chest. When you stop and let the weight go, you should feel an intense burn in the pecs, and no-where else!
- ✓ This is a perfect drop set exercise and should give you a crazy pump.
- ✓ As an alternative, you can bring the cables up from the bottom. There's not much difference, except that you need to keep your biceps and front delts out of it. The burn at the end will tell you how you're doing.

Dips

These are great for a few reasons. First, dip bars are at every gym and they're all the same. Second, if done correctly, they target the lower chest without having to use those crazy decline benches. Third, you don't need a spotter and can always go to failure.

- ✓ Positioning is everything and you can only go by feel. Having said that, this is a great "practice" exercise. There's no weight involved, which takes ego out of the equation so you can focus on isolating and pushing your chest.
- ✓ Your goal is to take the arms and shoulders out of the movement.
- ✓ Once up, cross your legs and push them back as you lean forward
- ✓ Stick your chest out and let your shoulders release back.
- ✓ Bend your arms just enough to take the weight off your elbows/shoulders and try and place it on your chest.
- ✓ Once you can feel it on your chest, start going down.
- ✓ At the bottom, you want to focus on sticking out your chest and feeling the pecs stretch.
- ✓ Coming back up, you want to push with your chest, not your arms.
- ✓ Don't lock out your elbows, keep your shoulders back and the weight on your chest.
- ✓ Down, stretch, squeeze the chest, don't lockout.

✓ As you get tired, instead of letting your triceps take over to finish the reps, keep stretching at the bottom and coming up halfway.

✓ While looking forward will help remind you to stick out your chest, once the move becomes natural, many people look down or at the floor a few feet ahead.

Bodybuilders will all tell you that dips are one of the best ways to finish off a chest workout. Here's a couple extra tips.

✓ If your gym has a good belt, you can add weight to the movement. Always make sure you can still focus all of the weight on your chest. On the last set, I would use the weight to failure, then drop the belt and bang out twenty reps with no weight. Even if I had to take a two second break, I would always get to twenty.

✓ If you do this exercise last, it is a great indicator of how hard you were able to punish your chest. If I struggled on the dips, I knew I'd had a good workout. If they were easy, then I blew it.

✓ Practice this move. Don't just bang them out. When you can't feel your arms doing any of the work, you've got it right. If your triceps are burning after a set, your positioning is off. Lean forward more and get those shoulders back.

A quick word on using spotters. I've recommended again and again that you shy away from getting help on your finishing sets. I don't want you to think I'm recommending you don't use a spotter. There's a big difference. A spotter is there to help you finish that last rep, or re-rack the weight once you fail. That way, if you're doing a flat or incline bench, you know if you get stuck at the bottom, there's help. That lets you comfortably practice going to failure. Don't be afraid to tell them to let you fail, to not touch the bar until you ask, or until it just stops moving. People will assume you want to do a few forced reps. If you really want to do one after you've failed then by all means try, but you shouldn't do it on your heaviest set.

Steve Foxall

Steve's Gym Rules

Don't be that guy (or gal) that doesn't respect the rack. The rack is for squats, rows, deadlifts, shrugs and shoulder presses...that's it! Taking it up for 20 minutes doing lunges or curls will not make you any friends.

Don't hoard five pairs of dumbbells for a half hour of drop sets: have some courtesy!

Don't use the gym for some crazy aerobic session running all over the place—it's distracting and annoying.

Don't be that guy that cuts his shirt up so there just enough material to keep it on your shoulders, nobody wants to see that shit. Really.

Don't be that guy that goes around giving advice to every girl in tights just to strike up a conversation. Just because they're too polite to tell you where to go, doesn't mean they're not thinking it. Respect the focus.

Don't be that guy that tells everyone what you 'used' to be able to lift. "Back when I was your age, I could bench twice as much for twenty reps!"...ya? Were gyms full of assholes back then too?

Don't load up the sled with twenty plates and then throw them all over the floor after the set...you look like a kid trying to piss off your parents.

Don't walk around the gym talking on the phone...hang up and get back to work!

Don't make fun of overweight people in the gym. They're busy lifting, and probably doing a better job than you are.

Don't be that guy that supersets three different machines all over the gym and then freaks out when someone jumps on your bench that's been vacant for five minutes.

Don't be that guy that stares at women like you're imagining shit. Go back to your ipad.

Don't be that guy that brings his girlfriend so she can video you and take pics for your Instagram. Nobody gives a shit that you lift and she has better things to do.

Don't be that guy with anger issues, the one that slams every plate and throws dumbbells on the floor. So you lost your job. Fine, take it out on the weights, but not every day, it's hard enough to concentrate without having to block out your crazy shit.

Chapter 20: Shoulders

If you look at a video of a bodybuilding competition, or if you've ever been to a competition, you'll notice that on stage, the competitors look massive. Look at those same competitors doing an interview after and they don't look anywhere near as big. The reason is that what they present on stage is an illusion, created by what's known as the bodybuilding physique. Two crucial elements create this illusion, size and symmetry. When all of the muscle groups are developed equally, you appear complete, everything fits together and the result can be very impressive. It is also rare. At the gym you'll usually see upper bodies that overpower legs or a big chest with little back development and so on. In competition, the ability to create the illusion is only a start, it's the entrance fee. To excel, to stand out and impress the judges, you need to have built upon certain characteristics, the ones you were born with.

There are a handful of professional bodybuilders that were able to take size and symmetry to a level that set them apart from the others. One of the more famous examples of this was Ken "Flex" Wheeler. Look up some pictures and you'll immediately see why. In his prime he had enormously full muscle bellies that tied into seemingly miniature joints. He had the waist of a scrawny teenager that made his shoulders appear as wide as the stage he stood on. What Flex displayed was extreme, mind-blowing, and it raised the bar. It resembled something from the pages of Stan Lee's sketchbook. It's likely what fascinates people about bodybuilding.

I had this great economics teacher in University, he was probably the only teacher I connected with in my four years there. He was a young guy and had a desire to make a real impact on those he taught. What I remember is how he motivated you to take control of accomplishing your goals. He encouraged you to create a path in life and use knowledge as a guide because without knowledge, you are left blind and guessing.

One of the concepts in economics that we carry with us for the rest of our lives is opportunity cost. The cost of any action is the opportunity we give up to do another action. In terms of money, if you spend a hundred bucks on boots, you give up the opportunity to buy a jacket. It's a concept that I think is very important in the gym when it comes to structuring your workouts.

What I see, especially when it comes to shoulders, is a lot of poorly performed dumbbell and cable moves. People are swinging weight all over the place and believe me, it isn't doing much for them. We're all rushed and we don't have two hours to spend training, and even if you do have that much time, one hour is plenty. Now in that time, your job is to pick the best exercises that will help you reach your goal. Any exercise you do comes at the expense of not doing another. So when I see people getting creative on the cables set after set, I think to myself, why aren't you doing presses? It's the same for all muscle groups, I just see it more with shoulders, in particular, with laterals.

People learning to lift have a hard time performing laterals correctly. Even those who have been lifting for years still don't manage to carry a large portion of the weight on their delts, it's all on their forearm flexors. Laterals certainly have a place, but they shouldn't represent the main focus of your workouts. You don't center your chest workout on flyes, or your leg workout on extensions, so put those shoulders to work...here's how.

Behind the Neck Smith Machine Presses

Everyone always told me that these are dangerous, that I'd tear up my rotator cuff. So I stayed away for years and now, looking back, I wish I hadn't. I started doing them a couple of years ago on the old school Smith machine and I can see that it's made a big difference. Watching videos of Kevin Levrone doing these with four plates a side in his prime just boggled my mind.

I always recommend the Smith machine for these. It makes this a safe exercise. Always select exercises that put you in the best position to safely take your muscles to failure.

What I like most about this movement is that it allows you to isolate the shoulder. I don't ever look at this as a "power" move and therefore moving big weight is never a concern or a focus. The more you can isolate a muscle, the lower the weight. It's important to appreciate that rather than continually selecting other exercises that put you in a stronger position. Essentially, you are taking your upper chest out of the equation.

The positioning of the bench is very important. The back needs to be straight up, all the way. Make sure you always start without any weight on the bar and adjust the bench back just enough so that you can comfortably get the bar behind your head without having to lean forward more than a couple inches. If the bench is too far forward you will be putting a great deal of stress on the shoulder joint which is what you want to avoid. Once you have the bench adjusted properly, you can begin to add weight.

This is one of those exercises that makes it tough to work out with a partner or worse, a group of friends. If you're always moving the bench then you'll lose that perfect position and you won't get as much as you can out of the movement.

Start light, very light. You want to make sure you can feel the delts moving the weight, you want to feel the contraction. That means lots of reps, down slow, up fast.

I bring the bar down to just below ear level and no lower. Letting the bar drop right down to the back of your neck is what can make this move a dangerous one. My method will allow you to stretch your shoulder muscles and then push them without putting them in danger, and you will get a great contraction. This exercise should feel very comfortable when done correctly, and it should make you feel like your shoulder muscles are the only muscles doing any work.

As you move up slowly in weight, it is very important to keep the rest of your body tight and your head forward. You never want to squirm during a movement and that's crucial here. Nothing else moves and your mind should remain 100% focused on moving the weight with your delts. At the top, another mistake is extending your arms all the way up and locking your elbows. As soon as you lock the elbows, all of that weight is instantly and firmly placed on your elbow joint, and there is absolutely no benefit to that whatsoever! Raise the bar enough to contract the muscles before allowing it to slowly come back down, probably about 90% of the way up.

The other element that excites me about this is the amount of mental focus you need to push yourself. It's very easy to get stuck at the bottom if you doubt your ability to lift the bar. A good rhythm will certainly give you the opportunity to practice staying positive.

This is also a great exercise for partial reps, pause sets and drop sets. If your shoulders aren't burning after using those then you need to focus more or adjust your positioning. These techniques can be done without a spotter which is a great benefit of the Smith machine.

You can also use lateral force here by trying to pull your hands apart on the way down. I find it keeps my delts engaged and in a better position to explode off the bottom.

Front Smith Machine Shoulder Press

While it is rare to see anyone hammering out behind the neck presses, it is all too common to see the front version being performed. Too often, they are performed incorrectly.

Remember in the last chapter when I talked about the incline bench on the Smith Machine, and how you needed to keep the elbows under the bar? The exact same lesson applies here. Let them come back and you're pushing into the mirror. On the Smith machine, we can fall into a trap of letting the rails allow us to use poor form.

Here's what you should do. The bench should be just one notch lower than vertical. It must be positioned so that when the bar comes down, it has to be as close to your face as possible. When done correctly, you should have to lean your head back a little in order to make room for the bar. This will allow you to bring it down while keeping your elbows directly under your wrists. This will help take your upper chest and triceps out of the exercise.

Once you have the positioning correct, the rest is pretty easy. With the Smith machine, I'll often use a false grip. It's safe and helps take the arms out of it. Give it a try. Bring the bar down just below your chin. Many people bring the bar right down to their chest and again, this is a mistake. Your goal is to extend the shoulder muscles and then contract them. When the bar is just below your chin, your deltoids are extended, or stretched and in the perfect position to contract with strength and power. Bring it down too far and you lose that isolation as other muscles have to help get it going again.

In a similar fashion to the behind the neck version, you have to believe 100% that you will return the bar to the top before starting to bring it down. Keep good rhythm, keep everything tight and focus on those shoulders. You should be a little stronger in this position. I know I'm repeating myself but these movements are so tough to do with a partner or group: that bench has to be in the perfect spot. One option is to keep a roll of painter's tape in your bag and put a piece on the floor to mark where the bench has to be for your sets. If you're unsure if the bench is set properly, you will not have that confidence you need to push yourself.

Free weight standing or seated front shoulder press

Unfortunately, a good Smith machine can be hard to come by now. If you feel the same way I do about the newer machines, then I suggest you get used to the free weight version. I've been performing front seated presses at the new gym I use down the street from my house and I really like them. Just keep in mind that whenever you try something new or different, it takes a few weeks for your body to get used to it, especially when it comes to free weights. Don't get frustrated.

With either seated or standing, the key with shoulders is always to start light and work your way up. It is one muscle group you don't want to start maxing out on, or getting too competitive about with your friends.

While you're getting used to a move, go slow on the negative and control the weight. Remember, when the muscle memory kicks in you can pick up the pace. Go too fast with these and the bar might run into your nose or chin (trust me).

When you bring the bar down, you want to flex your shoulder muscles as if you're doing a back double bicep pose. This helps keep the weight off the triceps. Again, try pulling your hands apart on the way down.

When doing standing presses, make sure your feet are shoulder-width apart. You need a good base. You have to lean back just a little to get the bar down in front of your face, but if you lean back too far, you could strain your lower back. It takes getting used to so keep the weight manageable until you do. If you're just learning, master the seated version before jumping to try the standing version. Rhythm plays a huge part in all shoulder presses, it will keep your set going. I find on both of these that it helps to grip the bar less than shoulder width, it tends to give you more control.

Seated Dumbbell Press

One quick word of caution with these, you have to be extra careful anytime you're lifting heavy dumbbells over your head, especially when you're learning.

- ✓ Don't do these as your first 'heavy' exercise. Again, it's tricky to get the weight up and control it. I would strongly recommend waiting until you're 'pre-exhausted' so you can drop the weight a little and maintain more control.
- ✓ Remember to flex your delts during the negative portion and contract them to get the weight back up.
- ✓ When you're coming down, make sure you keep a ninety degree angle in your arms, if the dumbbells are too close to your head, you'll be working your triceps. If the weight is too far apart, you risk losing control and you risk an injury. Be safe, please.

Machine Press

There's no shortage of options here, plenty to choose from. The big benefit? Going heavy. While I can't warn you enough to be careful with delts, machines give you a chance to really push yourself.

One word of caution though. Don't ever do a machine just because it's there. Remember the rule, you have to be able to push yourself, to take your muscles to the limit, and some machines just don't let you do that. They have to fit and feel right.

I almost always turn around and sit facing the bench on a standard machine press. This allows me to sit upright and position myself so that I can bring the handles down exactly where I want them. Often, if you sit facing the front, as they are designed, the bar seems to come down too far in front of you, which just isn't natural. Find what works for you, and if it doesn't work, move on.

Once you find a good machine and have it set up right, you've got some mental work to do.

This is a great place to practice what I've taught you. I sit there and stare at the equipment until I'm ready and then I get in. I close my eyes and force that weight up with a fast tempo. It's one of those moves where I'll do eight reps and think I've reached failure, and then I'll do six more. Then I'll drop the weight and do another fifteen. Practice staying positive and going to failure and I assure you, here you will see progress.

Side Laterals

I think the biggest problem with this exercise is that for some reason, people don't seem to understand it. It happens quite often. We focus on the path of the weight, we think about where the dumbbell has to travel in order to complete a rep. But in order to lift effectively, we need to focus on what our muscles are doing, we need to let *them* control how the weight moves. Laterals are the perfect example.

Essentially, when you stand straight up and hold a couple dumbbells at your side, there are two ways to lift them up.

1. The first way, and the wrong way, is to break your wrist by curling your hands up. This will place the weight on the top of your forearm. Then, you force the weight up using your hands and your forearms. This is quite easy to spot as your hands will always be above your elbows at the top. In the finish position, your arms and body will form a Y shape.

2. Now, starting in the same position, let's go over the right way. Stand with your arms at your sides. Keep

your hands and forearms relaxed. Lift your elbows out to the side so that your upper body and arms form a T shape. If you kept your forearms relaxed, your hands should be right in line with your elbows. Do it a few times and you should feel your shoulder muscles contract.

That's really all there is to it. Yet, as simple as it is, so many people go with the first option. Why? A few reasons. For starters, some people don't even know which muscle this exercise works. Some just feel that it's the right way because they watch so many others doing it wrong. Finally, it lets you use more weight.

1. Figure out the right way to do an exercise
2. Repeat the right way, over and over again
3. Slowly increase the weight
4. When you can no longer maintain form, lower the weight

Here are some more tips for laterals.

- ✓ Swinging the weight only makes things easier for your shoulders, and easy doesn't get results.
- ✓ When you set up, you should bend your knees just a little and "sit" in your stance.
- ✓ Lean forward a little to take your weight off of your lower back and place it on your quads for a more stable base.
- ✓ Turn your hands in a little, this makes it harder to use your forearms.

- ✓ Focus on holding the dumbbell with only your little finger, it helps keep the hands relaxed.
- ✓ Arms should be bent a little at the elbow, never straight.
- ✓ Don't let your shoulders come up as if you were doing shrugs.
- ✓ Keep your head and eyes straight ahead, don't ever look in a side mirror while you're doing a set, it flexes the traps and can make it harder to focus the weight on the delts, and you can wrench your neck.
- ✓ Lift your elbows, not the dumbbells.
- ✓ When you get tired, do strict partials, about half way up.
- ✓ Drop sets are great, but don't go hoarding all the dumbbells, one drop set is plenty.

Here are three variations of the exercise.

One-arm cable laterals

My favorite variation is the one-armed cable lateral. Here, I stand with one side facing the stack. I grab a handle behind my back. You want to lean your body away from the weight, because this makes it more difficult, and that's what we want. Use the other hand to hang on to the equipment. Everything else is basically the same. The benefit here is that it's harder to swing the weight. As long as your hand is not higher than your elbow, you should be able to really isolate those delts and keep tension on them longer than you can with the dumbbell. Forget six to eight reps here, just keep going to failure and use a weight that gets you around twelve to fifteen reps. A tip about weight, this is not a 'strong' exercise and sometimes, especially for women, the lowest weight on the stack is too much. This forces you to use your forearm to keep it moving. If you can't rely solely on your delt muscle then you'll have to build up your strength with the dumbbells first. Some stacks in the gym have 5 pound plates and some up to 15, see if you can find one with 5s.

Seated laterals

Seated side laterals are another option. I'm not a big fan. It is just too difficult to keep pushing yourself once you fail. The only way is to use drop sets. Everything is the same except you take your lower body out of it. It's a complete isolation exercise.

Machine Laterals

A great option here, and a great learning tool, is the seated lateral machine. This is the one with the pads that you put your elbows and forearms under. It's a great teaching aid as it forces you to keep your forearms in line with your elbows. It forces proper technique. Down slow, up fast and squeeze.

I would recommend doing a few sets of these first, and then throwing in a couple sets with the dumbbells in an effort to 'copy' the machine. It should feel the same and with your delts all warmed up, you'll have an easier time.

Front Raises

There are three deltoid muscles. Those side laterals work the side delts the most. Front raises work those front delts and rear laterals work the rear delts. Each one is vital in bodybuilding as different poses highlight one of the three. While you can isolate them with these dumbbell and cable moves, each gets worked when you train your larger muscle groups. For example, you use front delts on incline presses, and you use rear delts on most rowing movements.

Here's a tip, you want to limit how many moves rely on your forearm flexors. Those are the muscles along the top of your forearm. For example, if you do side laterals with dumbbells, you're using the flexors quite a bit. If you want to then do some front raises, try some of these variations.

1. Grab the 'handles' on a forty-five pound plate and lift it up in front of you. This is great because your palms are facing each other (as if you were driving and your hands were at three and nine o'clock on the steering wheel). Remember, just bring the weight out in front of your face, no higher.

2. The one I prefer is grabbing a cambered bar, placing my hands palms up in the middle of the bar and raising it up to the top of my chest. This is kind of like doing curls, only you bring your whole arm up, not just your forearm. Again, this takes those forearm muscles right out of it. They're both fine, I just prefer the feel of this one.

3. Another option is lifting dumbbells in the 'hammer' position. I don't do these as I feel it's too easy to swing the weight. To each his or her own but do include something, it's an important muscle that if missing, creates a big weak point.

Rear machine laterals

This move focuses on the rear delts, hence the name. It's pretty common and fairly straightforward but still requires some attention.

- ✓ Adjust the seat. You want to have the handles in line with your shoulders, meaning your arms should be parallel to the floor throughout the move.
- ✓ I prefer to keep my hands flat (like a motorcycle grip) with the outside of my hands pushing against the bars. This again keeps the forearms out of it.
- ✓ Make sure you don't get lazy, bring the handles back an extra couple of inches to really contract the muscle.
- ✓ This is a relatively easy exercise so push yourself.

Rows for rear delts

Here you can use dumbbells or a straight bar, either one is fine. My favorite version is the "incorrect barbell row," the one I wrote about in the section on training your back. I'll do these standing or on one of the rowing machines for back where your chest rests against a pad. The key is to get your elbows right up in line with your shoulders and pull back with your rear delts. Your grip should result in a ninety degree angle in your arms as you contract the muscle. No need for a great deal of weight here because you're isolating a small muscle. There are lots of variations that I'm sure you'll see in magazines or on the web, find the one that works for you. Whichever one you chose, make sure you resist the urge to move more weight by getting your back muscles involved. Focus on the delts and getting the weight all the way back so you can squeeze the muscle.

One last note on rear delts. Lately I've seen a lot of people using a rope attachment on a cable and they pull the rope into their chin or their forehead. Their hands are close together so they're forced to break their wrists. This is not an effective variation, the arm position is all wrong and you won't be able to push those delts anywhere near failure. Stick to the basics, again, think about the opportunity cost theory I mentioned.

Upright Rows

This is a move that is also frequently butchered and used far too often. It involves grabbing a bar with a close grip and pulling it up to your chin. I just think it focuses too much of the weight on the forearms and not enough on the delts. I feel you get a far bigger reward from the other exercises. It is a very popular movement and I see people swinging that bar all over the place to get it up. Some will even kick-start the bar with a push from the thighs. I rarely see a good strict set. Plus when your hands are too close together it creates a lot of tension in the wrists. On occasion, while I'm doing my front raises, I'll superset with a wide grip version where I keep the bar very close to my body and use my delts to pull it up to the bottom of my chest. I don't recommend this as a main shoulder exercise, there are many better options.

Steve Foxall

Chapter 21: Biceps

There's this woman at the gym, and for a while now I've been fascinated with her. I can't help but watch, not because of how she looks or what she's wearing, but because of how she lifts, it's perfect. Any exercise she does is a demonstration of the muscles moving the weight, rather than just her hands. It's hard to describe, it's just fluid, as if the bar wasn't even there. One day, I went up to her, which is very rare for me in the gym. I told her how impressed I was and that I was writing a book on how to lift. I wanted to know how she learned. I was then told that it was years of experience with yoga that taught her how to control, stretch and contract her muscles. When she started lifting, it was just a matter of adding weight to her movement. The yoga taught her how to use her muscles and what their different roles are. How to use her shoulders to lift her arms out rather than lifting her arms to use her shoulders. I thought it was brilliant. It reminded me of when I played hockey and they would bring in figure skaters to teach us how to skate. They would talk about eliminating all the things that are slowing you down, how to make your movements pure. It's a lesson in simplicity when we tend to over complicate so many things.

Why do I bring this up with biceps? Because curling weight is simple, it's basic, and yet we over-complicate it. I'm going to teach you how to train them by eliminating what everyone does wrong.

Before we get going, there is some crucial advice I must pass along when it comes to training arms. It took me awhile to figure this out, which is frustrating, but it won't happen to you. The problem I had in the first few years was that I couldn't get a good pump in my arms, not matter how hard I trained. The next day, my muscles weren't sore and I just felt like I was wasting my time. The solution to my dilemma came from a bodybuilder named Vince Taylor. One of the top contenders, Vince was a rare proponent of light weight, high rep training. He would talk about how it was actually harder to train with light weight but easier to effectively push the muscle fibers. I was far too addicted to heavy lifting to give in to it, but I did give it a shot with arms.

What I quickly discovered is that every time you train your arms, the warm-up determines the effectiveness of your session, more so than with any other muscle group. You want light weight, lots of reps and plenty of squeezing and flexing the muscle. There are many days when my warm-up takes just as long as the rest of the session.

Until your biceps or triceps are full of blood and burning when you flex them, you aren't ready to start working them.

Barbell Curls

Grab a forty pound bar, or even twenty, a weight that offers very little resistance to those pipes. Now, I want you to curl that bar *without* using your biceps. Just use your hands and your forearms, and when your forearms get tired, just swing the weight up enough while bringing your elbows forward and then use your forearms to finish. Do a few reps like that, you'll get the hang of it. After a couple sets, you might notice that those forearms are really burning. Now, obviously this isn't the right way to do curls but my point is this, that's what I see every day in the gym. Even with dumbbells and cables, it's all the same.

Now that you know what you shouldn't do, let's go over the right way. Grab that same bar, shoulder-width grip. What you need to do is get the weight on your biceps. *Get it off your hands and forearms* and on to those bis. In order to do this, you need a slight bend at the elbow, then loosen your grip and lean your weight forward just a touch. Now, don't curl the bar, just flex your biceps, and it will come up a few inches all by itself. That's how you should start every single rep of your bicep workout, with your biceps and not your hands and forearms.

Once the weight starts, just keep flexing. Your elbows should always stay at your side, don't let them flare out. Constant tension is key, don't bring the bar up to a point where the weight switches to your elbows, which is what will happen when your forearms are close to vertical. Don't let the bar just drop either, maintain control and don't straighten your arms at the bottom. Again, the weight will go right to those forearms. By keeping the weight on your biceps at the bottom, it's easier to keep it there rep after rep. Down slow, up fast, always.

The goal is to keep lifting the bar by flexing and squeezing your biceps as hard as you can through the whole set. The goal is NOT to see how much weight you can curl. After each set, your biceps should be burning, and nothing else

Going up in weight…

Heavy curls are something you need to work your way up to. You first need to master lifting the bar with your biceps, it has to be second nature. Because you don't need a spot and there's no risk, everybody tends to jump right in, and that's a mistake. You also need to have that ability to focus, to push yourself while maintaining your form. That's what Arnold did that most don't, while he looked like he was swinging two hundred pounds around recklessly, he was actually keeping the weight on his biceps and pushing them as far as they could go. Even on the last rep, he was still using his biceps to lift the bar. Once you get to that point, then heavy curls will be a staple in your routine

As far as which bar to use, straight or cambered, I prefer straight. While my hands remain somewhat relaxed, I focus on only using my pinky fingers to hold the bar. This seems to help get a good squeeze at the top. It works with dumbbells too. If the straight bar hurts your wrists, then use the cambered bar, or just mix things up now and then.

Standing Dumbbell Curls

This is a great exercise but you'll see where people go wrong. It's that all too common move of bringing your elbow out away from your side and 'flinging' the weight up. By this point, I hope I don't have to explain why this is wrong. Here's how you do it.

- ✓ Stand up straight with a dumbbell at each side, and start light, always start light.
- ✓ Relax your forearms and grip, just tight enough to hold up the weight.

- ✓ Starting with one side, turn the weight about thirty degrees to the curl position and flex that bicep. As you then bend your elbow make sure it stays tight to your body.
- ✓ While keeping your elbow in at your side, contract your bicep.
- ✓ The path should bring the weight out in front of you but not so high that it rests on your elbow. The top position should be where the weight is forcing your bicep into a hard contraction.
- ✓ Slowly lower the weight down, wait until it is all the way down before moving your head over to look at the other dumbbell.
- ✓ Don't start the other side until you complete that move, you want to avoid swinging the weight.
- ✓ This is not a fast exercise, take your time and focus on the squeeze
- ✓ This is a great move for drop sets, NOT forced reps.
- ✓ Remember to always try to keep your forearms out of it. If you can't lift the weight by contracting your bicep then grab lighter dumbbells.

Seated Incline Dumbbell Curls

This is a great exercise and perfect for beginners, I say that because it will help teach you how to move the weight by contracting the muscle. Simply follow the standing version but while seated on an incline bench.

- ✓ The angle here is key, the seat should be around 45%. Too high and it defeats the purpose, too low and you put your arm in a weak position which could lead to straining the muscle.
- ✓ Make sure your feet are flat on the floor.
- ✓ Again, loose grip.
- ✓ You can alternate arms or do both at the same time, up to you.
- ✓ One technique is to go to failure with both at the same time and then bang off a couple one at a time.
- ✓ Sometimes, I'll go to failure on the bench and then do a few more reps while standing.
- ✓ Keep squeezing those biceps.
- ✓ For both standing and seating, note that at the top, you don't want to bring the weight all the way up and rest it on your elbows! You should be going up about three quarters of the way to get that crazy contraction, do it right, and you'll feel what I'm talking about.

Preacher Curls - Seated with a bar or machine

The preacher bench is the one where you rest your upper arm on the angled bench while curling the weight. The first thing you need to do is adjust the seat. The goal is to position it in order to take your lower body out of it. Your upper arms should stay tight against the bench, rather than using your elbows as a leverage point. If you're down to a sleeveless shirt, then putting a t-shirt or towel on the bench helps.

- ✓ Grab the bar. Most use the middle of a cambered bar here to alleviate the stress on the wrists, a machine bar will be angled.
- ✓ It is essential to maintain a loose grip, just rest the bar on your palms with your fingers acting as hooks.
- ✓ Bend the arms slightly and do not fully extend your arms at any time, it will put a lot of stress on your bicep while in a weak position and that's dangerous.
- ✓ Get the weight on your bicep by keeping those forearms loose and then contract.
- ✓ Again, bring the bar high enough to get that contraction, no resting at the top.
- ✓ Slowly lower the weight, DO NOT let it drop, the position you're in will isolate the bicep and without supporting muscle groups you are always more susceptible to injury.
- ✓ While this isn't an exercise for heavy weight, it is one where you can just close your eyes and keep going.
- ✓ A prefect weight is one where you can do 7 or 8 reps with good rhythm and then just push through 3 or 4 more.
- ✓ This is a good one for the rest pause technique. Put the weight down and rest for ten seconds, then bang off a few more, then repeat.
- ✓ Remember, your goal is not to cheat the weight up, it's to pump and punish the biceps, that's it, that's your total focus.

21s

Here's an exercise I wish I had known about in the early years. It likely would have solved a lot of my problems. Grab a light barbell for some standing curls. The first 7 reps will be from the bottom up to the halfway point. The next 7 are from the halfway point to the top and the last 7 are full reps. Consistently, you'll find that the top exercises I rave about are the ones that take 'weight' and ego out of the equation, and this is one of them. Try to use too much weight on this move and 21 reps will be out of the question. You need a bar that gets you there, albeit with a little swinging at the end. The result will be an intense burn in the biceps and a great pump, two of the essential components of a good arm workout. Do three sets as a second or third exercise. I love finishing off with them.

Obviously there are many other movements to choose from but those are the basics. If you want to try concentration curls, cable curls, one-arm preacher curls and so on, wait until you learn how to properly curl the weight by contracting the bicep, then you'll know the feeling you need to get. If you struggle to get that feeling, then go back to what works. Stick to the basics, three exercises max and you should be done in about twenty minutes. The more you focus on that warm-up, the more effective your session will be.

The best advice you will ever get on biceps is to warm up until you get a crazy pump, *then* start your session.

A quick note on the Brachialis/Forearms. These are both important and you will read plenty of articles that say they get enough work from all those heavy back workouts, but I like working them.

Here's a simple way to incorporate them into your bicep workout. I start out with 5 supersets of the following two exercises, and that's it. It's quick and it gets the job done.

1. **Hammer curls** – This one is pretty easy, elbow tight to your side, hold the dumbbells with your palms facing in so each forearm and dumbbell look like a hammer. You can either bring the weight straight up, or bring it across your body up to your opposite side chest. You have to concentrate on using the muscle that's under your bicep. If you aren't sure of which muscle it is, look it up.

2. **Reverse Curls** – Here again, pretty simple, grab a cambered bar with a reverse grip. Don't grab it in the middle, your hands should be shoulder-width apart. Using the back of your forearms, bring the weight up in one solid pull to a point just above 90 degrees at the elbow, that's plenty. I usually do these fairly quickly.

Steve Foxall

Chapter 22: Triceps

"Always be yourself, express yourself, have faith in your-self, do not go out and look for a successful personality and duplicate it."

Bruce Lee

I started cycling about five years ago. I found a used moun-tain bike and hit the trails by the house. I loved it. I almost killed myself a few times but once I got used to the clips and the trails I was able to hit it pretty hard. A year later, the owner of the bike store in town sold me his road bike, a carbon fiber frame with all the latest gear on it. He gave me a great deal so I couldn't pass it up. I was skeptical and figured riding on the roads would be boring. Surprisingly, I found the opposite to be true. Before long I was getting up at five thirty to hit the country roads. I'd bike around thirty-five kilometers before work and it energized the shit out of me.

What I liked most about it was the climbing. If you've ever watched a Tour de France, you know that climbing is by far the toughest part of the sport. It's a definite challenge. You start up a hill, already tired, and it's a commitment that can't end half way up. You just deal with the pain and keep going to the top. That's what lifting does to you, it makes you crave challenging situations, it makes you want to achieve, to take something on and defeat it.

I absolutely hate doing cardio in the gym, but this was cardio that got my ass out of bed before the birds started singing. I live in a town called Ancaster, which is right next to a town called Dundas, and cyclists from all over come to Dundas for one reason, Sydenham Hill. It's a fairly steep 1.3 km climb, something that's hard to find when you don't live around mountains. My record is six repeats with no rest. It might not sound like a lot but you're welcome to come by and give it a shot, I'll have a go with you.

Back to the Tour, when it's on I always try and catch the climbing stages, or at least the highlights. It really is an amazing thing, you can actually see the pain in their bodies and faces. It's a display of incredible punishment. The Giro D'Italia is the second biggest race next to the Tour de France and in 2012, a Canadian rider named Ryder Hesjedal was going for what would be an historic win for his country. It was the second last stage with the final stage being a time trial, so a good showing would almost ensure a victory. It was a 219 km trek through a valley that finished with a monster climb on the Passo Dello Stelvio. The elevation was just over 2,700 meters and the last five kilometers were torture for Ryder. His team had left him by now, and he was exhausted in what was his twentieth stage. With nothing left in the tank, he dug deep, real deep, and found enough energy to push right through to the finish, and the next day, be became the first Canadian to ever win the race. Now, the message here is that even though I bust my ass cycling and push as hard as I can, my 1.3 km hill is a fraction of what it takes to complete one stage of a Tour. There's climbing Sydenham, and then there's climbing the Stelvio Pass, but I still love to climb.

The same thing applies to lifting. There's big, and then there's Ronnie Coleman big. There are a handful of people on the planet with 24 inch arms and I'll never be one of them, but I still love to lift, and I always will. For some, that can be a challenge.

So how do we accept mediocrity in the gym? It seems a lot tougher in bodybuilding than in any other sport. I think one of the main reasons is all of the advertising and promotion that's done. Every product we buy promises to make us bigger, and quickly. The ads have you believe you'll get huge and have ripped abs in no time. Another reason could be the unavoidable de-sensitizing. We are bombarded with pictures of the pros in mag-azines and videos. It's a constant image that slowly gets ingrained in our minds. It's easy to become discouraged after years of training and still seeing someone in the mirror that doesn't even come close to the physique of even an amateur bodybuilder, let alone a pro. Even when you *do* see progress, some massive dude walks by you at the gym and makes you feel about as big as the cast of *The Big Bang Theory*.

When your goal in the gym is just to get big, you can easily set yourself up for discouragement. In all of my time training, I've never considered myself to be 'big'. That's not all that un-common, I think a lot of guys and girls feel their physique isn't as good as it really is. Having said that, if you're going to gauge your success by how you compare to professionals, even your best accomplishments will feel like failures. Almost all pros are well on their way very early in life. If you're going to make the

NFL, you're running circles around the other players in high school. If you're going to be a pro bodybuilder, then there's a good chance people are staring at you before you even start lifting. My goals have always been based on becoming very good at lifting, it was never about getting huge or lifting massive amounts of weight. I'm passionate about lifting, I'm not passionate about the results. Any size I achieve is a side effect of doing something I love to do. It's like getting big calves from cycling. You cycle because you love to do it—the calves are just a side-effect. Get to that place and I think you will create a much more positive and encouraging environment for yourself. You will lift for a very long time and be a much better person for it. The rewards you experience will astound you, and believe me, the benefits go far beyond your measurements.

Now, when it comes to constantly trying to convince yourself that you are making progress and that you're bigger than everyone else at the party, we need to talk about your triceps. It's the gauge, the indicator, that one part of the body that you can quickly and subtly flex when you walk by that mirror. It tells you how much of a pump you're still hanging on to when you haven't been to the gym in three days. It always comes into play when deciding on that t-shirt or choosing an outfit for that date. It's a muscle that can make you look like you lift, it can legitimize your hobby and get you respect. It means you know what you're doing. I've always trained my tris, from day one they were always included. I didn't do a lot of fancy shit with cables, I used those just to warm up. For me, the close-grip bench, skull crushers and two-handed overhead dumbbell extensions did the trick. It's time well spent, as far as the physique goes. It's a very important piece of the puzzle and completes what big shoulders, traps and pecs can't do alone.

Now while I stuck to the basics, it wasn't about moving as much weight as I could, it was always about solid contractions and overloading the muscle in order to incorporate the maximum amount of fibers. As with biceps, the warm-up is absolutely essential. I don't go anywhere near those basic exercises until the back of my arms are so pumped they're in pain. I can't emphasize this enough: effective arm training can only come after a very thorough warm-up. I'd do cable pushdowns with light weight, I'd keep my elbows in tight and use only my tris to move the weight. I would squeeze as hard as I could for five or six sets and that would do it. This is also a great idea for the sake of your elbows. Once ready, here's what I do:

Close Grip Bench Press

This is your meat and potatoes lift for triceps, but it can be tricky to get right. The key is making sure your chest and shoulders aren't doing the work.

- ✓ Grip is where many people screw up. As the bar comes down, your arms should be tight at your sides and your forearms straight up and down. Most beginners have their hands too close together so when their arms come down, their forearms are angled in. This puts a great deal of stress on the wrists. Your thumbs should be a good eight inches apart.
- ✓ It's not the close grip that forces your triceps to work here, it's not using your chest. When you lie on the bench, do NOT stick out your chest or arch your back. Lie flat.

- ✓ As I've said before, you want to carry the weight with your tris before you start bringing the weight down. It's pretty easy on this one. Take the bar off the rack with a slight bend in your arm, this should immediately place the weight on the back of your arms.
- ✓ As you bring it down, go slow and focus on carrying the weight with your triceps, lateral force works very well here. Do not bring the bar down quickly and bounce the weight as you might do with bench presses.
- ✓ You should be using a path that brings the bar down to your lower chest. Again, from every angle, your forearms should be straight up and down. The bar should be in line with your lower chest.
- ✓ Once the bar reaches the chest, you have to really focus on contracting your tris. Starting light and working your way up will help a great deal.
- ✓ Don't lockout at the top, ever.
- ✓ One key here is to not grip the bar too hard, this is a bad tendency. You want to get into the habit of squeezing the muscle harder as you maintain a relaxed grip.
- ✓ I'm not one for drop sets or partials here. If I want to make it harder I'll go down slowly, while focusing on the negative, pause and then flex the triceps as hard as I can.

Skull Crushers

This is a great exercise that takes a lot of concentration.

- ✓ Use a cambered bar, it should be a little easier on the elbows.
- ✓ Make sure your feet are on the floor, don't sit them on the bench. This will help you keep your body tight, and engage your core, which is very important.
- ✓ There are a couple of options here. One is to keep your upper arm straight up and down while bringing the bar down to your forehead. The other is to bring the bar down behind your head allowing your upper arm to come back. I've always used the first option but it's your call.
- ✓ When I bring the bar down to my forehead, I make sure my tris are engaged and carrying the weight. Then I imagine that I'm pressing the weight straight up to the ceiling, almost like a bench press. It just gives me a feeling of being powerful.
- ✓ I don't lockout but I flex the muscle at the top of every rep. This is key to making this an effective move. As the set goes on, I'll hold that squeeze for a second or two which helps maximize the pump.
- ✓ One tip is to make sure you don't break your wrist on the way down, keep the back of your hands flat.
- ✓ Once you're done, you can always bring the weight to your lower chest and bang out some close grip presses. That's a great way to push your triceps past failure and force that pump.

✓ Don't go too heavy on these, and don't bring your elbows into play so you can lift more weight. Be strict and concentrate, focus on getting the tris to move the weight while keeping the rest of your body still and tight.

✓ You will be get better and better at incorporating your abs, and this will help you squeeze out extra reps when your arms get tired.

Two-Handed overhead dumbbell extensions

✓ I've always done these and I think that's one of the reasons my triceps have consistently developed. Allow me a quick review here about a couple of mistakes people make. The biggest one involves too much focus on the hands and moving the weight.

✓ First of all, you need to keep your elbows in and your upper arms straight. You don't ever want your elbows going out as the weight comes down, the only thing moving should be your elbow joint.

✓ As you start the weight down, think about bringing it back behind you, instead of down. It should travel in an arc while you maximize the distance between the dumbbell and the back of your head.

✓ Focus on your triceps and making the exercises as hard as you can. That's a crucial aid here. You should really feel the weight on the back of your arms, and not on your elbows.

✓ Go down enough to really stretch the tris and then focus on contracting them to get the weight back up.

✓ I like to pause at the bottom here while pushing the weight back behind me, it really accentuates the stretch. That's what makes this move so great, it's that stretch at the bottom. Most people don't even focus on it, they just go through an up and down motion. Trust me, it makes a huge difference.

✓ Always keep in mind that you're holding weight above your head. Always use a weight that's manageable, that allows you to stay in control. By purposely making this move as hard as you can you are able to use less weight while increasing the effectiveness.

✓ If you have a spotter, again, no forced reps above your head, just have them wait until you can't do any more reps and then they can take the dumbbell off your hands.

One hand overhead dumbbell extensions

✓ It's the same idea on these, make them as hard as you can and get that stretch at the bottom.

✓ You aren't using a lot of weight here so focus on just using the triceps and making sure the elbow joint is the only thing moving.

✓ I don't do these as I always incorporate the two arm version but they are definitely a good idea.

✓ Using the right weight will allow you to get into a good rhythm and bang out those extra reps.

✓ Don't do these standing, always sit, it just allows for better focus and keeping the body tight.

Cables

- ✓ There are all kinds of cable moves for triceps, from pushdowns to overhead extensions to underhand pushdowns and so on. The idea with all of them is very similar.
- ✓ Focus on the triceps, not your hands.
- ✓ Don't use a ton of weight. When you do that, you're just using other muscle groups. Pushdowns are the worst for this. Keep your elbows in and don't lean in-to it too much. You aren't pressing the bar down, you're contracting your tris.
- ✓ Two of the many benefits of cables are the stretch you can create and the constant tension they allow for.
- ✓ Drop sets are great for all of the cable moves. The first three tri moves were for mass. These are all for pump and working the inner head.
- ✓ It's a mistake to focus too much on the cables. Pick two out of the first three moves I've covered and fin-ish with a cable move. (You should have used a cable move to warm up, that doesn't count.)
- ✓ A good tricep workout for me means an insane pump, it means it actually hurts to flex the muscle. Get there and you'll be on your way to bigger t-shirts.

*The gym is a classroom, it teaches us that nothing comes easy,
and it reminds us every time we go to school.*

Steve Foxall

Chapter 23: Calves & Traps

Perseverance – *Steady persistence in a course of action, a purpose, a state, etc., especially in spite of difficulties, obstacles or discouragement.*

Dictionary.com

I've lumped these two muscle groups together because of the similarities. Both are very strong, dense and fibrous in nature. They can be extremely challenging when it comes to growth. There are those that naturally have big calves or traps. We'll call them the 'lucky' ones, but they are far the norm. For most of us it takes years of properly performed, consistent training. It takes perseverance.

A few years ago, my training evolved, and it became so much more effective. I'm a perfectionist so if I was going to spend all that time training, I wanted to be damn good at it. That's why I'd get frustrated with the lack of results. I kept thinking, "If I can bang out twelve reps of standing calf raises using the whole stack, what do the pros do? How do *they* push the muscle?" A few years back I figured it out, and it's an incredibly important lesson in lifting.

It's almost like a paradigm shift, which in the world of business means to take on a radically different way of thinking or a completely new direction. Every time you perform an exercise, there are two polar opposite ways to do it, with some in-between. The first is to use your body in a way that allows you to move the most weight. The second is using your body in a way that allows you to move the least amount of weight. My guess was that on some exercises, the pros stick to the latter, and given my theory on the benefits of learning from the best, I've been doing what I think the pros do, and it's been working. I'm going to use this way of thinking to explain the exercises in this section to show you exactly what I mean.

Standing Calf Raises

While this seems like a 'can't go wrong' exercise, believe me it is. Just look at how many guys walk around the gym with skinny calves. There's one big mistake that I think comes from simply watching others. It's focusing on the top 'double-pump'. It's where you get to the top, drop down a little and then come back up flexing your calves. I just think it's counterproductive, but it seems to be the norm.

Calves take a tremendous beating every day, walking, running, working out. You ever notice a woman walking with crazy high heels and how flexed her calves are? If you think about the range of motion of a calf raise compared to running or jumping, what part does everyday life work on? It's the top half. Imagine you're skipping rope, it's all top half. You can't stretch your calves at the bottom because the ground is flat. The result is that your calves are quite used to the top half and the 'double-pump' makes us focus on just that part of the range.

In order to shock the muscle, to get those fibers working and push them, you need to focus on the bottom. So, when doing any calf raise, it's crucial that you stretch as far as you can before bringing the weight back up, on every rep. Let's look at the hard way and the easy way.

Maximum weight – This is what I see most of the time. Shoulders are positioned under the pads, ahead of your feet. From the side, you're leaning forward a bit, and this brings in the back muscles. The soles of your feet are positioned forward on the foot plate. This increases your leverage (just think how hard it would be if only your toes were on the plate). Put those two together and you substantially increase the amount of weight you can use. In addition, when people don't go down all the way, they're able to get the weight moving and use their backs to help out with the top of the range. I did this for years and years so believe me, I know what I'm talking about.

Minimum Weight – Post evolution, I now do the opposite. When I set up, my shoulders are as far back as the pads will allow. I place my feet as far back as I can while keeping the balls of my feet on the plate. I stand straight up with a slight bend at the knee. This takes all of the weight and places it squarely on my calves. I stretch all the way down, pause, and then in one strong contraction, I squeeze my calves right up to the top.

Now, let's talk about sets. Given that calves are so dense, you'll find they take a while to get going. My goal with each session is to punish them, to make them burn, not just during the set but after. You can't do this with three sets, not a chance. For me, it's usually around seven or eight. Reps are anywhere from fifteen to thirty.

The heavy volume is essential. It's difficult to punish the muscle, it takes dozens of intense reps. It means forcing the calves to keep moving the weight. My way of thinking is that the harder I can make the exercise, the more efficient this punishment will be, and as a result, my job is done sooner. As a result, usually, around three quarters of the way through a set, I'll adjust to make it harder. I'll stand straight up and force that weight all onto the calves. You'll instantly feel the burn as you bang out three or four more. Apart from your calves contracting, nothing else on your body should move, especially the knee joint, which should remain slightly bent and stay that way.

As for principles you can use here, I mentioned earlier about the 'flex sets,' the one I picked up at the photo shoot. I've used it ever since and can only urge you to give it a try. On my last set, I'll do a few reps to get the pain going and then I'll get the weight up and flex my calves as hard as I can for as long as I can. Usually around thirty to forty seconds. I can't tell you exactly why this helps, only that I think it further shocks the muscle with a function that it isn't quite used to.

Aside from that, drop sets...lots of them.

Seated Calf Raises

Same philosophy here, find a good machine that you like, one that allows you to push to failure. When you set up, the same points apply. Feet and knees have to be back in order to place the weight on the calves. Full stretch at the bottom and squeeze that weight up. Follow that advice and again, you should be in for some serious burning.

The seated version works the outer calf and the standing one focuses more on the larger inner calf. That is why people tend to do both. You need to know that so you can focus on one or the other, so that you can use your mind to make those fibers work.

Stretching – Now with all that pain comes the need to stretch. This is an easy way to stretch out those fibers and re-lieve some soreness that will be waiting for you in the morning. Find a machine or bench that has a bar along the floor high enough to do a standard runner's stretch. Put your toes up and lean forward until you can feel that muscle strain, hold it for a good twenty seconds and then switch. If you find a good spot then keep using it for each workout. Take the time to do this, consider it part of your workout, make it your third exercise.

There are other ways to train calves. You can use the leg press, Smith machine (don't see the point of that one), or maybe you're lucky enough to have a donkey calf raise machine where you're bent over at the waist with the pads on your lower back. All the same rules apply, make it hard, make it as hard as you can and you will then start to make progress. The amount of weight you use for calves should be of little concern to you, trust me, it doesn't matter to anyone else in the gym.

Barbell Shrugs

I can never help but shake my head at all of those guys doing shrugs with four, five or even up to seven plates a side with a set of traps that even mine dwarf. It's the mother of all 'cheat' exer-cises. Heave the bar up with your legs and back while you try to hang on long enough to finish a set of four. I can honestly say that with all the stupid shit I've done, going crazy heavy on shrugs was never part of my workout.

Maximum Weight – The key here is moving the knee joint and the hips in one big motion. Almost as if you were finishing off a deadlift. It's not complicated, it just brings in the majority of your big strong muscles. That allows people to move crazy weight.

Minimum Weight – This one might take some practice because it's not as easy as the standing calf raise.

- ✓ Grip the bar so your arms are hanging straight down. Going wider than that is a mistake, it will encourage you to pinch your traps together at the top and it's less efficient.
- ✓ Stand with just a slight lean forward to keep the weight off of your lower back.
- ✓ Before you start, you need to purposely place the weight on your traps. Do this by letting the weight hang right down. This will stretch out the traps and let you 'feel' the weight with them and ensure they're carrying the load.
- ✓ This is the key: don't pull on the weight with your arms.
- ✓ Focus on using your traps to get it going.
- ✓ As you keep contracting your traps, make sure you bring your shoulders straight up, NOT up and in. When they come in it limits the contraction. Think up and out.

✓ This might be slower than you're used to because you aren't jerking the weight up, it should be very smooth from the bottom up to the top.

✓ Always let that bar go right down in order to stretch out the traps, it's the same rule that applies to calves. Your traps aren't used to that portion of the range and you need to incorporate as many fibers as you can.

✓ As you approach failure, you really need to focus on leaving your back out of it and forcing your traps to contract. This takes practice, it's not easy.

✓ Do lots of sets, as many as it takes to really exhaust the muscle. Weight isn't important. As soon as you can't get that contraction at the top with your traps alone, lower the weight. There is little benefit to letting your back do the work.

The best principle here is rest pause sets. I'll do these in the rack so I can just rest the bar on the cross beams. I'll rest for a few seconds and then bang out some more reps with that same weight. You can also do partials here, focusing on the stretch at the bottom and bringing the bar up as far as you can.

Dumbbell Shrugs

Similar tactics here. The difference is in how you bring the weight up. You can experiment and mix it up from session to session. The benefit of the dumbbells is that you can let your traps dictate the range of motion. To find out what's best, use light weight. Hang your arms down and focus on contracting your traps, let them pull the weight up and see where it goes. That is likely your ideal path.

If you don't already know, go straight up and down, don't roll your shoulders. The reason is that rolling while carrying that much weight can cause some serious damage to your shoulder joint. You can essentially 'grind' parts that should never grind. There's no benefit to it whatsoever.

Remember, take your time, there's no rush. With the dumbbells being lighter than the bar, you can hold them longer with your straps. This means your set can take longer and you can rest at the bottom before continuing. I find partial reps work great here. Once you're exhausted, just work the bottom half.

One variation is to bring the dumbbells back and up, it's an alternative to behind the back shrugs.

Shrug Machines – You'll usually find a shrug machine at your gym. Don't use it just for the sake of using it. I've yet to find a good one. I think it's very difficult for a machine to mimic the barbell shrug. The one at my gym now is no good because the handles are too far apart. I see people using it all the time and they're just pulling into the ears, instead of up. Sometimes, the best machines are those designed for something totally different. Sometimes if you watch other lifters, you might see someone turn another machine into a great trap machine.

Chapter 24: Hamstrings

There's a significant mistake that even experienced body-builders make. It has to do with recovery. I've already written about the importance of both mental and physical recovery and how overlooking that element of training will without a doubt, impede your level of progress. The mistake involves overtraining, but not in the sense of spending too much time in the gym or not taking enough days off or not eating enough food, that's separate. I'm talking about overtraining as a result of placing too much unnecessary stress on your body when you don't have to.

When it comes to hamstrings, stiff-legged deadlifts are a very common exercise. Quite often, I see this movement done with two plates, three plates and even four. Remember what I said earlier, if you're using a ridiculous amount of weight to train a muscle that isn't that strong, then you must be incorporating other 'big' muscles. In this case, the majority of people doing stiff-legged deads are basically doing deadlifts. It's something we just gravitate to. We'll do the exercise and position ourselves in a way that maximizes the weight we can use. Why use 135 pounds when I can use 315? Obviously 315 must be better. You have to lift heavy in order to get big, or so goes the myth. That line of thinking couldn't be more wrong. It's the same with 500 pound shrugs or 600 pound calf raises.

When working smaller muscle groups, adjusting your form to incorporate larger muscle groups in order to maximize the weight you can lift will reduce the effectiveness of the session and it will impact how those 'big' muscles are able to recover from workouts. It will also make it more difficult for your nervous system to consistently recover week after week.

Does that make sense? Whenever you are asking your body to lift hundreds of pounds, it is going to have a significant impact. That impact is something you have to respect and recover from. You want to limit how often you do that, you want to save it for those heavy back, chest and leg workouts. When you train your arms, shoulders, traps, calves and hamstrings, you want to isolate the muscle in order to let the big muscles rest. You have to remember that this is a game of repetition. We work these muscles over and over again, week after week, year after year, so the little details in how we go about that will determine our level of success.

When it comes to hamstrings, people tend to fall into one of two groups. The first are the ones that do the heavy stiff-legged deads and go heavy on the leg curls and then maybe a third exercise to really push the muscle. The second group are those who do a few sets of leg curls at the end of their usual leg workout.

I rarely do anything after training my big muscle groups other than drinking a shake and going home. There's just nothing left in the tank. Maybe I'm just getting too old but I find that my experience allows me to really push those muscles to the limit, and at the end, I'm just not able to push another muscle to that same limit. In order to ensure that I train my whole body, I now train calves, traps or hams first. Arms get their own day...every now and then. It allows you to really focus and hammer away at what are likely your weak points, while still having plenty of energy to hit one of the big muscle groups. We'll start out with the exercise that is often butchered for the sake of lifting heavy.

Stiff-Legged Deadlifts

The simple key here is mechanics. Whenever you bring the bar down close to your legs, like you do in regular deadlifts, your back is doing the work. Bring that bar out and away from your body, and instantly, your hamstrings are forced to carry the weight. Try it and you will feel the difference.

1. Rather than placing your feet at shoulder-width, try spreading them out, the farther the better.

2. Grab a light bar, something you would do curls with. Place your hands father apart than you normally would.

3. The key to this move is to engage the hamstrings. Before you start, get the weight on the back of your legs and off your lower back. Do this by leaning forward a touch and flexing your hams. Move around a little until you feel it, and focus your mind on the back of your legs.

4. As you lower the bar, you want to keep it far away from your body. Imagine there's a line on the ground a foot in front of you and you're trying to put the bar down on the other side of that line.

5. Keep lowering the bar and you should quickly feel an intense stretch in the hams. Go easy on the first couple of sets—you need to stretch them out before going lower. Now, this is the hard part. You want to bring the weight back up by pulling it with your hams and not letting your lower back take over. The wide stance and grip will help with this. Make sure as the bar comes up that you don't bring it in until the very end. You don't need to lean back at the top, just flex those hams. This takes a lot of practice and a lot of focus. Keep going slow and pause at the bottom. Remember, you're not moving weight, you're stretching and squeezing the back of your legs. The effect will be that you are pushing your hams to the limit while not involving your back, which is exactly what you want to do.

If you feel your back taking over then...

- ✓ Make sure you're keeping the bar away from you.
- ✓ Move your feet and hands a little wider out if you can.
- ✓ Keep the weight manageable.
- ✓ At the bottom, pause, and try to start the bar moving back up with your hamstrings. The muscle that starts the weight moving tends to be the one that keeps it moving.

✓ Use lateral force by pushing your feet outwards and behind you, as if you were skating.

Do these correctly and you will feel it the next day, both in your hams and your glutes. This is great practice for using your mind and body to control which muscle moves the weight. It is also a great way to incorporate stretching into your routine. You're bending at the hips and you'll be able to go lower on each set because of that stretch.

Lying Leg Curls

This is the one where you lie on your stomach and curl your legs up. It's a favorite of many and will enable you to really push those hams.

Again, depending on how you position your body and use your arms, you can definitely incorporate the lower back muscles. Start out light making sure the pads on the back of your ankles are positioned correctly so that at the top they are not too high up your leg or too far down by your shoes. You want to really stretch and squeeze the hams. The one thing about this move is that you can really extend and stretch the muscle at the bottom without having the weight go anywhere else. If you lock out your arms when doing bench press, the weight goes to your elbows. That won't happen here, it just stays on the hamstrings. Having said that, you need to go slow on the descent as you do not want to pull something.

The challenge here is to not get too aggressive with the weight to a point where you're pulling with your arms and incorporating your lower back muscles.

- ✓ If your gym has a leg curl bench shaped like an upside down V then hop on that one, the body position makes it easier to isolate the hams.
- ✓ Adjust the bar so it's closer to your feet than your butt. This also makes it tougher for the back to help out.
- ✓ As I mentioned up top, when it comes to the small muscle groups, mental focus is difficult but essential. With the movement, I focus on one quick, strong contraction using only my hams. Slow going down and fast going up.
- ✓ Get into a rhythm and keep it going, forceful contractions with a tight squeeze at the top. It's the rhythm that keeps the set going and allows you to push the muscle through those last couple of reps. Once you lose the rhythm, the set is over.
- ✓ Use a weight that allows you to complete 8-10 reps in rhythm using those quick contractions.
- ✓ If you have to pull the weight up with your arms and back then lower the weight.
- ✓ Forget forced reps. Use drop sets, they're perfect for this movement. On the last set, keep dropping the weight and doing as many reps as you can until your hams are crying for you to stop.
- ✓ Again, this is one of those exercises where you can just close your eyes and keep going if the weight is right. You want to get into that zone where you really push the fibers. That's what will have you walking funny the next day, not trying to do the stack with four other muscle groups helping out.

Seated Leg Curls

This is the one where you sit up as if you were doing seated leg extensions but instead, your feet go on top of the pad and you curl the bar under. Most gyms now carry this contraption and if they do, use it. It's a great exercise that will let you really punish the hams. The big benefit here is that by sitting up, you take your back right out of it and focus the weight right on the hams and the glutes.

It's tough to go wrong here. I think the only advice I can give is that it's not a simple move as far as effort goes, it's just not easy. Remember what I said about stretching your legs out at the bottom for lying leg curls? Don't do that here, it puts the muscle in a very weak position where it's vulnerable. Just below lockout will get the job done and keep things safe.

The same thing applies when it comes to quick strong con-tractions. You shouldn't be struggling through a rep, it's either there or it isn't. You'll find that if you really push yourself on the-se, they are actually quite painful. After you're done, you have to release the bar that goes across the top of your thighs and it's no easy task at that point. Many in the gym have heard my painful cries after a tough set on this torture machine. Give it a shot and you will see what I'm talking about. Again, the weight means everything. Too light and you can keep curling through thirty reps, too heavy and you won't be able to get into that rhythm and have good productive sets.

**I recommend NOT doing this movement first,
you really need the hams to be warmed up
and stretched out before taking this on.**

Leg Press with Feet High

This is definitely one worth mentioning. When you do the leg press, it's very important that you know how your foot position impacts the muscles being engaged. I covered this under the leg section and from that you should know that the higher up your feet are, the more emphasis will be placed on your hamstrings and glutes. Knowing that, if you place your feet as high and wide as you can you will place a great deal of stress of those hams and abductor muscles. Keep in mind this only works on presses with big plates that allow for a high foot position. Some models don't give you the option to go high.

You aren't going to use a great deal of weight here. You want to bring it down slowly and focus on stretching out the muscle before pushing the weight back up using just your hams. Focus on the muscle and keep those big quads out of it. You won't get that same forceful contraction at the top as you will with all those curls but you will place more weight on the muscle during the negative portion and at the bottom of the rep. It's a good move to complement the curls and involve the abductor muscles and the glute tie-in at the same time.

Lunges

I know what you're thinking, lunges are for quads. Well, yes and no. I don't like doing lunges after squats and presses as I have a tough time doing them when my legs feel like jello. For me, doing a few sets at the end of the hamstring workout is far more productive as the added control gives me the ability to really focus on stretching and squeezing both the hams and glutes.

Let's be honest, are you really going to take your quads to failure on these or initiate growth? The answer is no. Can you have an impact on your hams and glutes? Absolutely. In order to do so, you need to have balance and be able to place that front foot right where you want it.

Hamstring workouts are very tough, and very painful. I don't enjoy them at all but I keep on trucking because I know that there's no point in banging out all of those squats and heavy leg presses if I'm not going to take the time to build the back half of the leg. If you're a bodybuilder looking to compete, that thickness makes a huge difference in all of the side and back poses.

One last note. I have two leg workouts, one based on starting with heavy leg movements, the other one starting with hams and finishing with just one heavy quad movement. Without a doubt, the second option always gives me a better session. .Give it a try.

Steve Foxall

Chapter 25: Abs

Time to talk a little pop culture, and how the gym mirrors what society considers sexy.

When I hit the gym late at night, there are more guys training. Women procrastinate less and get shit done. One night, I was in finishing off an arm workout with some cable pushdowns. Halfway through my last set I noticed this kid standing right next to me. Just a little guy, early twenties and new to lifting. He was wearing those 'skinny' track pants and sporting a pair of Lacoste boat shoes. Guy was on his phone texting away, and then he faced the mirror, lifted his shirt, moved around while flexing his abs and started snapping pics. And he kept going until he was satisfied he had something worth posting.

Now I know social media is littered with gym selfies but what gets me is how accepted it is, how what used to be laughed at and considered self-centered is now just part of working out. It's actually part of a huge shift in gym culture. I gave the kid a look that said that phone was about to take its last selfie and moved on, and then I started thinking about my chapter on abs.

Pop culture is a very powerful thing, and the gym is the perfect place to see the effect it has on society. It wasn't too long ago that you would walk into a gym and see the majority of the women on the cardio equipment sweating up a storm, while the men were all lifting heavy in their track pants and t-shirts. Back then, women all wanted to be skinny and guys were busy building muscle. That was what pop culture dictated for years. Big like Arnold and Stallone, skinny like Kate Moss. The men were there to lift and the women were there to socialize.

Today, things couldn't be more different. Now, the guys are the ones sweating on the treadmills spending a fortune on their Under Armour outfits and shoes, while the women are all in the racks doing squats and deadlifts. Now guys all want to have abs and girls all want muscle, they want curves. Why? What caused the culture to shift? Easy: Ryan Gosling, or Ryan Reynolds, David Beckham and even that kid in Twilight that turns into a wolf. For the women, butts are in: JLo, Nicky and Kim, there's no shortage. Sexy is always in, and today, that's what sexy is.

The thing is, while pop culture always has an impact, social media has greatly magnified its effects. Facebook, Twitter and Instagram have all created this environment where you can actually create and edit your image and how people 'perceive' you. Look at our friend taking the selfie, he found that spot in the gym where the lighting was just right to create some definition, then he edited it and posted it. It's done to create the image of someone that has abs, even at a hundred pounds soaking wet.

You want an even better example? The other day I saw a guy on the bench press. He had three plates a side and with the help of his friends, brought the bar down to his chest. They snapped a few pics and then two of his buddies lifted the bar back up. An instant 'image' of a guy that presses three hundred pounds. It's all done to impress others, to create someone better, someone more impressive.

It's a dangerous path and there are books written on that subject alone. What I want to talk about is how it can come between you and your goals.

This is something more directed toward young guys. They tend to be the ones swinging around the gym for an hour training abs and texting between sets. Ever notice that most women who lift don't have their phones in the gym? They put their headphones on hoping it will keep the guys away and they get after it. They use good form, the right amount of weight and they get results. Their selfies are taken at home, albeit still with perfect lighting. I've seen some ladies completely change their physiques in two years. (Yes, I know that's a lot longer than the 21 days that magazine promised, but it actually does take time).

A few things to think about as you move toward your goals:

1. Why fitness models are fitness models and you're not. Unless you're naturally lean, you shouldn't want, or need visible abs.

2. Why focusing on abs will get in the way of you reaching your goals, even if your goal is to have abs.

3. Why most of the ab workouts I see are way too long, wasting limited gym time that could be far more productive.

4. Why most bodybuilders rarely train abs directly, but incorporate them into key exercises for other bodyparts.

Let's get started...

Tough to go a day now without seeing a picture of some guy or girl with crazy abs. It could be a magazine at the store, an ad on TV or a pop-up on the internet. The idea is constantly being reinforced, that in order to be 'in-shape', you better have abs.

Here's the thing, fitness models are fitness models for a reason: they're naturally lean. Or, you're probably looking at someone who just did a competition and dieted for four months. (Like the pic at the end of this chapter.)

Every single ad for a program or product that promises to give you abs in a few weeks is so full of shit it's not even funny. You want abs, then you diet down until your body fat level is low enough to show them off. Now, for some people that isn't too hard. Maybe you're naturally lean. Women tend to get abs way easier than men because they usually carry fat on their hips and legs rather than their stomachs.

My point to all of this is that if you don't naturally have abs, then you really have to look at your goals and why you go to the gym. As you may or may not know, it is extremely difficult to gain muscle and get rid of fat at the same time. So if you want to put on size and have abs all the time, you're going to have a problem.

Here's another thing to consider, your abs are a muscle, one big one actually. If you want to look anything close to those guys and girls on the cover shots, guess what, you'll have to build a lot of 'ab' muscle. So while you're spending all those hours doing all kinds of ab moves, if you're dieting to stay lean, your abs won't grow. It defeats the purpose.

Let's say you're happy with the level of muscle you have and you're in the gym to get a nice lean look for the summer. You want those abs so you spend 45 minutes working them. I know that's extreme but I see it. Guys hanging and swinging all over the place. Here's the thing, and once again, it's opportunity cost.

Whenever you're trying to get lean, you want to burn as many carbs and calories as possible. To do that, you want to work those big muscles. Now what do you think will do a better job, crunches or squats? Knee raises or deadlifts? All that time you're spending training abs *takes away* from the time you could be having much more effective, metabolism-boosting fat-burning workouts. Training abs probably burns the least amount of calories of any other body part, except maybe calves. So again, ask yourself: why are you *really* in the gym?

Last point. Let's say you're in the gym to build muscle, you're not dieting and you want to grow. How much time should you be spending on abs? Not that much. Bodybuilders and fitness competitors all know that it is quite easy to incorporate your abs when you work other body parts. There are certain exercises that rely on them and while doing those moves, if you focus mentally on your abs, it can have a significant impact.

I consider every tricep workout to be a tricep/ab session. Skull crushers, overhead rope extensions, even close grip presses: all rely heavily on the abs.

You will rarely see any bodybuilder spend more than 15 minutes on abs unless they're close to a show. You incorporate them to a point where it just becomes second nature and then you add a few sets of crunches or rollers or leg raises either before or after your workout.

It's all up to you. If you just love to train abs and go Rocky in the gym, hey, it's your time. I'm just trying to explain how you can get the most out of your time in the gym, how to train efficiently and be in a better position to reach your goals.

Crunches

- ✓ I typically do these lying on the floor with my feet up on a bench or an exercise ball. (Yes, I just admitted to using an exercise ball.)
- ✓ If you prefer, use the Roman chair, but it's easier to cheat and use your legs on that.
- ✓ The degree of difficulty depends on what you do with your arms.
  - ○ Easy = arms at your sides with hands by your hips
  - ○ Medium = arms across your chest
  - ○ Hard = hands at the side of your head (never behind your head!)
  - ○ Very Hard = hold a plate or a medicine ball on your chest
- ✓ Down slow, always keeping your abs flexed...constant tension is the key
- ✓ Pull your body up by contracting your core.
- ✓ Breathe out at the top while squeezing your abs.
- ✓ Look at the ceiling and imagine using your abs to pull your head up closer to the ceiling.
- ✓ Do lots of sets to failure, and there should be plenty of pain...good pain.
- ✓ If your back hurts, use a pad or perform the crunches at the start of your workout while your lower back muscles are still fresh.

Leg Raises

- ✓ Again, no swinging, you're wasting your time.
- ✓ Pull your legs up and focus on contracting and squeezing your lower abs.
  - ○ Easy = hands resting on the pads of the equipment, knees bent
  - ○ Medium = hand on the pads, legs straight
  - ○ Hard = hanging from a chin bar with legs bent
  - ○ Very hard = hanging from a chin bar with legs straight
- ✓ You want to work your way up from easy to very hard.
- ✓ Either way, do as many as you can with your legs straight and then bend your knees and crank out a few more reps.
- ✓ Again, no rest at the bottom, keep the abs tight.

That's all I've ever done, and it's really all you need. Once you master these two—and you will know by the pain you experience after ten reps—feel free to experiment with other moves. If you try something and you can't get that same burning, move on. There are plenty of new fancy machines that work abs and the same rules apply. Ab rollers are great to use at home and work them top to bottom.

Do all the crunches you want, abs are built in the kitchen

Chapter 26: Women, the Gym and all those Trainers

I knew at some point I wanted to devote a section of the book to all the women that lift, but I wasn't sure how. I've also been contemplating whether to 'vent' about personal trainers given the fact that I just might be asking gyms to let me hold events to promote this book. Then, it all became clear to me.

I was going about my business lifting away and a woman in her twenties (I later found out her name is Jenn) was going through a session with her trainer. Jenn was attempting to do step-ups with a weighted bar resting on her shoulders. This is an exercise for the glutes where you stand in front of a platform. Using one leg at a time you step up, pretty basic. What immediately caught my attention was that the platform was way too high, up around her waist. Jenn could barely get her foot on it before using all of her might to try and lunge her body up. Soon after I started watching, she lost her balance and fell, barbell and all. I just shook my head. The trainer was a young woman who bent down to help her client up. Once she was up, it was clear she had twisted her knee.

I figured that would be the end of it so I resumed my workout. A minute later, to my surprise, Jenn was back at it trying to do the exact same move. Long story short, I bit my tongue and minded my own business while Jenn fell again. Then, using dumbbells to keep things a little safer, she fell for the third time.

On my way out I saw Jenn leaving and couldn't resist letting her know that her trainer was a complete idiot and that was probably one of the most reckless things I've seen anyone do in a gym...and I've see some reckless shit. I told her that she may want to look at the qualifications of this person before continuing to employ her.

While it frustrates me to no end seeing people give up their hard-earned money to incompetent trainers, that's the business. I will, at the end of this chapter offer some advice for anyone considering that route. And no, I don't mean ALL trainers, there are plenty of good ones out there.

It did make me think about glutes and how many women train them without really understanding how to train them properly. So let's look at just that, and, in the process, incorporate some of the general mistakes women make that can get in the way of their progress.

It's been very difficult for me to write this book in a way that appeals to both men and women for a number of reasons. First of all, I'm a guy and I when it comes to training, I think like a guy. Most women lift for different reasons and therefore might not appreciate a great deal of the advice I'm handing out, or think that it doesn't apply to them. In addition, each group consistently makes a whole different set of mistakes, and it makes no sense to split them up in each section. I'm going to try, as best I can, to write about the mistakes I see women make and demonstrate how the majority of what I'm writing about can certainly help all women become more successful in reaching their own fitness goals.

Let's talk about goals in the gym, and how many times you've told someone that you're trying for more tone. Well, toning doesn't exist. Here are the main reality-based fitness goals you have to choose from:

Increase strength
Increase muscle size
Decrease fat levels
Increase flexibility/mobility
Improve cardiovascular health

I'm going over this because it's very important that you understand exactly what it is you're trying to accomplish. That way, you can better learn what each activity will contribute to, and what sort of outcome you should be expecting. If you're like most, you want to decrease fat and increase muscle. While this book doesn't focus on the goal of decreasing fat, I can certainly help with the muscle side. The biggest problem I have with 'toning' is that women tend to think they aren't trying to build muscle, so they steer clear of pushing themselves. They don't recognize that you need to learn how to train in order to build muscle.

We've all heard women say "I don't want to get TOO big from lifting weights." This is such a crazy misconception, and you need to get it out of your head. Women simply do not have the levels of testosterone required for any kind of substantial muscle growth, men do. The growth that you will experience will give your body that shape that you're looking for. If you want some context, look up a figure competition and you will see women that consistently go through very intense and challenging weight sessions. Are they too big?

Forget about the term 'tone' and accept the fact that your goal while lifting weights is to build muscle. Then, accept the fact that you will need to learn how to train properly and with enough intent in order to make the progress you're looking for. In other words, you need to follow the majority of the advice in this book. Let's dig into some common issues.

Not enough weight

From the book, you know that in order to make a muscle grow, you need to push it enough to cause damage (hypertrophy). The body will then repair that muscle, and if it feels you need more to keep up, it will make you a little more.

Essentially, you need to push your sets to failure. You also know that in order to learn how to lift weights, you need to learn how to isolate and contract your muscles. For example, you need to learn how to pull with your back and not your arms. The major problem with not using enough weight is two-fold. First, and I see this all the time, you complete sets where you could easily do thirty reps. In this case, you don't reach failure, you just get tired and figure "That's plenty of reps, I should stop now." On your working sets (after the warm-up), you should not be able to complete fifteen reps. If you can, grab a little more weight. When you have to quit around twelve, you're using a good weight. Ideally, you should be able to do around ten and then have to really push to get two more.

Second, when you don't use a lot of weight, it becomes very easy to just rely on your arms. If your arms are strong enough, they will do the work. As you increase the weight, you will find that you have to incorporate those other 'big' muscles and you will then be able to 'feel' those muscles more. That's what lifting is all about, engaging muscles. You need to work your way up and keep adding a small amount of weight until you can feel those big muscle working and ten reps becomes a challenge.

Big muscles vs. small muscles

Further to my point on the amount of weight you use, understand that some muscle groups will be much stronger than others, and adjust accordingly. For example, quite often I will see women doing dumbbell rows for their back with fifteen pounds, the same weight they then use for one arm bicep curls. In comparison, I use over a hundred pounds for my rows and forty for my curls. After all, your back muscle is way bigger and stronger than your bicep.

We all have our BIG muscles and our SMALL ones. When working back, chest, legs, you need to try using more weight. You need to work your way up and see what you're *really* capable of. You might be surprised at how strong those muscles are. I'll see women doing standing calf raises with thirty pounds. Your calves are very strong, just walking around they handle way more weight than that. Just give it a shot, move the pin down and see what you can do. No harm in trying, right?

Not focusing on one muscle group at a time

Here's another term that drives me crazy, circuit training. That's where you work your way down a line of machines in order to work your whole body in as little time as possible. That's great if you're a senior looking to keep your muscles active but that's about it. In order to build a muscle, you need to thoroughly warm it up and work through three to four exercises. Even out of the circuit area, I see many women jumping from one body part to another.

The goal of your warm-up is to pump the muscle you're working full of blood and in the process, oxygen. This will help you incorporate the muscle fibers and work them to create hypertrophy. Moving from muscle to muscle doesn't allow your body to maintain a good pump in those different areas. You will see people superset, but it's usually muscles in the same area like biceps and triceps, where your whole arm is pumped full of blood.

Come up with a split and stick to it. Review the section on Recovery to keep it foremost in mind.

Jumping to machines before learning with free weights

Machines can be a big stumbling block for women. In the chapter on machines vs. free weights I talked about how important it is to learn how to use your muscles with free weights before relying on machines. Women in particular will turn to those machines right away because it's pretty hard to go wrong, hop in and push or pull. The big issue is that a lot of these machines will not fit properly, and you won't know how they're supposed to fit. In that case, they can easily force you to perform the movement incorrectly, again, you'll have to rely on other muscles and joints to complete the moves.

In order to learn how to use and contract your muscles, you need to first master the free weights and cables. You will feel the difference, believe me.

Too much ab work

This applies to both men and women but I just want to repeat it here. Your abs get a great deal of work from the other exercises. Also, when you go through a leg or a back workout, you're burning a great many calories and you're boosting your metabolism with exercises like squats and deadlifts. Training your abs burns very few calories and doesn't have much of an anabolic or metabolism boosting effect. Basically, you're not making good use of your gym time. A few quick sets of crunches at the beginning or end of your workout is more than enough.

Lifting to lose weight

Following on the abs topic I just want to clear up a misconception that some of you might have that has to do with weight loss. It's a common one that is understandable given the decades of misleading advertising in the industry.

When your body stores food as fat, it decides where it wants to store it. Most women tend to see it in their thighs and hips, while men usually get the belly fat. Now, create the right scenario and your body will break down and use that stored fat for energy. Most often, our bodies work on the LIFO method, last in first out...regardless of what exercise you do. In other words, there is no such thing as spot reduction. All those ab machines in the infomercials will have you believe that crunches get rid of belly fat...that is completely wrong!

I say this because I think a lot of women structure their workouts around the idea of spot reduction. Say you want to get rid of the fat on your legs and butt, so you focus the majority of your lifting on those areas. Maybe you have fat on your arms that you could do without, so you train arms all the time. Your body just doesn't work that way.

Lifting is one of the best things you can do to increase your metabolism, which increases the rate at which you burn calories for energy. However, you are far better off doing a split that covers your whole body, so that you can give your muscles a chance to recover. Learn how to lift with the intent of building muscle on your whole physique. It will make a big difference in how you look and feel.

When it comes to getting rid of fat, remember the golden rule: You get strong in the gym, you get skinny in the kitchen.

Too many 'small' exercises

Continuing on the anabolic and metabolism boosting effects of lifting, another common error is focusing too much on 'small' exercises. For example, doing leg extensions instead of the leg press, or pulldowns for your back instead of rows. The big exercises are essential if you want to get the benefits that lifting can provide. Don't get me wrong, I'm not saying you have to move big weight and squat two hundred pounds. When you squat, you use your whole core, your quads, hamstrings, glutes, traps...all at the same time. When you do extensions, you use your quads. Which is better? I talked a great deal about opportunity cost in the book and in this case, I want you to make the most of your time in the gym. Going around doing all kinds of small exercises will leave no time for the compound moves. I know they can be more intimidating, but you have to give it a shot. You'll feel the difference: more soreness, more of a pump the next day and a bigger appetite for good food. These moves really kick your metabolism into gear and get your body burning more calories.

Eating/Supplements around your workout

This is a very important issue that I think a lot of women just ignore. Again, if you believe you're "just toning," then what difference does it make, right? But if your (realistic) goal is to build muscle, then you should know what to eat and drink around your workouts in order to meet that goal.

- ✓ You shouldn't eat a great deal right before you train, an hour before is good. It should be pretty obvious why.
- ✓ You definitely need to be hydrated. If you're training first thing in the morning have that big glass of water as soon as you get up. If it's at lunch or late in the day, make sure you're drinking your water.
- ✓ If you need a kick in the ass then take in some (moderate) caffeine, it will help.
- ✓ After your workout is when you really need to pay attention to what you do. If you don't have any protein powder, get some. As soon as your session is over, take in a half scoop with water. Not *after* you drive home or shower, but right away! I say a half scoop because that's all you should need. I'm 200 pounds and I use a full scoop. The benefit is a tub will last twice as long which is nice because the stuff isn't cheap.
- ✓ Oh, and for some reason, women tend to buy the worst tasting protein powder from some weird health food store. Go to a supplement store and find one you like, ask for samples, some of the chocolate ones are amazing. A shake with skim milk and a table-

spoon of peanut butter before bed is a great treat that will keep you full until the morning.

✓ Do not end your workout with juice, fruit or Gatorade, especially if you're trying to get rid of fat. Post workout, your body will continue to keep burning those extra calories and at this point, they are likely coming from fat stores. The second you ingest sugar, your body will stop burning that fat and start burning the sugar.

✓ Don't take any sugar in for an hour, then eat. Sugar at this point is actually good, it gets your system going and helps with the recovery. You should be eating carbs and protein. Remember my earlier advice, learn about nutrition, become an expert!

Lift first, cardio second

If you want to do both cardio and weights, do the weights first. You will have more food energy and focus. You'll be able to push through those reps and take your muscles further. Once you're done, you will likely be in a better position to burn fat while on the cardio equipment. Just remember, no sugar!

Straps/Gloves (weak wrists)

Last one: don't let a weak grip hold you back. If need be, grab a pair of lifting straps, they will make a huge difference and help you stop using those arms when you're pushing and pulling.

Advice for those seeking a personal trainer

1. Don't be intimidated by the gym, the trainer or the process, it's your money!

2. Ask to get a list of the available trainers at your gym with their qualifications, experience and time with the club. There's often a lot of turnover. Every gym has experienced trainers that have been there for years and those who just passed the course last week

3. Research them, check social media. Is this just a side job for them or are they passionate about fitness? Do they even work out? You'd be surprised, many don't. Would you pay for golf lessons from someone who doesn't play golf?

4. Select a few that you like and ask to interview them, ask them why they do what they do and why they consider themselves to be worth that $50/hour (even though they only get a portion). Then pick the one that's right for you. If you were hiring a trainer to come to your house, you'd be a lot more careful about who you chose. The same rules should apply at the gym.

5. Remember, you are going to class...so ask lots of questions and take notes. The idea is to learn how to lift so you won't have to keep paying for a partner.

6. If you need a trainer for motivation, find a training partner or join a class, it's much cheaper. I once put an ad on the internet to train people for some extra money and the first three people that answered simply wanted motivation. To me, that's ridiculous.

7. Don't get into social talk, it blows me away how many do...you're not paying for a friend. I see so many taking four or five minutes between sets to chat, that's crazy! If you want to pay $50 an hour just to talk to someone, call me.

8. Don't be afraid to question their advice when it comes to technique. On almost every trip to the gym I see all the mistakes I've talked about in this book being performed by people *with a trainer standing right next to them*. Don't assume they're right.

9. The majority of trainers work through a program that centers around how much you can lift and for how many reps. This is so they can easily track your progress in fancy charts. Your focus should be on learning how to isolate individual muscles, move the weight with those muscles and get a good contraction. Good trainers will work on your ability to do just that, rather than simply count reps.

10. Trainers tend to get creative with their exercises. This can lead to some pretty un-flattering body positions in the middle of a crowded gym. A good trainer will appreciate the need for discretion, some won't, don't be afraid to tell them if you're not comfortable with what they're asking you to do.

11. Whenever I'm asked, I tell people to consider hiring someone who doesn't work for a gym, someone who runs their own training business. You might find a much more committed and experienced individual and in turn, learn a great deal more and get your money's worth.

Steve Foxall

Conclusion

Before I wrap things up, I want to leave you with one more lesson, and it's one about life outside the gym. It's about having a path and getting wherever it is you want to go. I wrote a fair bit about my story in the book and I'm always fascinated to hear what others have gone through. It's my hope that this project will allow me to create an environment where I can interact with readers and hear their stories. When I look back at my own life, I see that it's always been a struggle. It's like I've had this opponent in my mind that I've had to fight every day. All I can do is keep battling, and I battle with drive and my unwillingness to settle. The battle I'm speaking of started one night about twenty years ago.

It was the middle of winter and I remember it like it was yesterday. There was a storm and it was coming down pretty hard. I left my shift at the bank late that night and missed the bus. The only way home was the train but my pockets were empty, I had no money. I was broke in a town where I knew no one. I've spent my fair share of nights on the street but it was cold so I headed over to the parking lot. Luckily it was dark enough for me to try and find an open car door and a few quarters on the dash, just enough for that ticket home.

Steve Foxall

The next morning, I swallowed every ounce of pride I had left and hit up social assistance. I think she felt sorry for me, maybe the suit helped. I went home with a cheque for $126, and three months later, I paid it back. I don't think I've shared that story before, but it's always in the back of my mind.

Fear is in all of us, and failure makes for a great spider. Successful people will tell you they've failed over and over and always learned from it, but at the time they were all fighting to stay alive. I was fighting that night and I was furious. Furious because I knew I would have to beg for help.

I've never smoked, I barely drink, and I went 40 years without a coffee. I don't want to have to rely on anything, even people...it's why I've never even considered steroids, I see it all as an addiction, and addiction scares the shit out of me. That's where my drive comes from, I don't ever want to beg for help again.

But drive is useless without a path. So where do you want to go? Who do you want to be? Where does your path take you? This book only exists because it was more important to me than sleep. Take some time and ask yourself what's important to you. We see it on social media over and over...you won't get anywhere without hard work, but I guarantee you won't get anywhere if you don't know where you want to go, and once you do know, you won't work hard unless it's important to YOU.

So I'd like you to create a new habit, and believe me, this is some of the best advice you will ever get. I want you to shut everything else out, grab a sketch pad, find a place to sit and focus 100% on yourself for an hour. I want you to ask yourself questions. Where are you now and where do you want to go? What's important to you in life? In what way do you want to be better? What are you passionate about? Then just write it down, throw your thoughts at the paper until you run out of room. Then I want you to stare at it, there's a path in there, you just have to find it. It might take a few tries but I promise you, it is time well spent and it should become a habit.

Then, once you know what you want, figure out what steps you can take now to get the ball rolling. It could be something very small, but it's still a step. We get intimidated by the sum of the effort, but any goal can be broken down into small steps, and anyone can take a step.

In today's society, the amount of time we spend focusing on other people is astonishing. People spending their nights looking at blogs telling you how to chase your dreams and work your ass off. Looking at pictures of people whose physiques they would love to have or sports cars they wish they could own. The irony is that people who are truly working toward their goals don't have time to sit around and look at everyone else.

It's all about becoming productive. It means managing your time and thoughts and it means going to sleep knowing you got shit done today, that you took that step.

Create the habit, get to know yourself and invest time in yourself, then one day, maybe all those people will be looking at what you've accomplished.

Start now, I dare you.

Notes:

www.ingramcontent.com/pod-product-compliance
Lightning Source LLC
LaVergne TN
LVHW051108080426
835510LV00018B/1961